TRAVELS, EXPLORATIONS AND EMPIRES

Volume 4

TRAVELS, EXPLORATIONS AND EMPIRES

WRITINGS FROM THE ERA OF IMPERIAL EXPANSION
1770–1835

Volume 4

MIDDLE EAST

Edited by Tilar J. Mazzeo

LONDON
PICKERING & CHATTO
2001

Published by Pickering & Chatto (Publishers) Limited
21 Bloomsbury Way, London, WC1A 2TH

2252 Ridge Road, Brookfield, Vermont 05036, USA

www.pickeringchatto.com

BRITISH LIBRARY CATALOGUING IN PUBLICATION DATA
Travels, explorations and empires: writings from the era of imperial expansion,
1770–1835
1. Travelers' writings, European 2. Discoveries in geography – European
I. Fulford, Tim   II. Kitson, Peter   III. North America   IV. Far East
V. North and South poles   VI. Middle East
910.9'4

ISBN 1851967206

LIBRARY OF CONGRESS CATALOGING-IN-PUBLICATION DATA
Travels, explorations and empires: writings from the era of imperial expansion,
1770–1835.
p. cm.
Includes bibliographical references and index.
Contents: v. 1. North America / edited by Tim Fulford with Carol Bolton –
v. 2. Far East / edited by Tim Fulford and Peter J. Kitson – v. 3. North and South
Poles / edited by Peter J. Kitson – v. 4. Middle East / edited by Tilar J. Mazzeo.
ISBN 1-85196-720-6 (set : alk. paper)
1. Voyages and travels – History – Early works to 1800. 2. Voyages and travels
– History – 19th century. 3. Travelers' writings. I. Fulford, Tim, 1962– II. Bolton,
Carol. III. Kitson, Peter J.

G465 T74 2001
910.4'09'033-dc21
00–051033

This publication is printed on acid-free paper that conforms to the American
National Standard for the Permanence of Paper for Printed Library Materials

New material typeset by
P&C

Printed and bound in Great Britain by
Antony Rowe Ltd., Chippenham

CONTENTS

ACKNOWLEDGEMENTS

This volume has benefited from the critical attention and intellectual generosity of many colleagues. Above all, I wish to thank Sandra Kroup and the Special Collections staff at the Suzzallo Library, University of Washington. My warmest thanks go to Jason Konig, George Erving and Thaine Stearns, whose scholarly insights have aided my research into the Romantic Levant.

INTRODUCTION TO VOLUME 4

THE INTIMATE ESTRANGEMENT:
ROMANTIC BRITAIN AND THE OTTOMAN EMPIRE

This volume on the Romantic 'Levant' encompasses the territories held by three Asiatic empires: the Ottoman Empire; the Persian Empire; and the independent kingdom of Afghanistan; as well as the Mediterranean island of Malta, the strategic 'key' to the Middle East.

THE OTTOMAN DECLINE

Amongst the three Asiatic empires comprising the territories of the Romantic-period 'Levant', the Ottoman Empire was by far the most important. Poised at the margins of Europe – and lying between Britain and its Indian empire – the Ottoman Empire and its holdings figured centrally in the foreign policies of the Russian, French and British empires. While in the late eighteenth century the Ottoman Empire was on the verge of collapse due to internal corruption and mismanagement, its territories were vast and of considerable strategic importance. During the Romantic period, Ottoman possessions included the entire Arabian peninsula; Palestine, Syria and Lebanon; Turkey, Greece and Albania; and parts of Iran and Iraq.

The janizaries

By the late eighteenth century, the Ottoman state was in precarious balance. Its precipitous decline was the result of longstanding internal frictions and increasingly indirect governance. During its imperial height in the late sixteenth century, the Sultanate had depended upon centralised military rule, and as central authority began to disintegrate in the seventeenth century, so did the empire. In theory, the Ottoman state consisted of two branches of government: the Learned Institution and the Ruling Institution. The former represented the state religious and legal establishment and was headed by Islamic religious authorities or Mufti, who issued decrees on Islamic law (*sharia*). The Sultan was charged with enforcing these sacred decrees, which he could supplement with additional secular laws (*gunun*). While there was chronic internal conflict over the appointment and exercise of religious authority, the central weakness of the Ottoman state stemmed from problems in the Ruling Institution. The military and political branch of the government, the Ruling Institution was led by the Sultan, whose authority was supposedly enforced by his élite military corps, the janizaries. In fact, however, the janizaries had exercised almost complete control over the Sultan since the late seventeenth century. In the Romantic period, *coup d'état* was a persistent threat, which crippled rule from Constantinople and ultimately led to the assassination of Sultan Selim III by the janizaries in 1807.

One result of janizary control was the disintegration of Ottoman military strength in an era of increasingly aggressive European imperial ambitions. Selim III (1761–1807), Ottoman Sultan from 1789 to 1807, recognised that drastic reforms were necessary to preserve the integrity of his empire from the imperial ambitions of Europe and in 1792 attempted to institute a series of military and political reforms known as the *nizam-i cedid* or 'new order'. Central to these reforms was a commitment to greater European contact – primarily in order to train Ottoman troops in Western political tactics and military technologies – which included the establishment of the first permanent Ottoman embassy in London in 1793. These efforts, however, drew a violent response from both the janizaries and the Islamic *ulama*, who were eager to retain control of the Ottoman state, and Selim was assassinated in 1807. His brother Mahmud II was established as Sultan, and, although janizary power was finally destroyed by Mahmud in the 'Auspicious Event' of 1826, it came too late to restore his empire.

The Wahabi

In addition to these internal conflicts within the centralised Islamic state, religious dissent further undermined the Sultan's ability to exercise control in the provinces of his empire. Although the Ottoman Empire had a largely homogenous Islamic population, important and potentially explosive divisions existed, especially between Shi'i and Sunni sects. While the majority of Ottoman Muslims identified themselves as Sunni, the majority of Persian Muslims adhered to Shi'i practice and, as always in the Islamic state, contests for theological authority and for political authority were inseparable. Throughout the Romantic period, this resulted in periodic military conflict along the Ottoman–Persian borders. The more important threat to the Sultanate, however, came from the Wahabi Islamic reform movement in the Arabian peninsula, which resulted in direct conflict between the province and Constantinople.

Despite its position at the religious and geographical heart of Islam, the Arabian peninsula was in fact governed by local groups which were openly hostile to rule from Constantinople. In 1800, the major political power in the region was the Wahabi sect. Strict Sunni Muslims, the Wahabi were a militant and puritanical Islamic reform order, whose members identified themselves as the followers of Muhammad ibn 'Abd al-Wahhab (1703–92). The group came to political power in the region with the conversion to Wahabite principles of Muhammad ibn Su'ud, the ruler of the Nadj province, in 1744. By 1800 the Wahabi, under the leadership of Su'ud's successor Abd al-Aziz I, had taken control of the shores of the Persian Gulf and of the Hedjaz. Over the course of the next few years, the Wahabi engaged in direct conflicts with Ottoman rule and managed to undermine considerably the Sultan's authority as protector of Islam's holy cities, disrupting the hajj caravan from Damascus to Mecca for most of the next decade and successively capturing Karbala (1801), Mecca (1803) and Medina (1804). The Wahabi movement was curtailed by 1812 and put down in 1818, but it was of little help to the Sultan: the conqueror of the Wahabi was Muhammad Ali, himself the renegade governor of Egypt.

The Bedouin Arabs

In addition to Wahabi challenges to Ottoman authority, tribal communities played an important role in disrupting centralised control throughout Arabia. In fact, almost the entire population of Arabia was comprised of tribal groups, while Iraq, Iran, Egypt, Syria and Albania had significant minority populations of nomadic peoples. In the late eighteenth century, there were periodic outbreaks of violence throughout Syria, Iraq and the Egyptian Delta, as the inhabitants of expanding settlements came into conflict with nomadic tribes. During the Romantic period, however, it was the Bedouins of the Arabian desert who posed the greatest threat to travellers in the Levant and who most fully captured the Western imagination. Loosely organised by tribal confederation, the Bedouin Arabs were divided into nomadic family groups, inhabiting the desert regions of Arabia, Syria and Jordan, and they had the reputation for being at once rapacious marauders and a fiercely 'noble' people. The Bedouins made travel and trade within Arabia or along the shores of the Red Sea a dangerous proposition; with limited resources and struggling to survive in a harsh environment, they took what they needed by force from settlements, caravans or individuals. However, the rugged independence of the Bedouin tribes and their often flagrant disregard for Ottoman authority also appealed – at least in the abstract – to Western travellers in the region. Cast as the 'true Arabs' and as an essentially democratic people, the Bedouins came to embody the biblical virtues of classical Arabia and its inhabitants. In the Romantic imagination, 'the Bedouin [were] no more like the [Ottoman] Arabs of Egypt than a free man is like a slave'[1] and, sprung from the 'original stock' of Moses and his people, they represented the golden age of Eastern antiquity. In this respect, the Bedouins were viewed

---

1 Giovanni Batista Belzoni, quoted in Katherine Sim, *Desert Traveller: The Life of Jean Louis Burckhardt* (London, 1969), p. 401.

by Western travellers in much the same way as the native Greeks were imagined – as positive representations of Europe's own cultural origins in Asia.

The Mamelukes

While the Arabian peninsula was in a state of anarchic disorder, the Sultanate had also lost administrative control of Egypt at the end of the seventeenth century. Although still held by the Ottoman Empire, Egypt functioned throughout the Romantic period as a semi-autonomous province, initially ruled by the Mameluke beys. Descended from the medieval dynasty of slave soldiers, the Mamelukes held Egypt independently and refused to pay taxes to Constantinople. Too weak to enforce his possession of the area, the Sultan was obliged to acquiesce. Mameluke unity and strength had been maintained in the eighteenth century under the rule of Ali Bey, but his death in 1773 left a power vacuum that factionalised the princes, and Napoleon took advantage of their weakened position when he invaded Egypt in 1798. The French occupied Egypt for three years (1798–1801), during which time Napoleon engaged in a brutal campaign against the Mameluke rulers of the province, considerably weakening their position but failing to establish secure administrative control himself.

Muhammad Ali

With the withdrawal of French troops from Egypt in 1802 and of the British navy in 1803, a second power vacuum was created when the Sultan was again unable to exercise his authority effectively in the region, and numerous local governors scrambled to secure power. Ultimately, Muhammad Ali (1770–1849), an Ottoman soldier and part of a force sent by Constantinople to oppose the French, established control of the Egyptian provinces – ostensibly in the name of the Ottoman Empire. By 1805, however, he had removed Selim's pasha from power, destroyed the remaining Mameluke authority and established a firm rule that was virtually independent of Constantinople. In 1807 the Ottoman government was compelled to appoint him Governor of Egypt, acknowledging his *de facto* administration of the territory. Over the course of the next thirty years, Muhammad Ali Pasha and the Ottoman Sultan were to negotiate constantly a delicate balance of power, with Ali performing periodic military favours for Constantinople but being left to rule Egypt independently. In 1811 Sultan Mahmud charged Ali with the task of putting down the Wahabi insurrections in Arabia, and Ali used this opportunity to extend his local control into the Hedjaz. By 1818 he had taken control of the Wahabi base in Najd, effectively ending the reform movement and expanding his territories into the heart of Arabia. In the 1820s, Ali's military support was called upon in Greece as well, where he was instrumental in putting down the fledgling independence movement. By 1831, Ali had gone to war against Constantinople, and in 1841 he and his descendants were granted dynastic hereditary rights over the rule of Egypt by the Ottoman government.

Ali Pasha, the 'Muslim Bonaparte'

The Romantic period also saw the collapse of centralised Ottoman rule in Albania and eastern Greece and the rise of Ali Pasha Tepelene (1744–1822) as the *de facto* ruler of the empire's European territories. A renegade governor initially appointed to the northern Albanian pashalic of Janina (now Ioannina), Ali ruled as Ottoman pasha from 1787 to 1820 but was able to secure autonomous control throughout the region, largely due to his willingness to negotiate privately with European heads of state. While Ali had steadily expanded his territorial responsibilities throughout the term of his governorship, his rise to independent power began in 1797 with the French possession of the Ionian Islands. These islands lay directly off the coast of Turkish possessions and, in a bold move, Ali Pasha signalled his desire to negotiate foreign policy directly with Napoleon. The French, hoping to divert Ottoman attention away from Egypt – which Napoleon was planning to invade – immediately sent an embassy hoping to encourage this renegade behaviour. By 1803 the British too were dealing directly with Ali on Mediterranean policy and had established an independent ambassador in his territories. Throughout the years of the Napoleonic Wars, numerous alliances and coalitions formed and unformed, and Ali Pasha, willing to negotiate with France, Britain or Russia, consistently expanded his own territories through strategic associations, while maintaining nominal loyalty to the Ottoman Sultan. By 1811, the time of Lord Byron and John Cam Hobhouse's visit to the region, Ali Pasha controlled an area that included most of southern Albania, Epirus, Thessaly and the Morea, and his reputation for irrational cruelty, keen imperial ambitions and despotic rule earned him from Byron the title of the 'Muslim Bonaparte'. By 1815, it had become clear that Ali's diplomatic objective was the secession of his territories from the Ottoman Empire and, when Sultan Mahmud II determined to re-establish centralised control of his empire in 1819, Ali Pasha was to pay the price for this bold independence. He was assassinated upon orders from Constantinople in 1822.

EUROPEAN OBJECTIVES IN THE OTTOMAN LEVANT

The rise of Britain's second empire

The Romantic period saw Great Britain's transition from the policies of the 'first empire' in the West to the administration of its 'second empire' in the East. One result of this shift in imperial focus was a renewed interest in the Levant and its regional stability. Under the first empire in North America, British imperial policy had been formed largely by market interests, and the result had been resentment and revolution. Indeed, as Adam Smith was to claim, in America 'A great Empire ha[d] been established for the sole purpose of raising up a nation of customers'[1] and, although for some time the North American colonies were an important source of revenue, the ultimate effect on Britain was negative. Theories of imperialism were naturally of considerable interest to eighteenth-century political economists, and there was an overwhelming consensus amongst them on this point; while Britain had made money in the North American colonies, it had not gained strength through expansion there. With the loss of the American colonies in 1783, new imperial priorities emerged and with them Britain's second empire. Developed primarily under the Pitt administrations, a new policy of imperialism emerged, one which proposed a model of horizontal national 'trusteeship' rather than vertical commercialism. And Britain's new empire would be in the East.

Britain's imperial objective was to establish an Anglo-Indian empire which would both compensate economically for the loss of possessions and trade in North America and contribute materially to Britain's national power. The turn to the East was perhaps inevitable. By 1783, the majority of Britain's colonial territories were in the Indies, and the expansion of administrative control in the region proceeded with relative ease. Throughout the Romantic period, however, Britain's problem was ensuring access to this eastern empire. There were essentially four routes to India in the nineteenth century and three of them ran through the Levant. By 1793, British concern over these routes dominated foreign policy and had placed the crumbling Ottoman Empire at the heart of European imperial concerns.

'To chase the English out of India': Napoleonic ambitions in the Levant
European interest in the Ottoman Levant became intensely focused after the French declaration of war in 1793. At the time there were three overland routes to India: one proceeding through Egypt and the Red Sea; one following the caravan routes through Syria and southern Persia; and one crossing the Black Sea to Tabriz. All three overland routes, however, began in the Mediterranean – and while the war with France lasted trade through the region would be difficult. The fourth route to India was around the Cape of Good Hope. While it necessitated a long passage – often seven or eight months by sea, the Cape Route was also independent both of the Mediterranean and of the Levant. The British moved immediately to secure it, withdrawing their fleets from the Mediterranean and engaging the Dutch in Africa. Meanwhile, the French saw an unparalleled opportunity. British possession of the Cape Route came at the cost of French dominance throughout

1 *An Inquiry into the Nature and Causes of the Wealth of Nations* (Oxford, 1993), p. 274.

the Mediterranean, and it left the overland routes and, finally, India vulnerable to Napoleonic ambitions.

At the end of the eighteenth century, the British objective vis-à-vis the Levant was straightforward: to keep the Ottoman Empire between British India and Britain's European competitors at any price. The Ottoman Empire would serve as a buffer, holding the French and Russian empires at a safe distance from Britain's increasingly important Indian possessions. This all depended, however, upon the Turks. The Ottoman Empire was on the verge of internal collapse and Britain feared the inevitable consequences of partition, which would give France and Russia opportunities to expand their empires eastwards and might allow France to establish permanent control of the Mediterranean. Thus the cornerstone of British foreign policy in the Levant throughout the Romantic period was support for the territorial integrity of Ottoman possessions – including, for some time, the Ottoman possession of Greece.

The situation regarding the territorial integrity of the Ottoman Empire came to a crisis in 1798 with Napoleon's invasion of Alexandria. Napoleon's ambitions in Egypt and the Middle East during the Romantic period were complex. He had claimed that 'The truly great empires and revolutions have taken place only in the Orient', and Napoleon hoped to establish his own empire beginning with a conquest in the East. In 1798 Napoleon understood two things about the situation in Egypt: first, that a Sultan too weak to retain control of the region would be equally unable to reassert it; second, that Egypt was the key to the Middle East and to Britain's imperial jugular.

Napoleon's grand plan was to destroy the British in a three-pronged attack; invasion at home, in Egypt and in India. This connection between Egypt and India, more than any other factor, established the Ottoman Levant as a critical region in respect to British imperial expansion. Control of Egypt would give the French not only assured dominance in the Mediterranean, but also the opportunity to control the overland route to India and the East. Napoleon intended to take control first of the Suez isthmus, Egypt and the Red Sea, thus interrupting British commerce and, more importantly, British mail. With the loss of the Red Sea to French control, Britain's ability to correspond efficiently with India would be seriously and perhaps disastrously compromised, opening the way for Napoleon's final ambition: an overland invasion of India itself. The stated French objective was 'to chase the English out of India'.

Malta

In order to possess Egypt, the French would first need to take control of Malta, strategically located between Europe and Africa. As the British realised immediately after Napoleon seized the island on 11 June 1797, French possession of Malta made the Mediterranean a 'French lake'. Ultimately, Malta would be placed at the crux of world policy and become, in Horatio Nelson's estimation, the 'most important outwork' of British India.[1]

In 1797 Malta was an independent principality, held by the Order of St John of Jerusalem. The knights had been granted the island in 1530 by the Habsburg Emperor Karl IV and had defended their possession from Ottoman attacks throughout the sixteenth century, leaving Malta extraordinarily well fortified. While the island was vulnerable only to extended siege, the membership of the Order was also overwhelmingly French. When Malta fell to Napoleon in a matter of days, collusion was widely suspected. In response to Napoleon's capture of the island, the British navy moved quickly to establish a blockade of Malta in the autumn of 1798, but the effort to wrest the island from French control would prove inefficient, unpopular and costly. Under the command of Nelson and Captain Alexander Ball, the British began the Siege of Valletta, which was to last two years.

Despite an enormous outlay of effort and expense, the British at first had little investment in Malta *per se*. The objective was simply to prevent French control of the island. In Nelson's assessment, 'the possession of Malta by England would be an useless and enormous expense; yet any expense should be incurred, rather than let it remain in the hands of the French'.[2] Ultimately, British policy toward Malta was determined by a much larger set of concerns, which focused on India and on the balance of power in the Middle East. Napoleon saw the Middle East as the key to the British Empire – and Malta was the key to the Middle East.

By 1800 Napoleon's expedition in Egypt had failed, and in the autumn of that year the French surrendered Malta to British control. The island's importance on the world stage might have ended there, had the Addington administration negotiated the Treaty of Amiens with more foresight. For, although Britain was bargaining from a position of formidable strength, the Treaty of Amiens (1802) and its Preliminaries (1801) were rife with ill-considered commitments and concessions. Most disastrously, the Treaty left the Anglo-Indian empire unprotected at both ends. The Cape of Good Hope was restored to the Dutch, Egypt was returned to the crumbling Ottoman Empire and Malta was granted its former independent 'neutrality'. While the French retained their naval conquests in the Caribbean, Britain gained important economic territories in Ceylon, Trinidad and the West Indies, but little of strategic value. By relinquishing control of Malta and the Cape, the British had foolishly given up the means of securing either the overland or the naval routes to India and had, as Lord Grenville put it, purchased 'a short interval

---

1 Quoted in Holland Rose, A. P. Newton and E. A. Benians, *The Cambridge History of the British Empire* (Cambridge, 1961), p. 125.

2 Quoted in Desmond Gregory, *Malta, Britain, and the European Powers, 1793–1815* (London, 1996), p. 66.

of repose by the sacrifice of those points on which [their] security in a new contest may principally depend'.[1]

In 1802, as the time came to evacuate Malta, the British government began to have doubts about the wisdom of exposing the Mediterranean and the overland routes to Napoleonic conquest a second time. The island was to revert to the neutral Order of St John, rather than to the protection of any imperial power, and there was little to prevent Napoleon from renewing his possession of the principality. These fears were heightened in 1803 when the 'leaked' news of refreshed French ambitions in Egypt appeared in *Le Moniteur*. Britain now demanded that it be allowed ten years additional occupation in Malta, in the absence of any other guarantee of the island's neutrality and independence. Napoleon and Tallyrand refused. On 18 May 1803, Britain went to war over the issue of Malta – and over the implicit threat to Egypt and India that it represented.

Throughout the years of the Napoleonic Wars and under the Continental System, the British decision to retain Malta proved invaluable. Possession of Malta allowed Britain to trade through Mediterranean routes despite Napoleon's blockade on land. During the final years of the Napoleonic Wars, Malta was amongst Britain's most profitable and strategically important territories, although it was not yet under colonial administration. However, the Treaty of Paris, which concluded the war with France on 30 May 1814, left Malta permanently in British hands, thus securing the first stage of the overland routes to India.

Egypt

As we know, one of the primary objectives of Napoleon's Egyptian campaign was the disruption of British communications with India, and his early successes in the region were startling. French troops seized Alexandria on 4 July and Cairo on 21 July 1798, and Napoleon was poised to establish control of Upper Egypt. When the British understood Napoleon's intentions, they responded quickly. On 1 August, Nelson engaged the French navy off the coast of Alexandria, destroying almost the entire French fleet in the Battle of the Nile. By the time the Ottoman Empire formally declared war, on 9 September, Napoleon had become effectively stranded in Africa. Although he held Egypt, it was not from a position of strength and he did not have the resources to secure administrative control permanently. The French Directory, justifiably anxious about Napoleon's ambitions at home, were content to leave him there as he was. Indeed, Napoleon's subsequent course of action in the East was largely determined by his domestic political objectives: returning to France as the republic's conquering hero, he planned to take control of the French government himself.

1 Quoted in Rose, Newton and Benians, *The Cambridge History of the British Empire*, p. 81.

In order to accomplish these objectives at home, Napoleon needed a stunning victory. Egypt, clearly, would not be that. Thus Napoleon turned his attention to invading the Middle East proper. On 31 January 1799, Napoleon's officers initiated a full-scale campaign against Syria, taking Gaza, al-Ramleh, Jaffa and Haifa by late March. However, as the siege of Acre dragged on into late spring, with officers and soldiers dying at an alarming rate, Napoleon was obliged to abandon the Syrian expedition on 20 May.

When Napoleon arrived back in Cairo on 14 June, he found the city gripped by plague and in full revolt against French rule. While Napoleon had made several genuine efforts to modernise Egypt and to respect Islamic customs, the populace was now clearly hostile and by the end of the summer he had had enough. Late on the night of 17 August, accompanied only by a handful of advisors, he deserted his command and troops, leaving an officer to negotiate peace with the Ottoman Empire. Contrary to all expectations, Napoleon was nevertheless received by the French people as a returning hero – and by early November 1799 he had seized control of the French republic in the coup of 18–19 Brumaire.

EUROPEAN EMBASSIES AND EXPLORATION IN THE OTTOMAN EAST

Arabia

During the Romantic period, the British government had little political or economic interest in the anarchic Arabian peninsula. However, these territories were of considerable interest to adventurers and explorers, who found amongst the desert nomads and in Islam's holy cities glimpses of the 'true' East. Europeans travelling in Arabia at the end of the eighteenth century were most often 'professional' adventurers or merchants and there were three major destinations for travellers in the region: the Islamic cities of Mecca and Medina; the biblical lands of the Sinai peninsula, Syria and Palestine; and the desert culture of the Bedouins.

Mecca and Medina were dangerous and tantalising places for Romantic-period travellers, who often considered seeing the annual hajj or pilgrimage caravan to the Islamic holy cities as the pinnacle of Eastern adventure. Forbidden to all but Muslims on penalty of death, journeys to Mecca and Medina by Christians had to be made incognito or in bondage, and they offered travellers an unparalleled insight into the Islamic 'character'. While the 'autobiographical' *Travels of Ali Bey* was a popular account of the hajj ostensibly recounted by a Westernised Muslim, the Romantic reading public was particularly interested in the perceptions of European pilgrims. The first recorded visit by an Englishman to Mecca was described in the seventeenth century by the merchant Joseph Pitts, who had been taken captive along the

Barbary coast and sold to an Islamic master, and Pitt's *Faithful Account of the Religion and Manners of the Mahometans* remained an important text. However, the most famous traveller to Arabia during the period was Johann Ludwig Burckhardt, who travelled to Mecca in the character of 'Sheikh Ibrahim' during the first part of the nineteenth century. Burckhardt's observations, *Travels in Syria and the Holy Land*, were published by his employers at the African Association after his death in 1817 and excerpts from his account are reproduced below (pp. 301–24).

Pilgrims to the Holy Land were another important category of travellers to the Levant from the time of the Crusades onward. The most important early account of the biblical sites was Henry Maundell's seventeenth-century journal, *A Journey from Aleppo to Jerusalem*, which was republished in numerous editions throughout the period. Once again, however, Burckhardt was the pre-eminent adventurer, making the first European expedition through Bedouin territories to Mount Sinai, the Monastery of St Katherine and the eastern shore of the Red Sea. A more established route for travellers in the Holy Land was into the northern Arabian regions of Syria and Palestine, which boasted the remains of the ancient cities of Petra, Bethlehem, Jericho, Nazareth and Jerusalem. During the period, several explorers left influential and widely popular accounts of the region, most notably: Constantin François Chasseboeuf, comte de Volney, author of *Travels in Syria and Egypt*; Carsten Niebuhr, author of *Travels through Arabia*; William Browne, author of *Travels in Africa, Egypt, and Syria*; and William Heude, author of *A Voyage up the Persian Gulf*. Excerpts from Burckhardt's account of Mount Sinai are included below, along with excerpts from the works of Volney and Niebuhr (see pp. 1–43 and 45–68).

Malta

The vast majority of Romantic-period travellers to Malta either were affiliated with the British government or were *en route* to final destinations in Asia. For while the region offered little to tourists, it was to play a central role in British imperial expansion and was a customary stopping point along Grand Tour itineraries. Indeed, at the end of the eighteenth century few travellers to the island ventured beyond the capital city of Valletta. Among the notable exceptions were Patrick Byrdone and Vivant Denon, both of whom toured Sicily and Malta in the 1770s. Byrdone's account of the tour, *A Tour through Sicily and Malta* (1774), was almost the only popular account of the region written in English before 1798. Meanwhile Vivant Denon, although famous for his travels with Napoleon in Egypt and for his accounts of that region, published a narrative of his *Travels in Sicily and Malta* (1789), offering an early account of French interests in the island. However, while tourists passing through the region since the early eighteenth century had left numerous brief accounts of Valletta and its port, the most important Romantic accounts of

Malta were written after Napoleon's Egyptian campaign, when the island's strategic importance for British national security became a subject of intense scrutiny and debate. In addition to Colonel Mark Wood's influential descriptions given in *The Importance of Malta* and reproduced below (pp. 91–115), important contemporary travel accounts of the island included: Lieutenant Francis Collin, *Voyages to Portugal, Spain, Sicily, and Malta … from 1796–1810*; Aeneas Anderson, *Journal of the forces which sailed from the Downs in 1800 … with a particular account of Malta* (1802); Thomas Walsh, *Journal of a Late Campaign in Egypt … Including Descriptions [of] Malta* (1801); and John Galt, *Voyages and Travels* (1813).

Egypt

Few Europeans toured the Islamic Levant simply for pleasure, and as an Ottoman possession Egypt was no exception. Indeed, Egypt's cities were particularly dangerous territory. While travellers were exposed to robbery, ambush and murder throughout the Middle East, Egyptians were particularly hostile toward the 'Franks', as Christian Europeans were designated *en masse*. As in Constantinople, foreigners were forbidden to live in the Turkish quarters of the city and they were frequently subject to verbal or physical abuse on the streets of Alexandria or Cairo, especially when appearing in Western dress. Finally, Egypt had periodic outbreaks of the plague. According to contemporary statistics, the worst epidemics – in 1785, 1791 and 1834–5 – killed just under twenty per cent of the entire population, with casualties highest in the urban areas. Yet, despite these risks, European merchants, antiquarians and adventurers were drawn to Egypt, and many of the Romantic period's most impressive 'discoveries' took place in the region.

The Europeans who came to Egypt at the end of the eighteenth century were perhaps more diverse than those visiting any other area of the Levant. In addition to travel accounts left by soldiers, merchants and resident ambassadors, significant records of exploration were recorded by travellers who went to the region with (or developed upon arrival) specialised interests in Egypt, including scholars, art collectors and professional adventurers. While the region was the point of departure for most explorers into the African continent, especially those in search of the sources of the Nile and the Niger, Upper Egypt was itself fertile ground for discovery and enterprise. Some of the era's most important travellers were merchants hoping to profit from discoveries and from the sale of artefacts and images, such as the renowned Robert Wood and James Dawkins, the British travellers who 'discovered' Palmyra and its ruins in 1751. Others had been sent to the region as part of diplomatic missions and turned their attentions to furthering the glory of the British Empire by stocking her museums with treasure, including William Turner, author of *A Journal of a Tour in the Levant* (1820) and Henry Salt, author of *A Voyage to Abyssinia* (1813). However, the most important antiquarian working in Romantic Egypt was the independent inventor turned Egyptologist, Giovanni Battista Belzoni (1778–1823), who made significant discoveries amongst the Pyramids. With the financial backing of other European travellers, including Johann Ludwig Burckhardt and Henry Salt, Belzoni arranged for the exportation to England of many important antiquities – including the vast statuary head of Ramses II known as the 'Young Memnon', so memorably described in Percy Bysshe Shelley's sonnet on 'Ozymandias'. Although Belzoni's most popular and influential work was not a travel journal, the *Narrative of the Operations and Recent Discoveries within the Pyramids* (1819) was amongst the most influential accounts of ancient Egypt in the Romantic period and remained an important text for subsequent archaeological expeditions to these sites.

Among adventurers in Egypt during this period, Lady Hester Stanhope merits individual mention. Lady Hester, whose family connections in England included the Chathams and the Pitts, was among the era's most extraordinary travellers and one of the very few women of the time to explore the Levant independently. With her young lover Michael Bruce in tow, Stanhope dazzled sheikhs and pashas with a combination of ostentatious display and sheer feminine audacity, and she was ultimately able to accomplish what several male adventurers had unsuccessfully attempted: a new expedition to the ancient city of Palmyra. Crowned by the local Bedouins as 'Queen of the Desert' upon her arrival, Stanhope's own behaviour soon grew correspondingly tyrannical and her considerable political influence at the Ottoman courts, often employed capriciously, earned her an unfavourable reputation amongst the British at Cairo.

Finally, French travellers and travel writers in Romantic Egypt are particularly important for our understanding of the geopolitical landscape of the early Napoleonic years. These excursions and researches reveal both the details of France's ambitions in the region at the end of the eighteenth century and the manner in which travel narratives were employed throughout the Romantic period as political propaganda, effective both at home and abroad. Although Napoleon occupied Egypt for only a brief period, his theory of imperialism was sophisticated and (by contemporary standards) 'enlightened'. While he held Egypt as a colonial possession, Napoleon had taken pains to modernise the region, initiating numerous cultural, economic and industrial reforms. In August 1798 he had established the Egyptian Institute and charged his scholarly advisers with researching and documenting French Egypt, in order both to further human knowledge and to advance the progress of colonisation. The members of the Institute wrote some of the period's most valuable travel accounts and histories of the region, most notably the works of Vivant Denon (1747–1825), including his *Travels in Upper and Lower Egypt … during the Campaign of General Bonaparte* (1803). Meanwhile, Napoleon himself had relied upon the earlier researches undertaken by order of the French government before the revolution, and these works offer an insight into France's investment in the territories of the Ottoman Levant in the late eighteenth century. The most important early texts include the works of Constantin de Volney, author of *Ruins of Empire* (1791) and *Travels through Syria and Egypt* (1788), and of Charles Sigisbert Sonnini, whose *Travels in Upper and Lower Egypt* appeared in an 1800 English translation (see below, pp. 69–89).

Constantinople

In an 1810 letter to his mother, Lord Byron indicated that any description of Constantinople would be superfluous; everyone, he observed, had 'read fifty descriptions by sundry travellers'.[1] Indeed, few places were as familiar to the Romantic imagination as the capital city of the Ottoman Empire or the Sultan's inner court. As Byron also observed, Romantic-period representations of Constantinople differed from one another very little – and almost all followed to some extent the pattern of observations made popular with the travel letters of Lady Mary Wortley Montagu (1689–1762). Lady Mary was, without question, one of the two or three most popular travel writers in the Romantic period, although her actual residence in the Ottoman Levant dated to the early part of the eighteenth century. From 1716 to 1718, Edward Wortley Montagu had served as the British ambassador to Turkey and Lady Mary had accompanied her husband to Constantinople. *The Letters of the Right Honourable Lady M—y W—y M—e*, however, was only published after her death in 1763, and was to remain popular throughout the Romantic period. Montagu's travel letters had imitators almost immediately as well, especially amongst women writers, with whom the epistolary travel genre became particularly associated. The introduction to the *Letters* suggests that because women travellers possess superior sensibility their accounts have unique value. She wrote with the intention

> that the world should see, to how much better purpose the LADIES travel than the LORDS; and that, whilst it is surfeited with Male-Travels, all in the same tone, and stuft with the same trifles; a lady has the skill to strike out a new path … as her ladyship's penetration discovers the inmost follies of the heart.[2]

Amongst those women travel writers who modelled either their itineraries or their narrative structures upon the model of sensibility set forth by Montagu were, most notably: Elizabeth Craven, author of *A Journey through the Crimea to Constantinople, in a Series of Letters* (1789); Ann Radcliffe, author of numerous Gothic novels and of *A Journey Made in the Summer of 1794* (1795); Mary Wollstonecraft, author of *Letters Written during a Short Residence in Sweden, Nor-*

---

1 George Gordon, Lord Byron, *Works* (London, 1898–1905), vol. 1, p. 274.
2 *Letters of the Right Honourable Lady M—y W—y M—e: Written during her Travels in Europe, Asia, and Africa* (Dublin, 1763), pp. iv–v.

way, and Denmark (1796); and Mary Shelley, author of *History of a Six Weeks' Tour* (1817).

˙ The voluminous accounts of Constantinople written during the Romantic period by male authors, meanwhile, are particularly interesting for the similar representations of the Turkish 'character' that emerge. These texts rank, undoubtedly, amongst the 'classics' of orientalism. European travellers found few points of comparison between the Ottoman 'Asiaticks' and themselves. Indeed, it comes as little surprise that authors of popular oriental tales in the Romantic period drew from contemporary travel sources, because the 'eye-witness' accounts of travellers in Turkey read much like Byron's *Giaour* or Southey's *Thalaba*. The tenor of these representations needs little rehearsal in our era either: contemporary narratives depict an Ottoman society oppressed by rapine, murder and terror of its rulers, who are themselves represented as effeminate, sexually degenerate, cruelly irrational and capricious in the administration of power. Amongst the numerous narratives describing tours in Romantic Constantinople, excerpts from a very interesting but entirely stereotypical account, F. C. H. L. Pouqueville's *Travels through the Morea, Albania, and Other Parts of the Ottoman Empire* (1806), are reproduced below (pp. 117–52).

Albania

Pouqueville's account is particularly interesting for the representation it offers of the Ottoman territories of Ali Pasha, who had established autonomous rule of Albania and eastern Greece during the Romantic period. As in Constantinople, 'European travellers who visited his lands were … greatly invested in seeing him in the most alien terms possible',[1] and this was particularly true of the British, whose sympathies with Greece depended in part upon its oppression by foreign Ottoman rule. The most informed traveller in the European provinces of the Ottoman Empire was William Martin Leake, who first visited Ali Pasha's territories between 1807 and 1810 in his capacity as British envoy to the independent governor. Leake was later appointed the British Resident at Janina and during his years of diplomatic service wrote several accounts of the region, including *Researches in Greece* (1814), *A Journal of a Tour in Asia Minor* (1824) and *Travels in the Morea* (1830). However, the most celebrated accounts of the region were John Cam Hobhouse's *Journey through Albania* (1817) and the second canto of Lord Byron's travel journal in verse, *Childe Harold's Pilgrimage* (1812), which describe their 1809–10 encounter with Ali Pasha. Selections from Hobhouse's account are reproduced below (pp. 183–223).

---

1 K. E. Fleming, *The Muslim Bonaparte: Diplomacy and Orientalism in Ali Pasha's Greece* (Princeton, 1999), p. 155.

PERSIA AND THE QAJAR EMPIRE

The Qajar administration

Like its Ottoman neighbour, Persia spent much of the eighteenth century on the verge of internal collapse. In Persia, however, there was no illusion of centralised authority. At the beginning of the eighteenth century there had been two major political figures in the region, each reigning independently: the Safavid Shah Sultan Husayn ruling throughout the north and Karim Khan Zand ruling an area in the south. In addition, diverse tribal groups held considerable autonomous or semi-autonomous regional territories; most significantly the Qajar and Afshar tribes and the Ghilzai of Afghanistan. In 1722, the Ghilzai, under the leadership of Mahmud Ghilzai, had overthrown the Safavid dynasty, and significant parts of the Persian Empire were placed under fleeting Afghani rule until in 1732 Nadir Khan helped to restore the Safavids for a brief time.

By 1736, however, Nadir Khan had risen to independent power and was declared Shah of the Afshar. During his subsequent rule of the empire, a brief interval of centralised authority and territorial expansion reigned. In 1736, Nadir Shah launched the first in a series of military campaigns against the Ottoman Empire and the Afghans that ultimately extended the borders of Persia as far west as Baghdad and Tabriz and as far east as Kabul, Peshawar and Mogul Delhi. Although Nadir Shah successfully united his empire, his rule became increasingly despotic and in 1747 he was assassinated. With his death, the short-lived Afshar dynasty also came to an end.

Out of the power vacuum created by the murder of Nadir Shah, the Zands of western Persia came to political prominence. Under the rule of Karim Khan from Shiraz, Persia enjoyed twenty-five years of stable and popular rule, which ended with Karim's death in 1779. Out of this second interval of dynastic instability, the Qajars came to power in Persia, under the successive leadership of Aga Muhammad Khan and, in 1797, his heir Fath Ali Shah. In the face of continuing problems with local factions, the Qajars ruled a united but increasingly weak Persian Empire throughout the Romantic period, with Fath Ali's heir, Abbas Mirza, playing an important role as Persia's ambassador to the West.

British India and the Qajar empire

By the late eighteenth century, the rough boundaries of the Persian Empire extended north–south from the Aral Sea to the Persian Gulf and east–west from the Hindu Kush to the Caspian Sea, incorporating much of present-day Pakistan, Afghanistan, Iran, Azerbaijan and Georgia. In the light of Persia's proximity to India, its strategic significance vis-à-vis British imperial ambitions was inevitable. However, the Qajar Empire posed little threat to the

British interests. By 1800, Fath Ali Shah was having difficulty retaining his own territorial possessions, which were threatened by any number of independent states in Afghanistan and by the Ottoman Turks. British foreign relations with Persia centred once again on a policy of buffer zones and containment.

Britain, of course, was concerned about its possessions in India and British policy in respect to neighbouring Persia developed out of two perceived threats to its colonial territories. In the local arena, Wellesley was worried about Afghanistan's Zeman Shah, who already held territories as far east as Peshawar and seemed ambitious. Meanwhile, the threat of a French campaign in the East loomed as a disturbing possibility, even despite the death in 1799 of Napoleon's Mysore collaborator, Tipu Sultan. The British strategy held that Persia, along with the Ottoman Empire, should be maintained as part of the buffer zone it desired between its European competitors and its possessions in India.

From the British perspective, there were several ways in which this Qajar buffer zone might be established. If Persia would co-operate, then Britain would propose a formal alliance, backed by the movement of British troops into Persia. However, if Persia refused what essentially amounted to protectorate status, then British objectives were to undermine Qajar rule, establishing in Persia an impoverished, disorganised and dangerous no man's land through which neither France nor Russia would choose to send troops. Naturally Wellesley preferred the first option – which would both expand British influence westwards from the Subcontinent and help to legitimise the Anglo-Indian empire he was trying to create.

In order to determine whether co-operation with the Qajar Empire could be established, Wellesley sent an embassy to Persia in 1799. This embassy – the first to Persia undertaken by a Briton since the seventeenth century – was led by Captain John Malcolm (1769–1833). Appointed Assistant to the Resident at Hyderabad in 1798, Malcolm had no experience as an envoy but was to become one of Britain's leading authorities on the region and one of the Romantic period's most important travel historians.

In the end, fortunate circumstances made Malcolm's first mission to Persia inconsequential. In 1799, the French were still in the Levant and Malcolm's primary objective was to prevent Napoleon's passage through Persia. The collapse of Napoleon's Egypto-Syrian campaign later that year made stopping the Corsican's advance unnecessary. The secondary objective of Malcolm's assignment was to encourage Persian aggression against the Afghani Zeman Shah's territories in the north, protecting Britain's Indian possessions in the south through a diversionary tactic. However, by the time Malcolm's embassy arrived in Tehran, Zeman Shah was already occupied with Afghani rebels and was in no position to launch a campaign against British India. Indeed, Malcolm's only concrete success was Fath Ali's guarantee by treaty in 1801 that Persia would contract no alliances with France – a guarantee that the Shah would break in 1808.

Malcolm's subsequent missions into Persia were similarly disappointing from a career perspective, although they chart the course of Anglo-Persian relations quite precisely. By 1807 the British again had reason to worry about Napoleon's objectives in the Levant, and in 1808 Malcolm was charged with a second mission to Tehran. Having occupied Vienna and established significant influence in Constantinople, Napoleon appeared to be marching eastwards in 1807. Diplomatic matters came to a crisis later in that year: Persia was at war with Russia and Fath Ali Shah was actively soliciting a French alliance against the Tsar. A French envoy arrived in Tehran in December 1807 to settle matters. In January 1808, with the continued absence of the expected British ambassador from London, Malcolm was hastily sent into Persia, in order to prevent a Franco-Persian alliance. In addition to this overarching objective, Malcolm had two specific charges on this second mission: to deliver to Fath Ali a British scolding in the form of Minto's *Declaration to the Shah's Ministers* and to negotiate a peace between Russia and Persia. Again, timing worked to Malcolm's disadvantage. In 1808, the French influence at the Shah's court was formidable and as a result Malcolm was not permitted even to travel into Tehran. The mission was scuttled before it began. By early 1809, however, news arrived in Tehran of the Franco-Russian alliance and it appeared that, for the moment, the European powers had lost interest in Persia. Later that year, to Malcolm's chagrin, the long-awaited British Resident to Persia, Harford Jones, arrived and Fath Ali at last agreed to formal cooperation with British interests. By 1810, however, Jones had resigned his post, and Malcolm was sent on a third disappointing mission to Persia, charged with executing the administrative details of Britain's new treaty with the Shah. In a humiliating final scene, Malcolm was recalled by London almost at the moment he reached Fath Ali's court and ordered again to await the arrival of the new London ambassador, Sir Gore Ouseley.

While frustrated as a career diplomat, Malcolm was more successful as a travel writer and historian of the East, and his subsequent publications were amongst the most important and most popular British Romantic accounts of the Persian Empire. During the period of his residency in the East, Malcolm researched and composed several important accounts of the region, including *Sketch of the Political History of India* (1811), which was to become a 'manual of modern Indian diplomacy'.[1] His works on Persia included *History of Persia* (1815) and the popular *Sketches of Persia* (1827).

However, while Malcolm's embassies to Persia played an important symbolic role in the history of Anglo-Qajar relations and while his writings

---

1 Quoted in Rodney Pasley, *'Send Malcolm!' The Life of Major-General Sir John Malcolm, 1769–1833* (London, 1982), p. 69.

contributed substantially to Romantic representations of Persia, he is particularly interesting for the group of younger travel writers who gathered around him. The vast majority of Romantic travellers in Persian territories were affiliated with the diplomatic service and several owed their first commissions in the region to Malcolm. Exploration and reconnaissance were, after all, standard objectives of any diplomatic mission, and envoys travelled with a large entourage of junior scouts, who often supplemented their meagre salaries with potentially lucrative travel writings. The membership of Malcolm's circle reads as a history of Romantic-period travel authorities on the Islamic East, including: John MacDonald Kinneir, author of *Geographical Memoir of the Persian Empire* (1813) and *Travels in Asia Minor* (1818); Henry Pottinger, author of *Travels in Beloochistan and Sinde* (1816); and Mountstuart Elphinstone, author of *An Account of the Kingdom of Caubul* (1815), an extract from which is reproduced below (pp. 271–99). Meanwhile, under rather less favourable conditions, Malcolm met another young man who was to become perhaps the pre-eminent Romantic travel writer on Persia. James Justinian Morier, author of *Journey through Persia* (1812), an extract from which is reproduced below (pp. 153–82), and later of the influential *Adventures of Hajji Baba of Ispahan* (1824), was one of the explorers sent to Tehran under the command of Malcolm's rival envoy, Harford Jones. In fact, Malcolm's *Sketches in Persia* was written in response to Morier's Hajji Baba tales, transforming this extended diplomatic rivalry into a literary combat. Later, Morier's *Adventures of Hajji Baba in England* (1826) was inspired by his experience escorting the Persian ambassador to London in 1809–10 and it became a widely influential literary representation of the Persian East.

While the accounts left to us by Malcolm, Morier and Elphinstone are the clear authorities within the field, several other Romantic travellers through Persia merit individual mention. Among the most important travellers in the eastern Levant, whose accounts represent the complexity of political ambitions in the region, are: Moritz von Kotzebue, author of *Narrative of a Journey into Persia in the Suite of the Imperial Russian Embassy* (1817); Guillaume Olivier, author of *Travels in the Ottoman Embassy, Egypt, and Persia, Undertaken by Order to the Government of France* (1801); and Sir Robert Ker Porter, author of *Travels in Georgia, Persia, and Armenia* (1821).

Although Romantic exploration of Persia was largely conducted as part of diplomatic or military service, travel accounts of the region were typically more entertaining than useful. If British policy toward the Islamic East as a whole was predicated upon keeping Europe and Asia separate, Romantic representations of the Persian Empire were often focused on exploring a limited range of cultural and historical similarities. While the most important single source of Romantic representations of Persia came from the writings of Sir William Jones and the *Asiatick Researches* project, travel writers as a group helped to shape and to popularise the Persian East – both for the general reading public and amongst poets and writers. Unlike the Ottoman Turks, who were viewed as irrational, effeminate, barbarous Oriental 'others', the Persians were seen as quasi-European. Much was made in travellers' accounts of their ethnic origins in the Caucasian Hindu Kush, their superior aesthetic sensibilities, especially in respect to poetry and music, and their love of hunting – which surpassed even that of the English aristocracy. Like the Greeks and the Bedouins, the Persians emerged as living remnants of a classical antiquity and as a more remote but still vital intermediary link between Europe and its imagined cultural origins.

INDEPENDENT AFGHANISTAN

Independent Afghanistan was the third government involved in the administration of the Islamic Middle East during the Romantic era and, although small, the Afghani kingdom exercised an important influence on British foreign policy in the Levant during the Napoleonic Wars.

During much of the eighteenth century, the Afghani tribes were engaged in a struggle for independence from the Persian Empire. Nadir Shah had expanded Persian borders to incorporate Afghanistan early in the century, but throughout his reign there were incursions into those territories by the displaced Abdali tribes, especially in the Herat. Eventually these local insurrections proved irritating enough for Nadir Shah to agree to return the Abdali to their ancestral homelands in Kandahar in exchange for their assistance in crushing his most determined enemies, the Afghani Ghilzai. Nadir Shah had wrested control of the Persian crown from the Ghilzai Mahmoud in 1732, but in 1738 the Ghilzai Husain still ruled at Kandahar. With the Nadir Shah's blessing, the Abdali took control of the territories and numerous Abdali tribesmen were released from Ghilzai imprisonment. Among these tribesmen was Ahmad Khan Sadozai, who was to become the founder of the Durrani dynasty and of independent Afghanistan.

Upon his release from Ghilzai imprisonment, Ahmad Khan quickly rose to military prominence, soon overthrowing the Mogul dynasty in Delhi and becoming the Afghani Shah's bodyguard. It was Ahmad's Persian officers who assassinated Nadir Shah in 1747. With Nadir's murder, the Afghani confederation decided to move for independence from Persia, guessing that Nadir's successor would not be able to preserve the territorial boundaries of his empire by force. Ahmad was appointed Shah of independent Afghanistan, and as Shah he undertook a series of very successful military campaigns aimed at extending the borders of the fledgling Afghani state. From 1747 to 1769, Ahmad conducted unrelenting attacks on the Moguls in Lahore and Delhi. He captured Kabul in 1741, taking Herat in 1749 and Kashmir in 1752.

By the time of Ahmad's death in 1772, he had established an independent Afghani empire and the Durrani dynasty.

Ahmad's successor was Timur Shah, who ruled from 1773 to 1793 and made Kabul the capital of the Afghani empire in 1776. His reign was followed by the rule of Zeman Shah, from 1793 to 1800. Throughout its history, the Durrani dynasty had been plagued by problems along its borders, including frequent clashes with the Moguls, Sikhs and Maratha to the east over contested territorial possessions. Zeman Shah had determined to end these skirmishes by firmly taking control of the territories, and he hoped to extend the borders of the Afghani empire into northern India. Zeman's ambitions alarmed both Persia's Fath Ali, who did not want a strong Afghani empire emerging along his own western border, and the Wellesley administration in India, which hoped to capture these same territories for the British Crown. An Anglo-Persian co-operative strategy was the objective of Malcolm's first embassy to Tehran and, although a formal alliance was not established at the time, Fath Ali did work to undermine Zeman Shah and his territorial ambitions. By 1800, Fath Ali had helped to depose Zeman in favour of his brother Mahmud Shah, but Persian influence at the Afghani court was short-lived: in 1803 Mahmud was himself deposed by another brother, Shah Shoja'. In 1809, Shoja' was again overthrown by Mahmud, whose second rule lasted until 1818, well after British interest in Afghanistan had faded.

It was during the brief reign of Shah Shoja' (1800–9) that British interest in the Afghani empire was at its peak. By 1807, the Shah was less ambitious and the British were less anxious about the Afghani threat to India. His empire was beginning to unravel as tribesmen in the outlying provinces began to assert their independence and Punjabi Sikhs intensified their aggression. The Afghani ruler was occupied with maintaining the territorial integrity of his state. Meanwhile, in Europe, Napoleon was at the height of his powers. In July 1807, the Franco-Russian Treaty of Tilsit had been signed, which dictated a commitment to mutual military support and divided the Continent between Napoleon and the Tsar. Soon the British learned that the French were again courting Tsar Alexander at Erfurt – and proposing a joint campaign against the Ottoman Empire and British India. In 1808, the British sent an embassy to Kabul, in order to discuss mutual defence in the event of a European campaign. On 7 June 1809, the diplomatic efforts of ambassador Mountstuart Elphinstone culminated in a formal Anglo-Afghani alliance. Fortunately for the British, the treaty was ultimately unnecessary, because by the end of 1809 Shoja' had been deposed and the alliance effectively nullified.

Britain's ambassador to independent Afghanistan, Mountstuart Elphinstone (1779–1859), went on like Malcolm and the adventurer-diplomats of his circle to create for himself a considerable reputation as a traveller and a travel writer. Although later a distinguished civil servant, whose posts included the Governorship of Bombay (1819–27), Elphinstone is important for Romantic studies because of the influence of his travel writing upon literary productions. Published in 1815, Elphinstone's *An Account of Caubul* was the only serious account of the region to appear in the period, and it has been identified as a source for poems that include Percy Bysshe Shelley's *Prometheus Unbound* (1818).

SUMMARY

Despite the complexity of Anglo-Islamic relations in the nineteenth century, Britain's investment in the Middle East was consistent and straightforward: it was the conduit of empire, and as such had to remain accessible to trade, exploration and development. The Levant was central to European interests because considerable economic and political capital lay just beyond its borders – both to the east in the Indian subcontinent and to the west in Africa. As liminal spaces, the empires of the Middle East also became sites of mystery, anxiety and fantasy. Throughout Romantic-period travel accounts of the region, European visitors struggled to articulate a coherent narrative description of a culture that remained largely inaccessible to them. Middle Eastern history became allegorical, in part because Western travellers were rarely able – or willing – to see beyond the symbolic and stereotyped elements of Islamic society. Harems and the Sultan's inner courts, the desert tents of Arabian Bedouins, and Islam's holy cities and veiled women preoccupied explorers to the region and tantalised Romantic reading audiences precisely because they tested the limits of European knowledge and understanding. In these accounts, largely written during the Napoleonic Wars by travellers keen to secure advancement or fame, the desire to know often becomes aggressive. Indeed, it is surprising to discover the degree to which Middle Eastern travel narratives were connected with war and the military expansion of empire, whether as propaganda or intelligence. Here, then, is orientalism at its most combative.

Collected in this volume are a series of Romantic-period descriptions of the Islamic East, covering the geographical extent of a region that reached from Africa to India and incorporated three empires. Taken from British and French accounts, they represent Europe's complex investment in the Levant and reflect European conflicts as they were manifested in foreign policy, scientific interest, literary representations and orientalist fantasy.

Volney:
Travels through Syria and Egypt

Constantin François Chasseboeuf, comte de Volney, *Travels through Syria and Egypt, in the Years 1783, 1784, and 1785. Containing the Present Natural and Political State of those Countries, their Productions, Arts, Manufactures, and Commerce; with Observations on the Manners, Customs, and Government of the Turks and Arabs. Illustrated with Copper Plates,* 2 vols (London: G. G. J. & J. Robinson, 1787), vol. I, pp. 369–85, 394–418.

Like the other texts reproduced in the present volume, Constantin François Chasseboeuf (1757–1820), comte de Volney's *Travels through Syria and Egypt* participated in the ideological partnership formed between travel writing and empire in the Romantic period. As such, it is a valuable record of European representational fantasies about the East and its native inhabitants. However, late eighteenth-century travel writing could also serve directly practical purposes in the expansion of empire, and a small number of these narratives were distinguished by their material contributions to European foreign policy. Volney's account of Syria and Egypt ranks amongst these texts. Just as Sir Mark Wood's account of Malta (see below, pp. 91–115) functioned as thinly veiled war propaganda, Volney's narrative descriptions of the character, climate and commerce within the region guided Napoleon's 1798 invasion of the East.

Volney's first published work, *Travels through Syria and Egypt* (1787) was warmly received by reading audiences throughout Europe, and it attracted the early attention of political leaders. Catherine the Great, Empress of Russia, awarded Volney a medal of gratitude for the publication in 1787, and in America both George Washington and Thomas Jefferson expressed admiration for the usefulness of the volume. Indeed, throughout the period, Volney's narrative was repeatedly cited for its pragmatic value, and contemporary reviewers praised 'the accuracy of his account and the justness of his observations' (see Count Daru, 'Life of Volney', in *The Ruins, or, Meditations on the Revolutions of Empire* (New York, 1926), p. xvi). Volney's descriptions were, of course, as romanticised as those of any other European traveller during the period, but what the contemporary reading audience seems to have responded to was the narrative's value as a political handbook. While to the Americans his account of Ottoman decline and his assessment of revolution offered the new republic a cautionary tale at a critical period in its political development, to the established empires of Europe Volney's narrative offered an invitation to expansion. The Ottoman East, he argued, was ripe for revolution. The Arab people had no commitment to the 'despoiling government' of their Ottoman Mameluke rulers. An 'enlightened' usurper might perhaps even be welcomed.

When Napoleon began his Egypto-Syrian campaign in 1798, he was in some respects taking up the invitation Volney's travel account had offered. Certainly, Napoleon occupied Egypt expecting some degree of popular support. Entering Cairo on 2 July 1798, Napoleon declared to the people: 'I have come to restore your rights and to punish the usurpers ... I respect God ... and the Koran far more than the Mamelukes do' (quoted in Alan Schom, *Napoleon Bonaparte* (New York, 1997), p. 111), and he anticipated a peaceful transition to French republican rule. To the degree that Napoleon had invested Egypt and Syria with Enlightenment fantasies of revolution, he was following in the spirit of Volney's text. Meanwhile, Volney's travel account also guided this effort at French colonial expansion in pragmatic and material ways. As contemporary reviewers had noted, it was full of precise geographical and cultural information on a region largely unfamiliar to European travellers at the time. Throughout both the Egyptian and the Syrian campaigns, Volney's narrative provided Napoleon with information that would be turned to concrete military advantage.

Volney, of course, was not an unwitting participant in these political realms. In fact, in the period after the French Revolution, Volney became a sometimes prominent politician, and his personal relationship with Napoleon dated to the early years of the Revolution. By 1789 Volney was serving as Deputy to the States-General; by 1790 he had been appointed Secretary in the National Assembly; in 1792 he travelled to Corsica. A critic of Robespierre, upon his return to Paris he was imprisoned for ten months during 1793 and 1794. Released after the coup of 9 Thermidor, Volney travelled for several years (1795–8) in North America, publishing an influential travel account entitled *On the Climate and Soil of the United States of America* (1803), which included the first geological map of the country. Upon his return to France, he again appeared briefly on the political stage during the events of 18 Brumaire (1799), where he strongly supported the Bonaparte–Sieyès coup. Subsequently appointed to both the Académie française and Napoleon's Senate, he was elevated to the title of count in 1808 in recognition of his service to the Bonaparte empire. In 1814 his peerage was confirmed by Louis XVIII.

Volney's other important publications include: *The Ruins, or, Meditations on the Revolutions of Empire* (1791); *Account of the Present State of Corsica* (1793); *The Law of Nature, or Physical Principles of Morality* (1793); *Lectures on History* (1800); and *New Researches on Ancient History* (1814).

C H A P. XXIII.

Of the paſtoral, or wandering Tribes of Syria.

S E C T. I.

Of the Turkmen.

THE Turkmen are of the number of thoſe Tartar hordes, who, on the great revolutions of the empire of the Califs, emigrated from the eaſtward of the Caſpian ſea, and ſpread themſelves over the vaſt plains of Armenia and Aſia Minor. Their language is the ſame with that of the Turks, and their mode of life nearly ſimilar to that of the Bedouin Arabs. Like them, they are paſtors, and conſequently obliged to travel over immenſe tracts of land to procure ſubſiſtence for their numerous herds. But there is this difference, that the countries frequented by the Turkmen being rich in paſturage, they can feed more cattle on them, and are therefore leſs diſperſed than the Arabs of the defert. Each of their *ordous*, or camps, acknowledges a Chief, whofe power is not determined by fixed laws, but governed by cuftom and circum- ftances. It is rarely abufed, becaufe the fociety is compact, and the nature of their fituation maintains fufficient equality among its members. Every man able to bear arms is anxious to carry them, fince on his in- dividual force depend both his perfonal fafety, and the refpect paid him by his companions. All their property confifts in cattle, that is camels, buffaloes, goats, and efpecially fheep. They live on milk, butter, and meat, which are in great abundance among them, and the furplus of which they fell in the towns and the neighbouring country, for they are almoft able alone to fupply the butcheries. In return, they take arms, clothes, money, and corn. Their women fpin wool, and make carpets, the ufe of which is immemo- rial in thefe countries, and confequently in- dicates their manner of living to have been al- ways the fame. As for the men, their whole occupation confifts in fmoking, and look- ing after their flocks. Perpetually on horfe-back, with their lances on their shoulders, their crooked sabres by their sides, and their pistols in their belts, they are expert horsemen and indefatigable soldiers. They have frequent differences with the Turks, who dread them; but as they are divided among themselves, and form separate camps, they do not assume that superiority which their combined forces would ensure them. The Pachalics of Aleppo and Damascus, which are the only parts of Syria they frequent, may be computed to contain about thirty thousand wandering Turkmen. A great number of these tribes pass, in summer, into Armenia and Caramania, where they find grass in greater abundance, and return to their former quarters in the winter. The Turkmen are reputed Musfulmen, and generally bear the distinguishing mark, circumcision. But they trouble themselves very little about religion, and they have neither the ceremonies, nor the fanaticism of sedentary nations. As for their manners, to describe them accurately, it would be necessary to have lived among them. They have, however, the reputation of not being robbers, like the Arabs, though they are neither less generous, nor less hospitable than they;

and when we confider that they live in plenty, without being rich, and are inured to war, and hardened by fatigue and danger, we may prefume they are equally removed from the ignorance and fervility of the peafants, and the corruption and felfifhnefs of the inhabitants of the towns.

S E C T. II.

Of the Curds.

The Curds are another national body, the divided tribes of which are equally difperfed over the Lower Afia, and have extended themfelves pretty confiderably, efpecially within the laft hundred years. Their original country is the chain of mountains from whence iffue the different branches of the Tigris, which, furrounding the upper part of the great Zab, paffes to the fouthward, as far as the frontiers of the Irak-adjami, or Perfian Irak *(a)*. In modern geography, it

(*a*) *Adjam* is the Arabic name for the Perfians. The Greeks were acquainted with it, and exprefled it by *Ache-men-ides.*

is known by the name of *Curd-eftan*. This country is mentioned in the moft ancient traditions and hiftories of the eaft, in which it is made the fcene of feveral mythological events. The Chaldean Berofus, and the Armenian Maribas, cited by Mofes Chorenenfis, affert that it was in the mountains Gord-ouæis *(b)*, that Xifuthrus landed after efcaping from the deluge; and the local circumftances which they add, prove, what was otherwife fufficiently evident, that *Gord* and *Curd* are the fame. Thofe were the fame Curds who are mentioned by Xenophon under the denomination of *Card-uchi*, and who oppofed the retreat of the Ten Thoufand. This hiftorian obferves that, though fhut in on all fides by the Perfian empire, they had conftantly braved the power of the *Great King*, and the arms of his *Satraps*. They have changed but little in their modern ftate; and, though, in appearance, tributaries to the Porte, pay very little refpect to the orders of the Grand Signior, or his Pachas. M. Niebuhr, who travelled in thefe countries in 1769, reports, that in their mountains they are fubject to a

(b) Strabo, lib. 11. fays, that the Niphates, and its chain of mountains, are called *Gordouæi.*

fort of feodal government, which appears to
me fimilar to that we obferve among the
Druzes. Each village has its chief, and the
whole nation is divided into different and
independent factions. The difputes infepa-
rable from this ftate of anarchy have detached from the nation a great number of
tribes and families, which have adopted the
wandering life of the Turkmen and Arabs.

Thefe are difperfed in the Diarbekir, and
over the plains of Arzroum, Erivan, Sivas,
Aleppo and Damafcus : all their tribes united
are eftimated to exceed one hundred and
forty thoufand *tents*, that is, one hundred
and forty thoufand armed men. Like the
Turkmen, thefe Curds are paftors and wanderers; but differ from them in fome particular cuftoms. The Turkmen give their
daughters a marriage dower : the Curds
receive a premium for them. The Turkmen
pay no refpect to that antiquity of extraction which we call nobility : the Curds honour it above every thing. The Turkmen
do not fteal : the Curds are almoft every
where looked upon as plunderers; on which
account, they are much dreaded in the neighbourhood of Aleppo, and of Antioch, where

they occupy, under the name of Bagdafhlia, the mountains to the eaft of Beilam, as far as near Kles. In this Pachalick, and in that of Damafcus, their number exceeds twenty thoufand tents and huts; for they have alfo fixed habitations. They are reputed Mahometans; but they never trouble themfelves about religious rites or opinions. Several of them, diftinguifhed by the name of Yazdia, worfhip *Shaitan,* or Satan, that is, the genius who is the *enemy* (of God). This notion, efpecially prevalent in the Diarbekir, and the frontiers of Perfia, is a relic of the ancient fyftem of the *good* and *evil principles,* which, varied according to the fpirit of the Perfian, Jewifh, Chriftian, and Mahometan doctrines, has continually prevailed in thefe countries. Zoroafter is generally confidered as its author; but, long before his time, Egypt acknowledged Orofmades and Arimanius, under the names of Ofiris and Typhon. It is no lefs an error, likewife, to fuppofe, that this dogma was not propagated prior to the reign of Darius Hyftafpes, fince Zoroafter, who taught it, flourifhed in Media, and was cotemporary with Solomon.

Language is the principal indication of
the confanguinity of nations. That of the
Curds is divided into three dialects. It has
neither the afpirations nor the gutturals of
the Arabic; and I am affured that it does
not refemble the Perfian; fo that it muft be
an original language. Now, if we confider
the antiquity of the people who fpeak it;
and that we know they are related to the
Medes, Affyrians, Perfians, and even the
Parthians *(c)*, we may be allowed to conjecture, that a knowledge of this tongue
might throw fome light on the ancient hiftory of thefe countries. There is no known
dictionary of it; but it would be no difficult matter to form one. If the government
of France fhould think proper to offer en-
couragements to the Drogmen, or to the mif-
fionaries of Aleppo, the Diarbekir, or Bagdad, proper perfons might foon be found to
accomplifh fuch an undertaking *(d)*.

(c) " On the Tigris," fays Strabo, lib. 16, " are
" many places belonging to the Parthians, whom the
" ancients called Carduchi."

(d) The Emprefs of Ruffia has lately given orders to
Doctor Pallas to make a collection of all the languages

S e c t. III.

Of the Bedouin Arabs.

A third wandering people in Syria, are the Bedouin Arabs, whom we have already found in Egypt. Of thefe I made but a flight mention in treating of that province, be-caufe, having only had a tranfient view of them, without knowing their language; their name fuggefted but few ideas to my mind; but having been better acquainted with them

fpoken in the Ruffian empire; and thefe refearches muft extend even to the Cuban and Georgia; and, perhaps, to Curdeftan. When this collection is completed, it will be neceffary to reduce all the alphabet of thefe languages to one; for this diverfity of Arabic, Arme-nian, Georgian, Iberian, and Tartarian alphabet is a great obftacle to the advancement of fcience. This will, perhaps, appear impoffible to many perfons; but, from fome experiments of the fame nature, which I have myfelf made, I think I may venture to pronounce it not only practicable, but eafy. It is fufficient to be well acquainted with the elements of fpeech, to be able to clafs the vowels and confonants of all the alpha-bets. It is proper alfo to obferve here, that the firft book of every nation is the dictionary of its language.

in Syria; having even made a journey to one
of their camps, near Gaza, and lived feveral
days among them, I am now able to treat
of them with more minutenefs and accuracy.

In general, when fpeaking of the Arabs,
we fhould diftinguifh whether they are cultivators, or paftors; for this difference in their
mode of life occafions fo great a one in their
manners, and genius, that they become almoft foreign nations, with refpect to each
other. In the former cafe, leading a fedentary life, attached to the fame foil, and fubject to regular governments, the focial ftate
in which they live, very nearly refembles
our own. Such are the inhabitants of the
Yemen; and fuch, alfo, are the defcendants
of thofe ancient conquerors, who have either
entirely, or in part, given inhabitants to
Syria, Egypt, and the Barbary ftates. In
the fecond inftance, having only a tranfient
intereft in the foil, perpetually removing
their tents from one place to another, and
under fubjection to no laws, their mode of
exiftence is neither that of polifhed nations,
nor of favages; and, therefore, more particularly merits our attention. Such are the

Bedouins, or inhabitants of the vaſt deſerts which extend from the confines of Perſia, to Morocco. Though divided into independent communities, or tribes, not unfrequently hoſtile to each other, they may ſtill be conſidered as forming one nation. The reſemblance of their language is a manifeſt token of this relationſhip. The only difference that exiſts between them is, that the African tribes are of a leſs ancient origin, being poſterior to the conqueſt of theſe countries by the Califs, or ſucceſſors of Mahomet; while the tribes of the deſert of Arabia, properly ſo called, have deſcended by an uninterrupted ſucceſſion from the remoteſt ages; and it is of theſe I mean more eſpecially to treat, as being more immediately connected with my ſubject. To theſe the orientals are accuſtomed to appropriate the name of Arabs, as being the moſt ancient, and the pureſt race. The term *Bedaoui* is added as a ſynonimous expreſſion, ſignifying, as I have obſerved, inhabitant of the *Deſert*; and this term has the greater propriety, as, the word *Arab*, in the ancient language of theſe countries, ſignifies a ſolitude or deſert.

It is not without reaſon that the inhabitants of the deſert boaſt of being the pureſt, and the beſt preſerved race of all the Arab tribes : for never have they been conquered, nor have they mixed with any other people, by making conqueſts; for thoſe by which the general name of Arabs has been rendered famous, really belong only to the tribes of the Hedjaz, and the Yemen; thoſe who dwelt in the interior of the country, never emigrated at the time of the revolution effected by Mahomet; or if they did take any part in it, it was confined to a few individuals, detached by motives of ambition. Thus we find the prophet, in his Koran, continually ſtiling the Arabs of the deſert rebels, and infidels; nor has ſo great a length of time produced any very conſiderable change. We may aſſert they have, in every reſpect, retained their primitive independence and ſimplicity. Every thing that ancient hiſtory has related of their cuſtoms, manners, language, and even their prejudices, is almoſt minutely true of them to this day; and if we conſider, beſides, that this unity of character, preſerved through ſuch a number of ages, ſtill ſubſiſts, even in the moſt diſtant ſituations, that is, that the tribes moft remote from each other preferve an exact refemblance, it muft be allowed, that the circumftances which accompany fo peculiar a moral ftate, are a fubject of moft curious enquiry.

In Europe, and efpecially in its more civilized and improved countries, where we have no examples of wandering people, we can fcarcely conceive what can induce men to adopt a mode of life fo repugnant to our ideas. We, even conceive with difficulty what a defert is, or how it is poffible for a country to have inhabitants, if it be barren; or why it is not better peopled, if it be fufceptible of cultivation. I have been perplexed, myfelf, with thefe difficulties, as well as others; for which reafon, I fhall dwell more circumftantially on the facts which will furnifh us with their explanation.

The wandering and paftoral life led by feveral Afiatic nations, arifes from two caufes. The firft is, the nature of the foil, which, being improper for cultivation, compels men to have recourfe to animals, which content themfelves with the wild herbage of the earth. Where this herbage is

but thin, a single animal will soon consume
the produce of a great extent of ground,
and it will be neceſſary to run over large
tracts of land. Such is the caſe of the
Arabs in the deſert of Arabia, properly ſo
called, and in that of Africa.

The ſecond cauſe muſt be attributed to
habit; ſince the ſoil is cultivable, and even
fertile, in many places; ſuch as the frontiers
of Syria, the Diarbekir, Natolia, and the
greateſt part of the diſtricts frequented by
the Curds and Turkmen. But it appears
to me that theſe habits are only the effect
of the political ſtate of the country, ſo that
the primary cauſe of them muſt be referred
to the government itſelf. This opinion is
ſupported by daily facts; for as often as the
different hordes and wandering tribes find
peace and ſecurity, and a poſſibility of procuring ſufficient proviſions, in any diſtrict,
they take up their reſidence in it, and adopt,
infenſibly, a ſettled life, and the arts of cultivation. But when, on the contrary, the
tyranny of the government drives the inhabitants of a village to extremity, the pea-
ſants deſert their houſes, withdraw with their
families into the mountains, or wander in

the plains, taking care frequently to change their place of habitation, to avoid being furprifed. It often happens even that individuals, turned robbers, in order to withdraw themfelves from the laws, or from tyranny, unite and form little camps, which maintain themfelves by arms, and, increafing, become new hordes, and new tribes. We may pronounce, therefore, that in cultivable countries, the wandering life originates ʾr the injuftice or want of policy of the government ; and that the fedentary and cultivating ftate is that to which mankind is moft naturally inclined.

With refpect to the Arabs, they feem efpecially condemned to a wandering life, by the very nature of their deferts. To paint to himfelf thefe deferts, the reader muft imagine a fky almoft perpetually inflamed, and without clouds, immenfe and boundlefs plains, without houfes, trees, rivulets, or hills, where the eye frequently meets nothing but an extenfive and uniform horizon, like the fea, though in fome places the ground is uneven and ftoney. Almoft invariably naked on every fide, the earth prefents nothing but a few wild plants, thinly scattered, and thickets, whose solitude is rarely disturbed but by antelopes, hares, locusts, and rats. Such is the nature of nearly the whole country, which extends six hundred leagues in length, and three hundred in breadth, and stretches from Aleppo to the Arabian sea, and from Egypt to the Persian gulph.

It must not, however, be imagined that the soil in so great an extent is every where the same; it varies considerably in different places. On the frontiers of Syria, for example, the earth is in general fat and cultivable, nay, even fruitful. It is the same also on the banks of the Euphrates; but in the internal parts of the country, and towards the south, it becomes white and chalky, as in the parallel of Damascus; rocky, as in the Tih, and the Hedjaz; and a pure sand, as to the eastward of the Yemen. This variety in the qualities of the soil is productive of some minute differences in the condition of the Bedouins. For instance, in the more sterile countries, that is those which produce but few plants, the tribes are feeble, and very distant; which is the case in the desert of Suez, that of the Red Sea, and the interior

of the Great Defert, called the Najd. When
the foil is more fruitful, as between Damafcus and the Euphrates, the tribes are more
numerous, and lefs remote from each other;
and, laftly, in the cultivable diftricts, fuch as
the Pachalics of Aleppo, the Hauran, and
the neighbourhood of Gaza, the camps are
frequent and contiguous. In the former
inftances, the Bedouins are purely paftors,
and fubfift only on the produce of their herds,
and on a few dates, and flefh meat, which
they eat, either frefh, or dried in the fun, and
reduced to a powder. In the latter, they
fow fome land, and add cheefe, barley, and
even rice, to their flefh and milk meats.

★ ★ ★ ★ ★

I have already faid, that the Bedouin Arabs
are divided into tribes, which conftitute fo
many diftinct nations. Each of thefe tribes
appropriates to itfelf a tract of land forming
its domain; in this they do not differ from
cultivating nations, except that their territory

requires a greater extent, in order to furnish
subsistence for their herds throughout the
year. Each of these tribes is collected in one
or more camps, which are dispersed through
the country, and which make a successive
progress over the whole, in proportion as it is
exhausted by the cattle; hence it is, that
within a great extent a few spots only are
inhabited, which vary from one day to another; but as the entire space is necessary
for the annual subsistence of the tribe, whoever encroaches on it is deemed a violator
of property; this is with them the law of
nations. If, therefore, a tribe, or any of
its subjects, enter upon a foreign territory,
they are treated as enemies, and robbers, and
a war breaks out. Now, as all the tribes
have affinities with each other by alliances of
blood, or conventions, leagues are formed,
which render these wars more or less general. The manner of proceeding, on such
occasions, is very simple. The offence made
known, they mount their horses, and seek
the enemy; when they meet, they enter
into a parley, and the matter is frequently
made up; if not, they attack either in small
bodies, or man to man. They encounter

each other at full speed, with fixed lances, which they sometimes dart, notwithstanding their length, at the flying enemy; the victory is rarely contested; it is decided by the first shock, and the vanquished take to flight full gallop over the naked plain of the desert. Night generally favours their escape from the conqueror. The tribe which has lost the battle strikes its tents, removes to a distance, by forced marches, and seeks an asylum among its allies. The enemy, satisfied with their success, drive their herds farther on, and the fugitives soon after return to their former situation. But the slaughter made in these engagements frequently sows the seeds of hatreds which perpetuate these dissensions. The interest of the common safety has, for ages, established a law among them, which decrees that the blood of every man who is slain must be avenged by that of his murderer. This vengeance is called *Tar*, or retaliation; and the right of exacting it devolves on the nearest of kin to the deceased. So nice are the Arabs on this point of honour, that if any one neglects to seek his retaliation, he is disgraced for ever. He, therefore, watches every opportunity of revenge : if his enemy perifhes from any other caufe, ftill he is not fatisfied, and his vengeance is directed againft the neareft relation. Thefe animofities are tranf-mitted, as an inheritance, from father to children, and never ceafe but by the extinc-tion of one of the families, unlefs they agree to facrifice the criminal, or *purchafe the blood* for a ftated price, in money or fn flocks. Without this fatisfaction, there is neither peace, nor truce, nor alliances between them, nor fometimes, even between whole tribes: *There is blood between us,* fay they, on every occafion; and this expreffion is an infur-mountable barrier. Such accidents being neceffarily numerous in a long courfe of time, the greater part of the tribes have ancient quarrels, and live in an habitual ftate of war; which, added to their way of life, renders the Bedouins a military people, though they have made no great progrefs in war as an art.

Their camps are formed in a kind of irregular circle, compofed of a fingle row of tents, with greater or lefs intervals. Thefe tents, made of goat or camels hair, are black or brown, in which they differ from thofe of the Turkmen, which are white. They are ftretched on three or four pickets, only five or fix feet high, which gives them a very flat appearance; at a diftance, one of thefe camps feems only like a number of black fpots; but the piercing eye of the Bedouin is not to be deceived. Each tent, inhabited by a family, is divided, by a curtain, into two apartments, one of which is appropriated to the women. The empty fpace within the large circle ferves to fold their cattle every evening. They never have any intrenchments; their only advanced guards and patroles are dogs; their horfes remain faddled, and ready to mount on the firft alarm; but, as there is neither order nor regularity, thefe camps, always eafy to furprife, afford no defence in cafe of an attack: accidents, therefore, very frequently happen, and cattle are carried off every day; a fpecies of marauding war in which the Arabs are very experienced.

The tribes which live in the vicinity of the Turks, are ftill more accuftomed to attacks and alarms; for thefe ftrangers, arrogating to themfelves, in right of conqueft, the property of the whole country, treat the

Arabs as rebel vaffals, or as turbulent and dangerous enemies. On this principle, they never ceafe to wage fecret or open war againft them. The Pachas ftudy every occafion to harafs them. Sometimes they conteft with them a territory which they had let them, and at others demand a tribute which they never agreed to pay. Should a family of Shaiks be divided by intereft or ambition, they alternately fuccour each party, and conclude by the deftruction of both. Frequently too they poifon or affaffinate thofe chiefs whofe courage or abilities they dread, though they fhould even be their allies. The Arabs, on their fide, regarding the Turks as ufurpers and treacherous enemies, watch every opportunity to do them injury. Unfortunately, their vengeance falls oftener on the innocent than the guilty. The harmlefs peafant generally fuffers for the offences of the foldier. On the flighteft alarm, the Arabs cut their harvefts, carry off their flocks, and intercept their communication and commerce. The peafant calls them thieves, and with reafon ; but the Bedouins claim the right of war, and perhaps they alfo are not in the wrong. However this may be, thefe depredations occafion a mifunderftanding between the Bedouins and the inhabitants of the cultivated country, which renders them mutual enemies.

Such is the external fituation of the Arabs. It is fubject to great viciffitudes, according to the good or bad conduct of their chiefs. Sometimes a feeble tribe raifes and aggrandizes itfelf, whilft another, which was powerful, falls into decay, or perhaps is entirely annihilated; not that all its members perifh, but they incorporate themfelves with fome other; and this is the confequence of the internal conftitution of the tribes. Each tribe is compofed of one or more principal families, the members of which bear the title of Shaiks, i. e. chiefs or lords. Thefe families have a great refemblance to the Patricians of Rome, and the nobles of modern Europe. One of the Shaiks has the fupreme command over the others. He is the general of their little army, and fometimes affumes the title of *Emir*, which fignifies Commander and Prince. The more relations, children, and allies he has, the greater is his ftrength and power. To thefe he adds particular adherents, whom he ftudioufly attaches to him, by fupplying all their wants. But befides this, a number of fmall

families, who, not being ſtrong enough to
live independent, ſtand in need of protection
and alliances, range themſelves under the
banners of this chief. Such an union is called *kabila*, or tribe. Theſe tribes are diſ-
tinguiſhed from each other by the name of
their reſpective chiefs, or by that of the ruling
family; and when they ſpeak of any of the
individuals who compoſe them, they call
them the *children* of ſuch a chief, though
they may not be all really of his blood, and
he himſelf may have been long ſince dead.
Thus they ſay, *Beni Temin, Oulad Tai*, the
children of Temin and of Tai. This mode
of expreſſion is even applied, by metaphor,
to the names of countries: the uſual phraſe
for denoting its inhabitants, being to call
them *the children of ſuch a place*. Thus the
Arahs ſay, *Oulad Maſr*, the Egyptians; *Oulad Sham*, the Syrians: they would alſo ſay,
Oulad Franſa, the French; *Oulad Moſkou*,
the Ruſſians, a remark which is not unim-
portant to ancient hiſtory.

The government of this ſociety is at once
republican, ariſtocratical, and even deſpotic,
without exactly correſponding with any of
theſe forms. It is republican, inaſmuch as

the people have a great influence in all affairs, and as nothing can be tranfacted without the confent of a majority. It is arifto-
cratical, becaufe the families of the Shaiks
poffefs fome of the prerogatives which every
where accompany power; and, laftly, it is
defpotic, becaufe the principal Shaik has an
indefinite and almoft abfolute authority;
which, when he happens to be a man of
credit and influence, he may even abufe; but
the ftate of thefe tribes confines even this
abufe to very narrow limits; for, if a chief
fhould commit an act of injuftice, if, for
example, he fhould kill an Arab, it would be
almoft impoffible for him to efcape punifhment; the refentment of the offended party
would pay no refpect to his dignity; the law
of *retaliation* would be put in force: and,
fhould he not pay the blood, he would be
infallibly affaffinated, which, from the fimple and private life the Shaiks lead in their
camps, would be no difficult thing to effect.
If he haraffes his fubjects by feverity, they
abandon him, and go over to another tribe.
His own relations take advantage of his mif-
conduct to depofe him, and advance themfelves to his ftation. He can have no re-

fource in foreign troops; his fubjects communicate too eafily with each other to render it poffible for him to divide their interefts,
and form a faction in his favour. Befides,
how is he to pay them, fince he receives
no kind of taxes from the tribe; the wealth
of the greater part of his fubjects being limited
to abfolute neceffaries, and his own confined
to very moderate poffeffions, and thofe too
loaded with great expences?

The principal Shaik in every tribe, in fact,
defrays the charges of all who arrive at or
leave the camp. He receives the vifits of the
allies, and of every perfon who has bufinefs
with them. Adjoining to his tent is a large
pavillion for the reception of all ftrangers
and paffengers. There are held frequent
affemblies of the Shaiks and principal men,
to determine on encampments and removals,
on peace and war; on the differences with
the Turkifh governors and the villages; and
the litigations and quarrels of individuals.
To this crowd, which enters fucceffively, he
muft give coffee, bread baked on the afhes,
rice, and fometimes roafted kid or camel; in
a word, he muft keep open table; and it is
the more important to him to be generous,
as this generofity is clofely connected with

matters of the greateft confequence. On the exercife of this depend his credit and his power. The famifhed Arab ranks the liberality which feeds him before every virtue, nor is this prejudice without foundation ; for experience has proved that covetous chiefs never were men of enlarged views : hence the proverb, as juft as it is brief, *A clofe fift, a narrow heart.* To provide for thefe expences, the Shaik has nothing but his herds, a few fpots of cultivated ground, the profits of his plunder, and the tribute he levies on the high roads, the total of which is very inconfiderable. The Shaik, with whom I refided in the country of Gaza, about the end of 1784, paffed for one of the moft powerful of thofe diftricts ; yet it did not appear to me that his expenditure was greater than that of an opulent farmer. His perfonal effects, confifting in a few peliffes, carpets, arms, horfes, and camels, could not be eftimated at more than fifty thoufand livres (a little above two thoufand pounds) ; and it muft be obferved that in this calculation, four mares of the breed of racers, are valued at fix thoufand livres (two hundred and fifty pounds), and each camel at ten pounds fterling. We muft not therefore, when we fpeak

of the Bedouins, affix to the words *Prince*
and *Lord,* the ideas they ufually convey; we
fhould come nearer the truth by comparing
them to fubftantial farmers, in mountainous
countries, whofe fimplicity they refemble in
their drefs, as well as in their domeftic life and
manners. A Shaik, who has the command of
five hundred horfe, does not difdain to faddle
and bridle his own, nor to give him barley
and chopped ftraw. In his tent, his wife
makes the coffee, kneeds the dough, and fu-
perintends the dreffing of the victuals. His
daughters and kinfwomen wafh the linen,
and go with pitchers on their head, and veils
over their faces, to draw water from the fountain. Thefe manners agree precifely with the
defcriptions in Homer, and the hiftory of Abraham, in Genefis. But it muft be owned
that it is difficult to form a juft idea of them
without having ourfelves been eye-witneffes.

The fimplicity, or, perhaps, more properly,
the poverty, of the lower clafs of the Bedouins, is proportionate to that of their chiefs.
All the wealth of a family confifts of move-
ables, of which the following is a pretty exact
inventory. A few male and female camels, fome
goats and poultry; a mare, and her bridle and
faddle; a tent, a lance fixteen feet long, a

crooked fabre, a rufty mufket, with a flint, or matchlock; a pipe, a portable mill, a pot for cooking, a leathern bucket, a fmall coffee roafter, a mat, fome clothes, a mantle of black wool, and a few glafs or filver rings, which the women wear upon their legs and arms. If none of thefe are wanting, their furniture is complete. But what the poor man ftands moft in need of, and what he takes moft pleafure in, is his mare; for this animal is his principal fupport. With his mare the Bedouin makes his excurfions againft hoftile tribes, or feeks plunder in the country, and on the highways. The mare is preferred to the horfe, becaufe fhe does not neigh (*), is more docile, and yields milk, which, on occafion, fatisfies the thirft, and even the hunger of her mafter.

Thus confined to the moft abfolute neceffities of life, the Arabs have as little induftry as their wants are few; all their arts confift in weaving their clumfy tents, and in making mats, and butter. Their whole commerce

(*) This ftrange affertion may be found in other authors. M. Chenier, in his *Recherches Hiftoriques fur les Maures*, Vol. III. page 139, affirms mares do not neigh. Mares in Europe, however, certainly neigh, as every body knows, or may know.

only extends to the exchanging camels, kids, ftallions, and milk; for arms, clothing, a little rice or corn, and money, which they bury. They are totally ignorant of all fcience; and have not even any idea of aftronomy, geometry, or medicine. They have not a fingle book; and nothing is fo uncommon, among the Shaiks, as to know how to read. All their literature confifts in reciting tales and hiftories, in the manner of the Arabian Nights Entertainments. They have a peculiar paffion for fuch ftories; and employ in them almoft all their leifure, of which they have a great deal. In the evening, they feat themfelves on the ground, at the threfhold of their tents, or under cover, if it be cold, and there, ranged in a circle round a little fire of dung, their pipes in their mouths, and their legs croffed, they fit a while in filent meditation, till, on a fudden, one of them breaks forth with, *Once upon a time*— and continues to recite the adventures of fome young Shaik, and female Bedouin: he relates in what manner the youth firft got a fecret glimpfe of his miftrefs; and how he became defperately enamoured of her; he minutely defcribes the lovely fair, boafts her black eyes, as large and foft as thofe of the gazelle; her languid and empaffioned looks, her arched eye-brows, refembling two bows of ebony: her waift ftreight, and fupple as a lance; he forgets not her fteps, light as thofe of the *young filley*, nor her eye-lafhes, blackened with *kohl*, nor her lips painted blue, nor her nails, tinged with the golden coloured *henna*, nor her breafts, refembling two pomegranates, nor her words, fweet as honey. He recounts the fufferings of the young lover, *fo wafted with defire and paffion, that his body no longer yields any fhadow* At length, after detailing his various attempts to fee his miftrefs, the ob-ftacles of the parents, the invafions of the enemy, the captivity of the two lovers, &c. he terminates, to the fatisfaction of the au-dience, by reftoring them, united and happy, to the paternal tent, and by receiving the tribute paid to his eloquence, in the *Ma cha allah* he has merited *(h)*. The Bedouins have likewife their love fongs, which have more fentiment and nature in them than

(h) An exclamation of praife, equivalent to *admirably well!*

thofe of the Turks, and inhabitants of the towns; doubtlefs, becaufe the former, whofe manners are chafte, know what love is; while the latter, abandoned to debauchery, are acquainted only with enjoyment.

When we confider how much the condition of the Bedouins, efpecially in the depths of the defert, refembles, in many refpects, that of the favages of America, we fhall be inclined to wonder why they have not the fame ferocity; why, though they fo often experience the extremity of hunger, the practice of devouring human flefh was never heard of among them; and why, in fhort, their manners are fo much more fociable and mild. The following reafons appear to me the true folution of this difficulty.

It feems, at firft view, that America, being rich in pafturage, lakes, and forefts, is more adapted to the paftoral mode of life than to any other. But if we obferve, that thefe forefts, by affording an eafy refuge to animals, protect them more furely from the power of man, we may conclude, that the favage has been induced to become a hunter, inftead of a fhepherd, by the nature of the country. In this ftate, all his habits have concurred to give him a ferocity of character. The great fatigues of the chace have hardened his body; frequent and extreme hunger, followed by a fudden abundance of game, has rendered him voracious. The habit of fhedding blood, and tearing his prey, has familiarized him to the fight of death and fufferings. Tormented by hunger, he has defired flefh; and finding it eafy to obtain that of his fellow creature, he could not long hefitate to kill him to fatisfy the cravings of his appetite. The firft experiment made, this cruelty degenerates into a habit; he becomes a cannibal, fanguinary and atrocious; and his mind acquires all the infenfibility of his body.

The fituation of the Arab is very different. Amid his vaft naked plains, without water, and without forefts, he has not been able, for want of game, or fifh, to become either a hunter or a fifherman. The camel has determined him to a paftoral life, the manners of which have influenced his whole character. Finding, at hand, a light, but conftant and fufficient nourifhment, he has acquired the habit of frugality. Content

with his milk and his dates, he has not defired flesh ; he has shed no blood: his hands
are not accuftomed to flaughter, nor his ears
to the cries of fuffering creatures, he has
preferved a humane and fenfible heart.

No fooner did the favage fhepherd become
acquainted with the ufe of the horfe, than
his manner of life muft confiderably change.
The facility of paffing rapidly over extenfive
tracts of country, rendered him a wanderer.
He was greedy from want; and became a
robber from greedinefs ; and fuch is, in fact,
his prefent character.   A plunderer, rather
than a warrior, the Arab poffeffes no fanguinary courage ; he attacks only to defpoil;
and, if he meets with refiftance, never thinks
a fmall booty is to be put in competition
with his life.   To irritate him, you muft
fhed his blood, in which cafe he is found to
be as obftinate in his vengeance as he was
cautious in avoiding danger.

The Arabs have often been reproached
with this fpirit of rapine; but, without
wifhing to defend it, we may obferve, that
one circumftance has not been fufficiently attended to, which is, that it only takes place
towards reputed enemies, and is confequent-

ly founded on the acknowledged laws of almoft all nations. Among themfelves they are remarkable for a good faith, a difintereftednefs, a generofity which would do honour to the moft civilized people. What is there more noble than that right of afylum fo refpected among all the tribes? A ftranger, nay, even an enemy, touches the tent of the Bedouin, and, from that inftant, his perfon becomes inviolable. It would be reckoned a difgraceful meannefs, an indelible fhame, to fatisfy even a juft vengeance at the expence of hofpitality. Has the Bedouin confented to eat bread and falt with his gueft, nothing in the world can induce him to betray him. The power of the Sultan himfelf would not be able to force a refugee *(i)* from the protection of a tribe, but by its total extermination. The Bedouin, fo rapacious without his camp, has no fooner fet his foot within it, than he becomes liberal and generous. What little he poffeffes he is ever ready to divide. He has even the delicacy not to wait till it is

(i) The Arabs difcriminate their guefts, into gueft *moftadjir*, or *imploring protection*; and into gueft *matnoub*, who fets up his tent in a line with theirs; that is, who becomes naturalized.

afked: when he takes his repaft, he af-
fects to feat himfelf at the door of his tent,
in order to invite the paffengers; his generofity is fo fincere, that he does not look
upon it as a merit, but merely as a duty:
and he, therefore, readily takes the fame liberty with others. To obferve the manner
in which the Arabs conduct themfelves
towards each other, one would imagine that
they poffeffed all their goods in common.
Neverthelefs, they are no ftrangers to property; but it has none of that felfifhnefs
which the increafe of the imaginary wants
of luxury has given it among polifhed nations. It may be alleged, that they owe
this moderation to the impoffibility of greatly multiplying their enjoyments; but, if it
be acknowledged, that the virtues of the
bulk of mankind are only to be afcribed to
the neceffity of circumftances, the Arabs, perhaps, are not for this lefs worthy our efteem.
They are fortunate, at leaft, that this neceffity fhould have eftablifhed among them a
ftate of things, which has appeared to the
wifeft legiflators as the perfection of human
policy: I mean, a kind of equality in
the partition of property, and the variety

of conditions. Deprived of a multitude of
enjoyments, which nature has lavished upon
other countries, they are less exposed to
temptations which might corrupt and de-
base them. It is more difficult for their
Shaiks to form a faction to enslave and im-
poverish the body of the nation. Each
individual, capable of supplying all his
wants, is better able to preserve his character, and independence; and private poverty becomes at once the foundation and
bulwark of public liberty.

This liberty extends even to matters of
religion. We observe a remarkable difference
between the Arabs of the towns and those
of the desert; since, while the former crouch
under the double yoke of political and religious despotism, the latter live in a state
of perfect freedom from both : it is true that
on the frontiers of the Turks, the Bedouins,
from policy, preserve the appearance of Mahometanism; but so relaxed is their observance of its ceremonies, and so little fervor
has their devotion, that they are generally
considered as infidels, who have neither law
nor prophets. They even make no difficulty
in saying that the religion of Mahomet was

not made for them ; " for," add they, " how
" fhall we make ablutions who have no
" water ? How can we beftow alms, who
" are not rich ? Why fhould we faft in the
" Ramadan, fince the whole year with us is one
" continual faft ? and what neceffity is there
" for us to make the pilgrimage to Mecca,
" if God be prefent every where ?" In fhort,
every man acts and thinks as he pleafes, and
the moft perfect toleration is eftablifhed
among them. Nothing can better defcribe,
or be a more fatisfactory proof of this than
a dialogue which one day paffed between
myfelf and one of their Shaiks, named Ahmed, fon of Bahir, chief of the tribe of
Wahidia. " Why," faid this Shaik to me,
" do you wifh to return among the Franks ?
" Since you have no averfion to our manners ;
" fince you know how to ufe the lance,
" and manage a horfe like a Bedouin, ftay
" among us. We will give you peliffes, a
" tent, a virtuous and young Bedouin
" girl, and a good blood mare. You fhall
" live in our houfe."—" But do you not
" know," replied I, " that, born among the
" Franks, I have been educated in their re-
" ligion ? In what light will the Arabs view

" an infidel, or what will they think of an
" apoftate ?"—" And do not you yourfelf
" perceive," faid he, " that the Arabs live
" without troubling themfelves either about
" the Prophet, or the *Book* (the Koran) ?
" Every man with us follows the direction
" of his confcience. Men have a right to
" judge of actions, but religion muſt be left
" to God alone."—Another Shaik, converfing with me, one day, addreffed me, by miftake, in the cuftomary formulary, " Liften,
" and pray for the Prophet." Inſtead of the
ufual anfwer, *I have prayed*, I replied, with
a fmile, *I liften*. He recollected his error,
and fmiled in his turn. A Turk of Jerufalem, who was prefent, took the matter up
more ferioufly : " O Shaik," faid he, " how
" canft thou addrefs the words of the true
" believers to an infidel ?" " The tongue is
" *light*," replied the Shaik, " let but the
" heart be *white* (pure) ; but you, who
" know the cuftoms of the Arabs, how
" can you offend a ftranger with whom
" we have eaten bread and falt ?"——Then,
turning to me, " All thofe tribes of Frank-
" eftan, of whom you told me that they
" follow not the law of the Prophet,

" are they more numerous than the muſſul-
" men ?" "It is thought," anſwered I, "that
" they are five or ſix times more numerous,
" even including the Arabs."—"God is juſt,"
returned he, " he will weigh them in his
" balance *(k)*."

(k) M. Niebuhr relates in his *Deſcription de l'Arabie*,
tome II. page 208, Paris edition, that, within the laſt
thirty years, a new religion has ſprung up in the Najd,
the principles of which are analogous to-the diſpoſition
of mind I have been deſcribing. " Theſe prin-
" ciples," ſays that traveller, " are, that God alone
" ſhould be invoked and adored, as the author of all
" things; that we ſhould make no mention of any
" prophet in praying, becauſe that too nearly re-
" ſembles idolatry : that Moſes, Jeſus Chriſt, Maho-
" met, &c. were in truth great men, whoſe actions
" are edifying; but that no book was ever inſpired by
" the angel Gabriel, or any other celeſtial ſpirit. In
" ſhort, that vows made in the time of imminent
" danger are neither meritorious nor obligatory. I
" do not know," adds M. Niebuhr, " how far we
" may truſt the veracity of the Bedouin who told
" me this. Perhaps it was his peculiar way of think-
" ing; for the Bedouins, though they call themſelves
" Mahometans, in general, care very little about either
" Mahomet or the Koran."
The authors of this new ſect were two Arabs, who,
having travelled, in conſequence of ſome commercial
affairs, into Perſia and Malabar, reaſoned on the di-

It muſt be owned, that there are few po-
liſhed nations whoſe morality is, in general,
ſo much to be eſteemed as that of the Bedouin Arabs; and it is worthy of remark
that the ſame virtues are equally to be
found in the Turkmen hordes, and the
Curds. It is ſingular alſo, that it ſhould be
among theſe that religion is the freeſt from
exterior forms, inſomuch that no man has
ever ſeen, among the Bedouins, the Turkmen, or Curds, either prieſts, temples, or
regular worſhip. But it is time to continue
the deſcription of the other tribes of the inhabitants of Syria, and to direct our attention to a ſocial ſtate, very different from that
we are now quitting, to the ſtate of a cultivating and ſedentary people.

verſity of religions they had ſeen, and thence deduced this general toleration. One of them, named
Abd-el-Waheb, in 1760, erected an independent ſtate
in the Najd; the other, called Mekrami, Shaik of
Nadjeran, had adopted the ſame opinions; and, by
his valour, raiſed himſelf to conſiderable power in thoſe
countries. Theſe two examples render ſtill more probable a conjecture I have already mentioned, That
nothing is more eaſy than to effect a grand political
and religious revolution in Aſia.

Niebuhr:
Travels through Arabia

Carsten Niebuhr, *Travels through Arabia, and Other Countries in the East*, trans. Robert Heron, 2 vols (Edinburgh: R. Morison & Son, G. Mudie and T. Vernon, 1792), vol. I, pp. 213–33.

Carsten Niebuhr (1733–1815) was the author of two travel accounts, both originally published in German and quickly translated into English as *A Description of Arabia* (1772) and *Travels through Arabia and Other Countries of the East* (1774). While Niebuhr's works provide a valuable account of European discoveries in and attitudes towards the territories of 'Felix Arabia', the complicated political and personal context within which his explorations were conducted offers the modern reader a rich portrait of the material realities of Romantic travel.

Born to an undistinguished working-class German family, Carsten Niebuhr was not 'a typical Romantic-period traveller and his career as an explorer and surveyor began largely by chance. A student of mathematics and astronomy at the University of Göttingen in 1758, Niebuhr was recommended by a professor as a possible addition to an expedition to Arabia then being proposed. Niebuhr was accepted and in 1760 the project was granted a commission from Frederick V, King of Denmark. With four other travellers and a Swedish servant, the royal expedition departed from Europe in 1761. In 1767 Niebuhr returned alone, the only member of the team to survive the hardships of the mission.

The object of the Danish mission was to investigate Egypt, Syria and Arabia, and the composition of the team reflected the diverse objectives of the expedition. While Niebuhr was sent as a surveyor and charged with producing maps of the region, other members included a botanist and naturalist (Petter Forskal), a physician (Christian Kramer), an artist and engraver (Georg Baurenfeind) and a linguist (Frederik von Haven). The first group commissioned to explore Arabia during the Romantic period, the enterprise promised to be both productive and popular. In addition to advancing European knowledge of the East, the Danish government had also hoped to profit materially and culturally from these orientalist researches, particularly anticipating the acquisition of valuable Arabic and biblical manuscripts.

The Danish government originally planned to publish the collective researches of the members and to this end each traveller was commissioned by Frederick V to keep a daily log of his personal observations. The collective account these journals record is unique amongst Romantic descriptions of the Middle East. In addition to providing the anticipated information on scientific and historical subjects, the journals testify to the material conditions of eighteenth-century travel in the East. Running throughout the accounts are allusions to the explosive personal tensions which undermined the expedition, anxious remarks about the physical dangers of caravan travel and records of the shocking death rate amongst these European travellers. A selection from Niebuhr's account, itself only part of a more extensive and dynamic possible record of this Arabian mission, is reproduced below.

The selection reproduced here records events that took place along the Red Sea, in the period of the tour immediately preceding the group's encounter with malarial fever, when personal tensions were running high. Travelling from Europe via Malta and Constantinople, the group had explored Egypt from 1761 to 1762, tracing sections of the Nile and then following the coast of the Red Sea as far as Jiddah. Early in the trip the conflict between von Haven and Forskal had become so intense that murderous plots were feared. Niebuhr had aligned himself with Forskal, and his distaste for von Haven is hinted at in the description of von Haven's dangerous interference with Islamic politics (see below, pp. 65–6). By 1763 the expedition had reached Arabia proper, and at Mokka the group encountered a malarial fever that killed von Haven and Forskal in rapid succession. By 1764, arriving in Bombay, Niebuhr was the only survivor.

Presumed dead by his Danish employers, Niebuhr followed the overland route from India to back to Syria, travelling incognito. Upon his unexpected arrival in Aleppo in 1766, he enjoyed a brief period of celebrity in European circles. Later that year, he left Syria to conduct an expedition into Palestine and Turkey, returning to Europe via Constantinople in 1767. Although it was a failed mission from the perspective of the Danish government, his account of the expedition, along with several superb maps, was published at his personal expense in 1772.

SECTION VII.

VOYAGE FROM SUEZ TO JIDDA AND LOHEIA.

CHAP I.

Departure from Suez.

During our absence, several small caravans had succeffively arrived at Suez; and the arrival of the great caravan from Cairo, followed foon after our return from Mount Sinai. Although from pirates properly fo called, there is little to be feared in the Arabic gulph, yet, fo unskilful are the mariners in thefe latitudes, that they dare not venture to any diftance from the coafts. This timorous mode of failing might expofe a fingle veffel to the robbery of the Arabs;—to a-void which, thefe fhips fail in little fleets; four always fetting out together, that they may join to defend themfelves.

After the arrival of the caravans, Suez feemed more populous than Cairo; and as fuch a multitude could not long find fubfiftence there, all were eager to fet out without delay. We were recommended to the mafters of two fhips that were to make the voyage. Although now accuftomed to live with the Mahometans, yet, in our paffage to Jidda, we fuffered a degree of uneafinefs, which we had not felt upon occafions of greater danger. Some Greeks had hinted to us, that the Muffulmans thought Chriftians unworthy of making this voyage in the company of the pilgrims who were journeying to the holy city; and that upon this account we fhould not go aboard with fhoes upon our feet. Some of the pilgrims, indeed, feemed to look upon us little lefs unfavourably than a Capuchin going to Jerufalem would regard a Proteftant. But, to be obliged to walk without fhoes upon the deck, was not an humiliating diftinction, confined to Chriftians: it was a reftraint to which all on board were fubjected. Nobody in thofe veffels but muft walk upon deck without fhoes.

To avoid the company of the Mahometans, we had hired an apartment which we thought the beft. In a chamber oppofite to ours, lodged a rich black eunuch, who was going to Mecca ;

and, ufelefs as it could not but be to *him*, was accompanied with his feraglio, like a Turkifh lord. In a large apartment under ours, were forty women and flaves, with their children, whofe crying and noife gave us no little difturb-ance. Every one of the other paffengers had hired a place upon the deck, where he remain-ed with his bales and parcels around him, hav-ing only a fmall fpace vacant in the middle, where he might drefs his victuals, fit, and fleep. Our Greek failors, who were very unfkilful, were perplexed by thefe incumbrances, and could not go about to manage the veffel, without trampling upon the goods of the merchants, which produced endlefs difputes.

Our veffel, although large enough to have carried at leaft forty guns, was very deeply la-den. Befides her own freight, fhe towed after her three large fhallops, and one fmall ; the three larger filled with paffengers, horfes, fheep, and even women of pleafure.

The mafter, an honeft merchant from Cairo, whofe name was *Schoreibe*, would not have been diftinguifhed among the feamen of Europe. He took upon himfelf the tafk of pilot to the veffel ; but was indeed a very unfkilful pilot. Between the two compaffes, where European navigators fet a light, he had placed a large magnet, to re-ftore, imperceptibly, as he faid, their magnetic virtue to the needles. It was with difficulty that I perfuaded him to remove it.

With fuch feamen, however, we were obliged to fail; although they durft not venture out into the open fea, but coafted round the fhores, at the rifk of being dafhed in pieces upon jutting rocks, or ftranded upon banks of coral. We had paid the mafter for our paffage, immediately after agreeing for it. But, according to the cuftom of the country, we were obliged to give an *acknowledgement* to the failors before going on board, which, in other places, is not expected till paffengers be leaving the veffel.

To avoid any difagreeable rencounters with the other paffengers, we had taken care to go firft on board. We had yet feveral days to wait, till the Governor fhould infpect the fhips, to fee whether they were not overladen. This duty he never fails to perform; for a fum of money is payable to him from each veffel, upon the occafion, which conftitutes a part of his revenue.

At length, after all thefe delays, the four fhips weighed anchor about midnight, on the 10th of October. The fide upon which we paffed would have been dangerous, if the wind had not been favourable; for it is covered all over with coral rocks. The fhips caft an-

chor every night; and we had then liberty to
go on fhore, if we chofe to run the hazard, in
order to fee any object of curiofity.

Chap. II.

Of the Harbour of Tor.

The harbour, in which we happened to caft
anchor, was once a place of fome confideration:
but the fmall fort of *Kalla and Tor* is now ruinous, and without a garrifon. In its neighbourhood, however, are fome remarkable villages;
the inhabitants of which, as of all this barren
coaft, live by fifhing.

The inhabitants of *Beled-en-Naffara* are Greek
Chriftians. In the neighbourhood is a convent,
but only a fingle ecclefiaftic in it. At *Bir* is a
well, the water of which is better than that at
Naba, but not equal to what the Arabs bring
upon camels from the hills. All the pilots who
fail between Suez and Jidda live in the village
of *Jebil.* Each of thefe pilots receives five
hundred crowns for the voyage; and gains
fomething, befides, in the courfe of it, by inftruct-
ing young perfons who accompany him, to
learn his art, which confifts merely in diftin-

guifhing where the fand-banks and beds of coral ly.

Mr Forfkal went on fhore to vifit the pretended *Valley of Elim*.   The ecclefiaftic belonging to the Greek convent, fent a guide to conduct him thither.   He found it overgrown with
date trees.   As he did not immediately return,
a report arofe in the veffel that he had been detained by the Arabs, for attempting to take
draughts of their hills.   Some merchants, who
were alfo janiffaries, fet inftantly out, to relieve and bring him back.   Happily, the report
turned out to have been falfe; and Mr Forfkal
returned, without having met with any unpleafant accident.

In this place, we had an opportunity of
feeing that whole range of mountains which
terminates with Jibbel Mufa, and forms a
mafs of which the mountain of St Catharine's
is the higheft peak.   One of thofe mountains rifes near Tor.   We had a diftinct view
of St Catharine's, and perceived how high it
towers above Sinai.   This vaft pile of mountains fills the whole tract between the two arms
of the Arabic gulf.   Near the fhore, thofe
mountains fink into fmall hills, which flope into fandy plains.

Chap. III.

Voyage from Tor to Jidda.

We continued, till we had failed as far as *Ras Mahommed,* to caft anchor every night. But, between that cape and the coaft of Arabia, we had to crofs the Red Sea at its full breadth. The Europeans think this the fafeft route, as there is not, through the whole, one rock on which a fhip can be wrecked. But, the Turks think themfelves undone, whenever they lofe fight of land.

So many misfortunes happen, indeed, from the ignorance of their feamen, that they have reafon for their fears. Out of four veffels that had fet out rather too late, in the foregoing year, two had perifhed in thefe latitudes. Some perfons, who had made the voyage in thofe veffels, narrated to us the particulars of that event, which afforded no bad fpecimen of the nautical fkill of the Turks. When the ftorm arofe, all the failors and paffengers leaped into the boats, and betook themfelves to the fhore. The two fhips being thus abandoned to the ftorm, one was dafhed againft a rock, and the other fank.

The mafter of the third cut away the cords of his boats, for which the paffengers threatened to cut him in pieces. But, by explaining to them their danger, and promifing to extricate them, if they fhould not perplex and impede him, he prevailed upon them to affift him in faving the fhip.

In our paffage, we found ourfelves in danger of a worfe misfortune than fhipwreck. The females, who were lodged under us, more than once fuffered linen, which they were drying, to catch fire, in confequence of which the veffel muft have been burnt, if we had not been alarmed by their fcreams, and haftened to their affiftance. The fecond time when this happened, our captain was enraged, and fent down an inferior officer into the feraglio, to beat the women for their careleffnefs. The infliction of this punifhment produced, at firft, no fmall noife among them ; but it was followed by four and twenty hours of a fweet filence. Thofe women were indeed extremely troublefome and indifcreet. Hearing their voices fo very near us, I was tempted to look through a chink, and faw three or four of them naked and bathing.

Nothing remarkable appeared upon the track by which we failed, unlefs a few fmall and defart iflands, and the fummits of fome diftant hills. The laft objects that remained within our view,

upon the coaſt of Egypt, were the famous mountains of emeralds, called by the Arabs *Jibbel
Sumrud.*

On the 17th of October, an eclipſe of the ſun
happened, which had been foretold to our Captain by Mr Forſkal. I ſhewed this phænome-
non through glaſſes to the Captain and the principal merchants, with which they were much
pleaſed ; for, among the Mahometans, a perſon
who can predict an eclipſe, paſſes for an univer-
ſal ſcholar, and eſpecially for a very ſkilful phy-
ſician. Mr Forſkal was conſulted by ſeveral of
the paſſengers, who fancied themſelves ſick upon a ſudden. He mentioned ſome harmleſs medicines to them, and recommended exerciſe and
a peculiar regimen. At length, one of the pilgrims complaining that he could not ſee by
night, my friend adviſed him to light a candle.
This humourous preſcription did him better ſer-
vice than the moſt profound ſkill in medicine
could have done : Thoſe Muſſulmans were pleaſed to find him thus accommodate himſelf to
their manners, and became very fond of him.

When we came near to the ſmall iſle of *Kaſſa-
ni*, the Turks began to expreſs their joy at having eſcaped the dangers of ſuch a paſſage, and
having ſo nearly reached the coaſt of Arabia.
Cannons and muſkets were fired ; the ſhip and

the boats were illuminated with lamps, and lanthorns; and all was exultation and jollity. The failors went round with a box, afking a dole from the paffengers; every one gave fome trifle; and they then threw into the fea,—not the money,—but the box in which they had collected it.

Continuing our courfe, we incurred confiderable danger, in doubling a cape furrounded with banks of coral, becaufe our pilot was drunk. He had frequently afked us for brandy, on pretence that he could not fee the hills, or the outline of the coaft, unlefs his fight were cleared by the drinking of a little ftrong liquor. We had refufed him, for fear of giving offence to the other Muffulmans; but we foon faw that they are not fo fcrupulous, for the Captain fent to us every morning for a quarter of a bottle of brandy to his pilot. The Greek merchants might perhaps have made him drunk, by adding to the dofe which he received daily from us.

We arrived foon after at *Jambo*, a walled town near the fea, and having a fafe harbour. Not having feen a fingle houfe, fince we had left Tor, we felt no fmall pleafure at the fight of Jambo.

Such as meant to take Medina, on their way to Mecca, went on fhore here. Three of our party alfo landed, and took their fabres in their hands, like the other paſſengers. An inhabitant of Jambo, ſuppoſing them Turks, gave them the ſa- lutation of peace, *Salam Alicum*, and entered fami- liarly into converſation, with them. But learn- ing that they were Franks, he became vexed at having profaned his form of ſalutation, by ad- dreſſing it to Chriſtians, and paſſionately railed at the inſolent audacity of theſe infidels, who dared to wear arms in Arabia. But the other Arabs not ſeconding his complaint, my fellow- travellers came on board, without meeting with any other unpleaſant accident.

After ſtopping for one day in this harbour, we proceeded upon our voyage, retiring by degrees. from the coaſt, near which many beds of coral rocks were ſcattered. We had an opportunity of ſeeing the town of *Maſtura*, which ſtands at the foot of a hill of the ſame name. We doubled Cape *Wardan ;* and anchored near *Rabogh*, a per- manent habitation of a body of Arabs, who live there in tents. We purchaſed from them a plentiful ſtock of proviſions.

Pilgrims, in their firſt journey to Mecca, are obliged to aſſume the *Ihhram* immediately after paſſing Cape Wardan, if the ſtate of their health permit. This is a piece of linen, which is wrap- ped round the loins. The reſt of the body is naked ; and in this ſtate, they proceed through the reſt of the pilgrimage, till they have viſited

the *Kaaba*. The only other garment they are
fuffered to wear, is a linen cloth upon the fhoul-
ders, which hangs down in the fafhion of a fcarf.
But many, under pretext of indifpofition, retained their ordinary drefs. Others, more devout,
affumed the Ihhram, although they had been
formerly at Mecca ; fo that by the evening, we
faw moft of thofe Muffulmans dreffed in a garb
different from what they had worn in the morning.

It may feem ftrange, that Mahomet fhould
have enjoined the obfervance of ftripping, which
is fo injurious to the health of the pilgrims. But
this law was inftituted at a time, when his followers were all Arabs, and there was little probability, that his religion would be propagated
in more northern regions. His defign was to
make the pilgrims appear with due humility,
and in the common drefs of the Arabs. Thofe
linens are ftill the only drefs worn by the inhabitants of this province. But the Turks, who
are accuftomed to wear warm clothes, and even
furred cloaks, find it extremely uncomfortable
to change thefe for the Ihhram. Superftition
maintains local cuftoms and inftitutions, even after circumftances have fo changed, as to make
them counteract the purpofes for which they
were originally intended. The members of feveral religious Orders retain, in cold countries,

the common drefs of the warm countries in which their Orders were inftituted. In a chilling cli-mate, we fee them repair, in the middle of win-ter, to damp, icy churches, becaufe the primitive Chriftians, in the mild climate of Afia, affembled through the whole year, in fuch buildings, which were there agreeable by their coolnefs.

At length, on the 29th of October, we arrived in the harbour of Jidda. The fame reafon which had induced us to enter the fhip before the other paffengers, difpofed us to remain in it till they had all gone on fhore. Every one was eager to get away with his goods affoon as poffible, and to conceal them as much as he could from the officers of the cuftoms. They were particularly at pains to conceal their ready money, which pays two and a half *per cent*, of duty. One of the paffengers failed in the attempt to fecrete his money; for his purfe burft as he entered the boat, and his crowns fell into the fea. Thofe who defraud the cuftoms, fuffer no confifcation of their goods upon detection; they are only laughed at. In feveral places in Turkey, thofe detected in thefe practices are compelled to pay the duties double,

All who had been this way in the former year, and were now returning from the city, complained bitterly of the harfhnefs with which they had been treated by the cuftomhoufe officers. We were therefore perplexed about our ready money, not that we were unwilling to pay the duties, but we were afraid of being plundered by the Arabs. As the Mahometans are unacquainted with the ufe of letters of exchange, we had been obliged to carry with us in Venetian fequins, the whole fum that we intended to expend on our journey. After various thoughts, we refolved to put our money in the bottom of our medicine-cheft, referving only two hundred fequins, where we expected the officers of the cuftoms to fearch. Our ftratagem fucceeded; and no perfon offered to move our medicines.

The other three veffels which had fet out with us from Suez, did not reach Jidda till a confiderable time after our arrival. One of them, by the ignorance of the failors, had been in great danger in the courfe of the paffage. She was even overturned in the road, the failors having, in order to gratify the impatience of the merchants, in difcharging the cargoe, placed too great a weight of goods upon the ftem of the fhip. She was again raifed upon her keel, but a great part of the goods had fallen into the fea, and were much damaged, a new inftance this, of the unfkilfulnefs of the Turkifh feamen.

CHAP. IV.

Of Jidda and its Vicinity.

WE entered this city under ſtrong apprehen-
ſions of ill-treatment from its inhabitants. Re-
collecting with what contempt Chriſtians are regarded at Cairo, and how our companions had
been inſulted by the Arab at Jambo ; we feared, that we might experience ſtill more of the
inhoſpitable inſolence of the Muſſulmans, as we
approached nearer to their holy cities. But we
found ourſelves agreeably diſappointed. The
inhabitants of Jidda, who are much accuſtomed
to Chriſtian merchants in the European dreſs,
were not ſtruck with any thing ſtrange in our
appearance, and did not ſeem to take much notice of us. We went freely to the coffee-houſes
and markets, without ſuffering any inſults. But
we underſtood, that none except Muſſulmans,
are permitted to paſs through the gate that opens
towards Mecca, or even to approach it ; and
kept therefore carefully at a diſtance from that
gate, leaſt we might be diſcovered.

Our letters of recommendation were of great
uſe to us. Mr Gœhler had been perſonally ac-

quainted with the Pacha of Jidda, at Conftantinople, and had accordingly recommended us to
him.   We had letters from two confiderable
merchants at Cairo, to two of the principal merchants in Jidda.   A poor Schech had given us
one to the Kiaja, the Pacha's lieutenant: a recommendation from which we had not expected
much, but which was, neverthelefs, of more fervice to us than all the reft.

That Schech was fecretary to one of the principal members of the academy of *Jamea-el-A-
fbar*, at Cairo.   He had been born in European
Turkey, and having often heard of the fuperio-
rity of the European Chriftians in matters of fcience, he came frequently to fee us, and was eager to receive information from us.   He was a
truly worthy man, perfectly free from fuperftition, and a friend to the whole human race·
Mr Forfkal and I inftructed him in the elements
of botany and aftronomy.   He, for his part, was
very ufeful to us, exercifing us in the Arabic
language, and explaining to us many things of
which we muft otherwife have remained ignorant.   In his youth, he had given the Kiaja
fome leffons.   He had written, without our
knowledge, by the laft caravan, to prepoffefs his
old friend in our favour : and gave us, befides,
this letter to him.

As we had not time to deliver all our letters with our own hands, we sent thofe to the two merchants by our fervant, in hopes that they might find us lodgings. But when they under-ftood that we were fo many, they excufed them-felves, alleging that it was not poffible to find a houfe large enough. Had we been fewer, we might have taken chambers in the public *Kan.* Our Greek fervant, when we were thus at a lofs for lodgings, applied to one of his countrymen, who was goldfmith to the fheriffe of Mecca, and in great credit with the principal men in the ci-ty. This goldfmith informed him, that the Ki-aja, having had previous intimation of our com-ing, had given him orders to do us any fervice in his power. He even offered us the ufe of his own houfe for a night, and promifed us a whole houfe to ourfelves, by next day.

Upon receiving this notice, we went inftantly to deliver the Schech's letter to the Kiaja; who received us with great politenefs. We went af-terwards frequently to fee him ; and in our an-fwers to his queftions concerning the cuftoms and manners of Europe, we communicated to him and his friends, more juft and favourable i-deas of the Europeans, than they feemed to have before entertained. The Arabs confider us in the fame light in which we regard the Chinefe. They efteem themfelves the more enlightened and ingenious people; and think they do us great honour, when they rank us in the fecond place. The Kiaja was fond of converfing about aftronomy. Mr Forfkal, who often vifited him, perfuaded him to form a garden for plants near his houfe, and to bring from the interior parts of the country, the fhrub which produces the balm in Mecca. The Arabs looked upon this as a happy thought; and the more fo, becaufe the balm is not to be obtained pure at Jidda, but is commonly corrupted with an intermixture of extraneous fubftances, before it comes there.

After a few days, we delivered our letter of recommendation to the Pacha. He had alfo fome knowledge of aftronomy, and wifhed to fee our inftruments. He thought them better than thofe ufed in the Eaft, and fhewed them to a *Schech*, a learned Turk, whom he had with him. The Pacha and the Schech fpoke no language but the Turkifh, to which I was a ftranger. But we had enough of interpreters; and, among others, three French and Italian renegadoes in the fervice of the Pacha. Yet they knew not the terms of fcience, either in their native language, or in the Turkifh. I could not, of confequence, make myfelf well underftood by the Pacha; and our converfation upon thefe fubjects was not long nor profound. With the Kiaja I was obliged to fpeak Arabic, which

I found not a little difficult, being still ignorant
of the terms of science in that language.

On the 1st of November, after hiring a house,
we made our effects be carried to the custom-
house, before we should remove them into the
city, and had the pleasure ro obferve, that we
were not the less kindly dealt with for being
known to the Kiaja. That officer sat, in an e-
levated situation, with his clerks around him,
and directed the goods of the merchants to be
examined, piece by piece; but he was fatisfied
with opening our trunks, and did not make them
be emptied. The officers of the customs expect
a gratuity when they behave with discretion.
The Sherriffe's goldsmith, who had taken upon
himself the direction of our expence, gave them
a trifle in our name publicly.

The news of the arrival of a party of Europeans, among whom was an astronomer, soon
reached Mecca. The brother of the reigning
Sherriffe was at that time advancing with an
army, to attack the city. With the Mahometans, an astronomer is always deemed an aftro-
loger. The Sheriffe, therefore, directed his
Greek goldsmith to enquire of me, Whether he
should remain in possession of the sovereign
power, or be compelled to give place to his
brother? I excused myself from returning an
answer, as being ignorant of future events, and

and as cultivating aftronomy only to improve
the art of navigation. But Mr Von Haven replied, that, of the two brothers, he who bore the
greateft refemblance to Haffan, the founder of
the family, fhould remain victorious. This re-
fponfe turned out the more happily, that the
reigning Sheriffe was enabled to maintain himfelf upon the throne.

A nobleman in Jidda afked me to difcover to
him the thief who had ftolen two hundred fequins which he had loft. I alleged the fame
excufe as in the former cafe. He then applied
to a famous Schech, who was a better *aftrolo-
ger* than I. The Schech gathered all his fervants, ranged them in a line, and, after a long
prayer, made each of them take into his mouth
a bit of folded paper, telling them, that
they who were innocent might fwallow it with
fafety, but that the guilty perfon would be
choaked by it. They all fwallowed the paper,
fave one, who, being thus furprifed, and em-
barraffed, confeffed the theft, and made refti-
tution.

He is faid to have been Sultan *El Guri*, fove-
reign of Egypt, who, in the year 1514, furrounded Jidda with walls, to protect it from
the Portuguefe, then beginning to become formidable on the Red Sea. Thofe walls are ftill
ftanding, but are now fo ruinous, that a perfon

may, in-many places, enter over them on horſe-
back. The bridge is in an equally defencelefs
ſtate ; a ruinous battery, with one diſmounted-
cannon, is all that remains to ſhelter it. Some
cannons before the palace of the Pacha, are
good. for nothing but to return the ſalute of
ſhips.which enter the harbour. This palace
is but an indifferent building, like the houſes
of the other Paçhas through the Ottoman empire. In the city, however, are ſeveral fine
buildings of coral ſtone. But the other houſes
are ſlight wooden fabrics, like the ordinary
dwellings of the Arabs through the country.

The city is entirely deſtitute of water. The
inhabitants have none to drink, but what is collected by the Arabs, in reſervoirs among the
hills, and brought by them from thence upon
camels.

People of diſtinction in this place dreſs nearly as the Turks in Cairo. But, the poorer ſort
wear only a ſhirt without breeches. The Bedouins in the neighbourhood wear only the
Ihhram upon their loins. The dreſs of the women among the lower ranks is the ſame which
is worn by the Arabian females in general;
large drawers, a flowing ſhirt, and a veil. Many of the poorer people are employed in fiſhing,
by which they ſeem to earn but a ſcanty living.

The country lying immediately around this city, is fandy and barren. If we may believe tradition, thefe regions have undergone no change fince the creation; for the tomb of Eve is ftill fhewn in a fpot at no great diftance from the fea. But, I have remarked fome fure indications of the fea having receded from the furface of the land here as well as in other places. At a certain diftance from the fhore, are hills entirely compofed of coral-rock, and having a perfect refemblance to the banks of coral lying along the coaft.

As I was walking by the harbour, I had an opportunity of obferving a fingular practice, which the Arabs ufe for taking up wild ducks. The perfon, who is in fearch of the game, ftrips, puts fea-weeds upon his head, and approaches the bird. The duck, not being alarmed at the fight of the fea-weeds, ftirs not till the Arab feizes it by the feet.

Pococke, and fome other travellers, were not credited, when they fpoke of this mode of taking wild-fowls as practifed in China. But no fact can be more certain (AA).

Sonnini:
Travels in Upper and Lower Egypt

Charles Sigisbert Soninni, *Travels in Upper and Lower Egypt, Undertaken by Order of the Old Government of France* (London: J. Debrett, 1800), pp. 254–72.

Charles Sigisbert Sonnini de Manoncourt (1751–1812) was the author of two important travel accounts, published in English as *Travels in Upper and Lower Egypt, Undertaken by Order of the Old Government of France* (1800) and *Travels in Greece and Turkey, Undertaken by Order of Louis XVI* (1801). As his subtitles indicate, Sonnini spent his early career in the service of the French *ancien régime*, where he was employed as an engineer and naval officer. From 1774 to 1780, Sonnini travelled throughout Egypt and Syria in this capacity, and his second journey into the Ottoman Empire kept him in the East until 1793. He returned to Egypt for a brief period around 1800, reputedly discovering the ancient medical manuscript subsequently known as Napoleon's 'Book of Fate' in 1801.

As a traveller, Sonnini's passion was science, and his reputation in the Romantic period largely rests upon the research that he incorporated into his exploration accounts and later developed in a series of scientific publications, most notably his *Histoire naturelle, générale et particulière* (1802). As an example of eighteenth-century scientific method showing its relationship both to imperial rhetoric and to contemporary exploration literature, *Travels in Upper and Lower Egypt* is unparalleled. The account narrates the author's 'inspection' of Islamic Africa and discovers for the Western reader's gaze the culture's most private parts – from its sexual diseases to its operations of female circumcision. Indeed, Sonnini's descriptions are often profoundly disturbing in a way that many Romantic-period travel accounts are not. For while these preconceptions and attitudes were shared by many late eighteenth-century travellers, the clinical descriptions of suffering in Sonnini's account demonstrate forcibly the extent to which these 'orientals' were viewed as dehumanised 'Others'.

While Sonnini's rhetorical strategies are distinctively clinical, *Travels in Upper and Lower Egypt* was nevertheless part of a significant body of exploration literature discussing intimate subjects within an Eastern context. Contemporary travel accounts often examined the Islamic Levant as an object of medical interest, particularly in respect to sexual dysfunction and pestilential disease. Sonnini's interest in viewing native genitalia and their circumcision, for example, had its origins both in the travel writing of James Bruce, Carsten Niebuhr and Jean de Thévenot, and in the scientific speculations of Georges Buffon. His notes, meanwhile, offer valuable references to popular scientific texts on subjects related to Eastern disease.

One notable example of the relationship between science and empire in Sonnini's narrative is the distinction he draws between the Orient and Egypt. In terms of political resonance, the contrast is critical, because it reveals both the complexity of his representation and the ways in which it engages with late eighteenth-century European attitudes toward the Ottoman Empire. Ruled by Ottoman Turks or 'orientals', the African and Arabian 'natives' are, in at least one metaphoric instance in Sonnini's account, contaminated by their despots. While Egypt had long been accounted the 'cradle of the plague' in the scientific literature, Sonnini breaks with tradition to argue that the more probable source of the plague is Constantinople. Thus, portrayed as inherently licentious and corrupt, the oriental people become the originary source for the ills threatening Europe – a view that was later reiterated in Romantic literary representations of Constantinople, most notably Mary Shelley's novel *The Last Man* (1826). Meanwhile, in Sonnini's account, the native Egyptian inhabitants are represented as fundamentally irrational and unscientific, and as such they become unwitting participants in the production of their own misery. For Sonnini suggests that Western scientific measures might easily tame this inhospitable climate and render it productive were the locals amenable to such an enlightenment. By the turn of the century, as French imperial expansion in Egypt failed, this representation had also become a popular stereotype of the Eastern character. Thus, prepared for publication during the period of Napoleon's Eastern expedition and released in 1800, Sonnini's *Travels in Upper and Lower Egypt* perhaps anticipates, but more probably reflects, these contemporary anxieties of empire.

If the ufe of the Nile water has been reckoned the primary caufe of feveral complaints, the climate of Egypt has long been confidered as the focus of the moft terrible difeafes. A multitude of writers, and particularly M. Pauw, the conftant depreciator of Egypt, have afferted that this country was the cradle of the plague, that irrefiftible inftrument of death, and the theatre of its moft cruel ravages. This opinion has been fucceffively repeated and propagated even to our days. So late as the year 1773, a phyfician of Paris affirmed, that Egypt was the cradle of the plague *. Dr. Samoïlovitz, a Ruffian phyfician, alfo wrote, much about the fame time, that the plague habitually reigned in Afia, and efpecially in Egypt. It is only fince the travels of Savary and of Citizen Volney that the public has been undeceived, and perhaps fome partial doubts may ftill exift on the fubject.

It is neverthelefs very certain that the plague, which is endemical in feveral other countries of the Eaft, is not fo in Egypt, and that it never originates in that country. Whenever it makes its appearance, it has been brought thither, either from Conftantinople, from fome other part of Turkey, or from the interior of Africa. This latter kind, which is called *the Said plague*, becaufe it comes from Upper Egypt, is exceedingly dreaded. It is, in fact, more deftructive that that which is brought from other quarters.

And what proves that the climate of Egypt, far from producing the moft fatal of contagions, appears, on the contrary, to oppofe it,

---

* Expériences pour parvenir à déterminer la Nature du Venin peftilentiel, &c. par Mauduit, D. M. (Journal de Phyfique, du mois d'Août 1773).

is, that, at the period of my travels, it had not been felt there for upwards of twelve years, although the inhabitants took no precaution to secure themselves againft its introduction. Ships from Conftantinople, the real focus of a contagion inceffantly exifting, frequently touched at Alexandria; the caravans from Africa arrived at Cairo feveral times a year, and no peftilential fymptom had been perceived. It was even known that, in 1780, a caravel belonging to the Grand Signior had entered the old port of Alexandria with the plague on board. A man who was ftanding near a cheft that was opened, being ftruck with the peftiferous *miafmata* iffuing from it, fell down dead upon the fpot; neverthelefs all the Turks belonging to this ship came on fhore, and went into different parts of the town, without exciting the fmalleft anxiety; they even mixed with the inhabitants, and no bad confequence refulted from this intercourfe.

We may, therefore, banifh all uneafinefs refpecting the fate of our interefting countrymen, by whofe exploits and labours Egypt is at prefent honoured, as it was formerly by its civilization and its monuments. This country is by no means the *cradle of the plague*; the Arabs and the Turks who inhabit it, are not the *authors of this epidemical difeafe*; they do not fuffer it to *take birth, in a manner, under their feet**; and the moft fimple precautions will fuffice to banifh it from thence for ever. In the unfrequent inftances in which it appeared there, it occafioned great ravages; and this circumftance is alone fufficient to prove that it is not habitual in the country. Its effects were propagated in a manner equally fudden and terrible; the Turks confidered it far more deftructive than that in the midft of which they lived. It was always in the month of April that it made its appearance, and what was very fingular, is that the contagion never failed to ceafe at once at the fummer folftice. This epoch was alfo the term of the precautions which the foreign

---

* Recherches Philofophiques fur les Egyptiens et les Chinois, tome i. p. 91.

merchants took at Alexandria. The houfes were then again opened, intercourfe was refumed, even before inquiries were made refpecting the ftate of the difeafe; fo certain did they think themfelves that the period of its rage was at an end. The Alexandrians exprefs in *lingua Franca* the adage which their experience has made them adopt— *Saint-Jean venir, gandouf* andar* (Saint John is come, adieu to the plague).

It muft neverthelefs be admitted, that if the plague and the other difeafes which originate from putrid *miafmata*, were fo unfrequent, it was not that the then Egyptians did not do every thing in their power to render them common. They neglected the moft ordinary precautions. Under the hand of thefe barbarians, not only the traces of the grandeur of ancient Egypt were almoft all effaced, but fuch works as were the indifpenfable foundation of the fertility of the foil, and of the falubrity of the air, were daily difappearing. Marfhes had ufurped the place of ufeful lakes; fome canals were choked up; others, upon the point of being fo by the quantity of mud that was fuffered to remain in them, were nothing more, during a part of the year, than fheets of ftagnant water, diffufing afar a f id effluvium. The bodies of dead animals infected the plains, and fometimes the interior of the cities; in fhort, it feemed as if the inhabitants made it their ftudy to render their country unwholefome. And what opinion may not be conceived of the falubrity of a climate which, in fpite of the efforts of the demon of deftruction, in fpite of the mifchiefs of ignorant indifference, had not contracted any dangerous influence?

In fact, no epidemical difeafes there prevail. The new comer is not attacked by thofe violent and inflammatory fevers which, in our Weft India colonies, compofe the tribute of death; he is not there tormented by long intermittent fevers which, in thofe countries, are followed by numerous obftructions and dropfy. Frequent dif-

---

* Plague. In Arabic, *toubb*.

eafes come not to threaten the life of the ftranger, or of the native. Of us four Frenchmen, two only experienced any indifpofition. In Upper Egypt I was attacked by the ophthalmia in one of my eyes; and my draughtfman could not for a long time get rid of a cutaneous diforder which he had brought with him: the reft of the time we conftantly enjoyed a good ftate of health. We faw Turks arrive from Conftantinople, emaciated by debauchery and its attendant complaints, and after fome ftay, refume, at leaft, the appearance of health. No reafoning whatever can poffibly overturn facts; and differtations may be heaped upon differtations, as has been done by M. Pauw, in order to prove that Egypt contains the feeds of an infinite number of difeafes; experience, the cleareft of all demonftrations, will atteft the purity and falubrioufnefs of its atmofphere.

Some traces of the precautions taken by the ancient Egyptians in the burial of the dead, are ftill employed by the moderns. The art of embalming is unknown to them; but the care with which they arrange dead bodies, a care which is inculcated, it is true, by the precepts of the Mahometan religion, is ftill the veftige, or, at leaft, the fhadow of an ancient and forgotten practice.

As foon as a perfon is dead, the Egyptians prefs the different parts of the body, in order to make it difcharge all its impurities: they wafh it repeatedly, fhave it, pluck out all the hair, and ftop all the apertures clofely with cotton; they then pour upon them odoriferous waters, and the perfumes of Arabia penetrate into all the pores. After having lavifhed thefe attentions of cleanlinefs, and marks of refpect, upon inanimate remains, they commit them to the earth, and depofit them in the bofom of eternity. A fmall ftone pillar, crowned with a turban, is erected upon the fpot where repofes the head of the deceafed. Every Friday, at the foot of this fepulchral monument, they renew their mournful adieus. The women fail not to repair thither, and with devout enthufiafm, to exprefs their forrow and their hopes: the tears of the daughter bedew the face of the mother; while the groans of the mother, accompanied by painful recollections, prolong in her mind the exiftence of the children fhe has loft. I do not fpeak of the tears of hufbands; there are in this country none but mafters and flaves.

The exercife of this piety towards the dead, fo neglected in our weftern hemifphere, is a facred duty among the people of the Eaft; and no where is it better fulfilled. The idea that in dying we muft renounce every token of the affection of thofe who were deareft to us, appals the foul and drives it to defpair; but, when we are affured that regret and the marks of the moft tender fentiments attend us to the grave; that there exifts an affecting and durable intercourfe between the living and the dead; that on clofing our eyes to the light, we fhall not be the lefs furrounded by the objects we loved, it feems that the enjoyments of the foul are about to be perpetuated, and that they will be more perfect, becaufe they will be lefs fubject to interruption; and we boldly enter into this career of immortality, which fenfibility prepares.

Whatever may be their refpect for the dead, the Orientals think that they have no right to injure the health of the living. Befides, folitude and filence beft fuit the frequent and melancholy vifits they receive. The laft retreats of men are placed without the limits of any habitation. They are large, folitary, and filent enclofures: a thick layer of earth covers the bodies, and protects them from the derangement and confufion that the courfe of time might produce; a delicate precaution which the moft refined feelings alone can have fuggefted.

Coffins covered with fome fort of cloth, the colour of which is optional, are employed in Egypt to convey the dead to the place of interment. A turban, the privileged head-drefs of the Muffulmans, is placed upon the carpet above the head; and that their cuftoms may in no refpect agree with thofe of Chriftians, the dead are carried with the head foremoft. They are preceded by priefts reciting paffages of the Koran; and women fcreaming, crying, and moaning, for money, follow the coffin. It will readily be conjectured, that the better the pay, the more priefts and hired female mourners fwell the proceffion.

There being no places deftined for the interment of the French at Roffetta, thofe who died there were conveyed to Alexandria, where they were buried in the convent of St. George. The corpfe was accompanied by the vicar, a drogueman, and a janizary. Thefe funeral journies being made by land, they were very expenfive.

After having fpoken of the cemeteries of Egypt, it is natural to fay a word of the moft common difeafes that fend men thither. Though neither frequent nor epidemical, putrid and inflammatory diforders there attack thofe whofe conftitution is bilious. Dyfenteries occur in that country, though not fo frequently as in Europe. Herniæ are by no means uncommon; but it is not the Nile water which occafions them, as fome authors have fuppofed: they originate from the relaxation occafioned by the ufe of warm baths, from the exercife of riding without proper precaution, and, above all, from the extraordinary widenefs of a part of the Egyptian drefs. Cutaneous difeafes are common, and would be ftill more prevalent but for the ufe of the bath. The leprofy, and that horrible malady the elephantiafis, fometimes make their appearance; but they do not feem to be very contagious, for perfons afflicted by them are feldom met with.

This laft fpecies of leprofy, to which the ancient Egyptians alfo were fubject, deficcates and hardens the epidermis of the legs, and makes them very big, rugous, and fimilar in appearance to thofe of the elephant. It is peculiar to the northern part of Egypt, feldom appearing at any diftance above Cairo; a circumftance which the ancient Egyptians had likewife remarked *. Hillary, who had ob-

* *Eft elephas morbus qui propter flumina Nili*
 Gignitur, Egypto in medio neque præterea ufquam.   LUCRET.

ferved this dry leprofy at Barbadoes, never faw both legs fwelled at the fame time *. The contrary is the cafe in Egypt, where they alike acquire a frightful and prodigious fize. No remedy was there known for this difeafe: fome will, doubtlefs, be difcovered by the refearches and talents of the French phyficians, who will alfo have an opportunity of afcertaining the efficacy of the method employed by the Indian phyficians in the cure of the elephantiafis, and which is very minutely defcribed in the fecond volume of the Afiatic Refearches, printed at Calcutta.

There is, perhaps, no country in the world where the difeafes which corrupt the fources of generation are more widely fpread than in Egypt. The ravages of the *fyphilis*, although checked by the heat of the climate, abundant perfpiration, and warm baths, are not the lefs dreadful; and no remedy being employed to ftop its progrefs, it fometimes produces the moft frightful effects.

But a malady truly endemical, is the ophthalmia, or inflammation of the eyes. Egypt is the country of the one-eyed and blind. Eyes perfectly found, or which are not fwelled or watery, are rarely to be feen. Misfortune has likewife its bodies corporate; and the corporation of the blind at Cairo has fometimes revolted, and carried matters fo far as to make the government tremble.

If Haffelquitz † may be credited, the vapours which exhale from the ftagnant waters are the principal caufe of thefe complaints of the eyes. But the ancient Egyptians kept the canals in the higheft order: they cleanfed them, and never fuffered the water to ftagnate; they were, neverthelefs, afflicted with the ophthalmia. On this principle, the fame traveller accounts for the greater number of diforders of the eyes at Cairo, than in other parts of Egypt, by the exhalations of the canal which croffes that city. I have paffed almoft

---

* William Hillary on the Glandular Difeafe of Barbadoes. London 1759.

† Voyage dans le Levant.

whole days at the window of an apartment that overlooked this canal, in the month of Auguft, that is to fay, at the time when the moft fetid vapours exhale from it ; and excepting the offenfive fmell, I felt no fort of inconvenience. If there be more blind people at Cairo, it is becaufe its population is very confiderable, and befides, the poor flock thither from all parts, in hopes of finding more relief. But the difeafes of the eyes are equally common in the reft of Egypt. I preferved my eyes found at Cairo, and had like to have loft one of them in the Saïd.

The exceffive heat, the air impregnated with nitrous particles, the acrid and burning duft which the winds fcatter in the atmofphere, are the principal caufes of the diforders of this organ. When the wind was a little ftrong, I could not expofe myfelf for a moment, in the middle of the day, on the terrace of the houfe in which I refided at Cairo, without experiencing a very violent inflammation in my eyes. Thefe fharp pains I often felt for feveral days; and I fucceeded in getting rid of them only by the ufe of cooling lotions.

Among the caufes of the cecity fo general at Cairo, and in all the great towns, may be reckoned the frequent watering of the ftreets and houfes. In order to temper the heat, a great quantity of water is thrown about them feveral times in the courfe of the day. The ground, for the ftreets are not paved, being exceffively heated, emits nitrous and fiery exhalations that are pernicious to the eyes. When I was cured of the ophthalmia with which I had been afflicted, my eyes were exceedingly weakened; and I obferved, that whenever the ground, or the gallery in which I ftaid, was wetted, they became painful, and for fome moments I loft my fight. This remark, I think, has not yet been made. It is certain that water, thrown abundantly and frequently upon a burning foil, containing a great many faline particles, produces acrid vapours, which may be confidered as one of the principal caufes of blindnefs.

There exift alfo fome fecondary caufes that render the diforders in the eyes more frequent than they were in the time of the ancient Egyptians, as the bad quality of the food on which the prefent inhabitants fubfift, and which communicates to the humours an acrimony that neceffarily occafions feveral complaints, and particularly thofe affecting the fight; and to thefe may be added the exceffive propenfity of the Egyptians to pleafures which are feldom thofe of love*.

* *Multiplicatio coïtûs eft nocibilior res oculo.* Avicen. iii. cap. 5.

CHAPTER XXIII.

CIRCUMCISION OF THE WOMEN.—SECT OF THE SAADI, OR SERPENT-EATERS.

No perfon is unacquainted with the nature of the circumcifion of men; no perfon is ignorant that the Jews and Muffulmans are circumcifed. Among the ancient Egyptians this practice was confidered as indifpenfable. Whether it was really fo in their climate, is a queftion which I will not at prefent undertake to refolve; although I am pretty well convinced that circumcifion, if not altogether neceffary, is at leaft of very great utility among a rude and flovenly people. It is likewife in ufe among the Copts, who, not thinking themfelves fufficiently fure of admittance into paradife by virtue of the baptifm they receive as Chriftians, reckon it alfo neceffary to fubmit to circumcifion, following, in this refpect, as in feveral others, the precepts of the religion of the Mahometans among whom they live. How extraordinary is a religious practice which nature difavows, and which cannot be mentioned without modefty taking the alarm! The particulars of an operation, which is the fame among all thofe who follow the religion of Mahomet, will find their place in my Travels in Turkey; but in Egypt, it is not peculiar to the men: the women alfo undergo one of a fomewhat fimilar nature.

This latter fort of circumcifion was likewife practifed by the people of ancient Egypt. It has been tranfmitted to their defcendants alone; for thofe women who have come from other countries to fettle in this, have not undergone it, nor, indeed, have they occafion for the operation. I am fenfible how difficult it is to treat fubjects of this nature, without awaking other ideas than thofe which occupy the naturalift in his refearches; but this point of the natural hiftory of man is too important to be paffed over in filence; and no traveller, before me, has inveftigated and determined it with precifion. I fhall confine myfelf to fuch terms as anatomy has adopted. If it be, in any cafe, allowable not to be very intelligible to the generality of readers, it is, no doubt, on fo delicate a fubject.

It was well known that Egyptian women fubmitted to circumcifion; but authors were not agreed as to the motive of this cuftom. The greater number of thofe who have written on this practice, have confidered it as the retrenchment of a portion of the nymphæ, which grow, it is faid, in thefe countries, to an extraordinary fize. Others, among whom is to be diftinguifhed that illuftrious traveller James Bruce *, have imagined that it was nothing lefs than the amputation of the clitoris, the elongation of which is, according to the fame authors, a difgufting deformity. Mr. Bruce calls it *excifion*, an expreffion which his able tranflator has introduced into our language, and for which it is, in fact, not eafy to find a proper fubftitute.

Before an opportunity occurred of my afcertaining the nature of the circumcifion of the Egyptian women, I alfo imagined that it confifted in the amputation of the excrefcence of the nymphæ or of the clitoris, according to circumftances, and according as thofe parts were more or lefs elongated. It is even very probable that thefe operations take place, not only in Egypt, but likewife in feveral other countries of the Eaft, where the heat of the climate, and other caufes, may produce too great an increafe of thefe parts; and I had the more reafon to be of this opinion, from having confulted feveral Turks fettled at Roffetta, refpecting the circumcifion of their women, as they gave me no other idea of it than that of a painful mutilation of this kind, the motives of which they alfo explained. Being, as has already been feen, great admirers of a fmooth and polifhed

* Travels in Nubia and Abyffinia.

furface, every inequality, every protuberance, is, in their eyes, a forbidding defect. At the fame time they alleged that, by one of thefe operations, the women loft, with the ardour of their conftitution, the facility of procuring themfelves illicit enjoyments. A barbarous refinement of tyranny, and the loweft degree of debafement of the one half of the human fpecies, which, by cruel means, the other half moulds to its pleafures at the will of its jealous defpotifm !

M. Niebuhr relates that Forfkal, and another of his fellow-travellers, having expreffed to a man of confequence at Cairo, at whofe villa they ftopped, a very anxious defire to examine a circumcifed girl, their complaifant hoft inftantly ordered that a country girl of eighteen years of age fhould be brought in, and allowed them to examine every thing at their eafe. Their painter made a drawing of the parts from nature, in the prefence of feveral Turkifh fervants ; but he worked with a trembling hand, on account of the confequences to be dreaded from the Mahometans *. M. Niebuhr has not publifhed the drawing made with a trembling hand ; nor does he give any other information concerning this circumcifion ; but, from what precedes, it is clear that this traveller confiders it only as the amputation of the nymphæ and clitoris, the enormous excrefcence of which is fo difpleafing to hufbands in thefe countries.

I fufpected that there muft be fomething more than an excefs in thefe parts, an inconvenience which, far from being met with in all women, could alone have given rife to an ancient and general practice. At length I refolved to leave no doubt upon this fubject, and formed the defign, which muft appear fufficiently bold to any perfon acquainted with the inhabitants of Egypt, not of having a drawing made of a circumcifed girl, but of having one circumcifed in my own apartments. M. Forneti, whofe intelligence and obliging difpofition had fo often been ufeful to me, had the goodnefs to

* Defcription de l'Arabie, par Niebuhr, tome i. p. 71.

affift me in this enterprife; and by the mediation of a Turk, who ferved as a broker to the French merchants at Roffetta, I fucceeded in getting to my room a woman, whofe profeffion it was to perform circumcifion, and two young girls, one of whom had been circum-cifed two years before, and the other who was now to undergo that operation. M. Forneti, the Turkifh broker, the conful's janizary, and myfelf, were the only men prefent at the ceremony.

I firft examined the young girl that was to be circumcifed; fhe was about eight years old, and of Egyptian origin. I was very much furprifed to fee her with a thick, flabby, and flefhy excrefcence, covered with fkin. This excrefcence grew from above the commiffure of the labia, and hung down it about half an inch. A tolerably correct idea may be formed of its fize, and even of its fhape, by comparing it to the caruncle pendent from the bill of a turkey-cock.

The operatrix fat down upon the floor; made the little girl fit down before her; and, without any preparation, took out a bad razor, and cut off the fingular excrefcence which I have juft defcribed. The child did not fhew any figns of fuffering much pain. A pinch of afhes was the only topical application employed, although the wound difcharged a confiderable quantity of blood. The operatrix touched neither the nympha nor the clitoris; and thofe parts were not externally vifible, either in this girl, or in the other older one, who had already been circumcifed.

Such is the nature of the circumcifion of Egyptian females, and it may eafily be conceived that it is a neceffary operation; for this fort of elongated caruncle increafes in proportion to a girl's age, and if fuffered to remain, it would entirely cover the os externum. The woman who performed the operation affured me, that at the age of five and twenty, the excrefcence would be more than four inches in length. It is peculiar to the women of Egyptian origin; all others being exempt from it, though belonging to nations that are fettled in the country, and, in a manner, naturalized.

In general, this circumcifion is not deferred to the age of puberty, which takes place earlier in Egypt than in our northern climates; but the Egyptian girls are deprived of this troublefome fuperfluity at feven or eight years old. The women of the Saïd are thofe who are in the habits of performing this operation, which is attended with little difficulty, as the reader may have conceived. They go about the towns and villages, crying in the ftreets : *Circumcifer! Who wants a circumcifer?* A fuperftitious tradition has fixed the period in which circumcifion is to be praĉtifed, at the commencement of the increafe of the Nile. To find parents who would allow their daughter to be circumcifed in a feafon fo remote from that which is reckoned the moft favourable, was one of the difficulties I had to furmount: it was then winter; but money removed this obftacle as well as the others.

Now, if we confider the nature of an excrefcence, a diftinguifhing charaĉteriftic of the women indigenous in Egypt, we fhall difcover fome conformity with that which is peculiar to the inhabitants of the other extremity of Africa. Buffon was unwilling to give credit to the teftimony of the only traveller who has afferted, that the Egyptian women had a fort of hard fkin growing above the os pubis, and hanging very low; but which they deftroy by cauterization *. There was neverthelefs fome truth in the account of Thevenot, and much lefs exaggeration than in thofe of the Jefuit Tachard, and of Kolben, who, from imagination alone, had been led to defcribe the natural apron of the female Hottentots.

If this fort of natural veil be not what has been reprefented, it appears, at leaft, that its exiftence cannot abfolutely be denied; and if it be not a general appendage to the women of the fouth of Africa, it cannot be contefted that it is found among fome of the nations inhabiting that country. A celebrated modern traveller had at firft

* Hift. Nat. de l'Homme.

confidered this conformation as fabulous, becaufe he had not feen it in thofe parts which he vifited; but he has fince met with it among the favage Hottentots, at a great diftance from the Cape of Good Hope. He has given a drawing of one of thefe Hottentot women: it feems to indicate an elongation of the flefhy fubftance which covers the os pubis; and which, in falling perpendicularly over the labia, is divided into two parts. However, Le Vaillant, who confiders this fingularity only as the effect of art, or rather a caprice of fafhion, adds, that it is an elongation of the labia, the diftenfion of which is firft produced by rubbing and pulling them, and afterwards continued by the fufpenfion of weights, till they fometimes attain the length of nine inches *. Had Le Vaillant beftowed a little more time in the purfuit of his obfervations, upon a point fo interefting to the natural hiftory of man, he would probably have difcovered that this extraordinary extenfion, which was reprefented to him as the effect of art, was the work of Nature alone. It is, in fact, very difficult to conceive how the fuperior commiffure of the labia can acquire any confiderable length, whatever means may be fuppofed to be employed for that purpofe. And when we reflect, that at the other extremity of the fame continent, there exifts a people whofe women have a natural excrefcence, which differs from that of the female Hottentots examined by Le Vaillant only in being fingle, and not bifurcated; when we are affured, that this excrefcence is not the effect of any friction or pulling, or of any other factitious means; fince the women are born with it, and are anxious to have it removed, we cannot avoid thinking that it is not confined to the Egyptian women alone, but extends from their country as far as the Cape of Good Hope, by a line which includes the tawny women only, and not the female negroes, who have no fuch characteriftic. This conjecture acquires additional weight from the certainty we

* Voyage dans l'Interieur de l'Afrique, tome ii. p. 347, &c.

have, that the Abyſſinian women undergo circumciſion as well as the Egyptian; and though we have no poſitive information concerning the motive of this operation in Abyſſinia, it is more than probable that it is a conſequence of a ſimilar conformation in both; and we have the more reaſon to be of this opinion, as the women who make a trade of circumciſing girls in Egypt come from that part of the country which is immediately adjoining to Abyſſinia.

I alſo contrived to procure myſelf, in my own apartments, a ſight of another kind. Nature alone had provided the ſubject of the former; the latter was a remarkable inſtance of the folly of men. The race of the Pſilli, a people who were perſuaded that they poſſeſſed the power of ſetting ſerpents at defiance, of charming them, of making theſe reptiles follow them at their call, and of curing their bites, has been perpetuated in Egypt. There exiſts a ſect called *Saadis*, from the name of their founder, a ſaint highly venerated among the Mahometans of that country. This *Saadi* had an uncle, a great man in Syria. Having one day ſent him for ſome branches of the buſhes in the deſert, when the lad had cut the faggot, he was very much at a loſs to tie it. After a fruitleſs ſearch, he bethought himſelf of knotting together ſeveral ſerpents, and with this living cord he bound his faggot. The uncle, delighted with his nephew's acuteneſs, ſaid to him: *Well, you may now make your way in the world, for you are more knowing than me.* Immediately on this the ingenious youth began travelling about the country, charming ſerpents by his wonderful and ſupernatural ſkill; and he had a great number of diſciples, to whom he communicated his art. His tomb is near Damaſcus; it is filled with ſerpents and other venomous animals, among which a perſon may lie down and ſleep, without their doing him the ſmalleſt injury.

Such is the ſuperſtitious origin of a very numerous ſect in Egypt, each individual of which inherits the ſkill of its founder. Every year they celebrate his feftival in a manner analogous to the inftitution. They march in proceffion through the ftreets, each holding in his hand a living ferpent, which he bites, gnaws, and fwallows piece-meal, making, at the fame time, frightful grimaces and contortions. But this feftival, which I was defirous of feeing, was celebrated only in the fummer; and I was extremely anxious to examine clofely one of thefe ferpent-eaters. On this occafion, M. Forneti and myfelf had recourfe to the fame means that we had employed refpecting the circumcifion; and a *Saadi* came to my apartments, accompanied by a prieft of his fect. The latter carried in his bofom a large ferpent, which he was continually handling. After having recited a prayer, he delivered it to the *Saadi*. I obferved that the reptile's teeth had been drawn; however, it was very lively, and of a dufky green and copper colour.

The *Saadi*, with a mufcular hand, feized the ferpent, which en-twined itfelf round his naked arm. He began to be agitated; his countenance changed; his eyes rolled; he uttered terrible cries; bit the animal in the head, and tore off a piece, which we faw him chew and fwallow. At that moment his agitation became convul-five; his howlings redoubled; his limbs writhed; his afpect bore the marks of madnefs; and his mouth, diftended by horrid grimaces, was covered with foam. From time to time he devoured frefh pieces of the reptile. Three men in vain exerted themfelves to hold him; he dragged them all three round the room, throwing his arms violently about on all fides, and ftriking every thing within his reach. To avoid him, M. Forneti and myfelf were fometimes obliged to cling to the wall, to let him pafs and efcape his blows. We could have wifhed the maniac far enough off. At length the prieft took the ferpent from him; but his fury and his convulfions were not at firft appeafed; he bit his hands, and his paffion continued. The prieft clafped him in his arms, put his hand gently upon his back;

lifted him from the ground, and recited fome prayers. His agitation gradually fubfided, and he became completely exhaufted, in which ftate he continued a few moments.

The Turks who were prefent at the abfurd and difgufting ceremony, were fully convinced of the reality of this religious frenzy. It is certainly true that, whether reality or impofture, it was impoffible to exprefs the tranfports of fury and madnefs in a more ftriking manner, or to fee a man in a more terrific fituation.

The great number of thefe ferpent-eaters had induced fome authors, and particularly Dr. Shaw, to believe that they fubfifted entirely upon thefe reptiles. According to this Englifh traveller, there are at Cairo and in its environs, more than four thoufand perfons who live on nothing but ferpents *. This, however, is a miftake; ferpents are not a difh among the *Saadis*; and if in their ceremonies they gnaw a few raw and alive, they are far from making them an article of food. In Egypt thefe men are very much refpected; but among the Turks of the other parts of the Ottoman empire they are only objects of laughter.

I had an opportunity of converfing with a fheick, or prieft of this fect. He was of an open difpofition; for, though he affured me that feveral of his fraternity had an extraordinary power over ferpents, he confeffed that he had not the fmalleft claim to it; but, on the contrary, was exceedingly afraid of thefe animals. By him I was informed of fome particulars which I fhall relate. In order to have ferpents ready, upon every occafion, they keep them in their houfes; but they previoufly take the precaution of extracting their teeth. If any perfon be bitten by a ferpent, he runs directly to a *Saadi*, who mutters a few words over the wound, fcarifies it with a razor; and, after having filled his mouth with lemon-juice, fucks the blood from it repeatedly. Thefe men alfo cure the *ferpent's*

---

* Shaw's Travels, vol. ii.

breath, an appellation given by them to inflammatory puftules which fometimes break out on thofe who fleep in the open air with any part of the body uncovered, and which they pretend are caufed by the poifonous breath of a ferpent. The remedy they employ is oil of fefamum mixed with cerufe, or white lead. With this liniment they rub the puftules, never failing, at the fame time, to mutter a few words, without which every remedy would be perfectly ineffectual. Such is the lot of mankind, that there is no nation in the univerfe, of whofe hiftory many pages are not appropriated to fuperftition !

Wood:
Importance of Malta

Mark Wood, *The Importance of Malta Considered, in 1796 and 1798; also Remarks which Occurred during a Journey from England to India, through Egypt, in the Year 1779* (London: John Stockdale, 1803), pp. 3–23.

When Samuel Taylor Coleridge described Malta in 1803 as 'the dreariest of all dreary islands' (*Collected Letters of Samuel Taylor Coleridge*, ed. E. L. Griggs (Oxford, 1956–71), vol. II, pp. 143–4), he was articulating a typical British response to this rugged principality. Yet, despite Malta's aesthetic limitations, the island and the Romantic-period travel accounts that described it were to play a central role in early nineteenth-century foreign policy and in the eastward expansion of British imperialism.

Malta was thrust onto the world stage on 11 June 1797, when Napoleon captured the island in the name of the French republic. Although it was an island of few natural resources or immediate economic advantages, the seizure of Malta was amongst Napoleon's most ambitious moves, indicating the scope of his imperial aspirations in the East. For the island was, as Nelson put it, the 'most important outwork' of British India and by taking control of Malta Napoleon was threatening to establish control of the overland routes through the Middle East to India. Because French Malta posed a considerable threat to the security of British colonial possessions in the East, the British response was determined. After two years' siege at Valletta, Malta's former neutrality was re-established in 1800, and its independent status was further guaranteed by the Treaty of Amiens (1802).

In the years following the siege at Valletta, the British maintained administrative control of Malta, and the most important Romantic travel accounts of the island date from this period. Indeed, there was considerable popular interest in Malta in the early years of the nineteenth century, largely as a result of the island's recent international importance, and numerous travel accounts were written by British bureaucrats employed in the region. When Malta once again became a subject of diplomatic controversy in 1802, travel writers were amongst the most important contributors to the debate surrounding Malta and its relation to British colonial security.

With the establishment of British administrative control at the turn of the century came a flurry of new travel accounts and new visitors to the island.

Malta had long been an established stop on the Grand Tour itinerary, but few eighteenth-century travel accounts had focused particularly on the island. For most travellers, Malta had been a way station on their journey eastwards to final destinations in Africa or Asia. Patrick Brydone's *A Tour through Sicily and Malta* (1773) was perhaps the only notable exception and even he remarked upon the island's limited attractions for tourists. After the Treaty of Amiens, travellers continued to pass through the island's ports, including figures as familiar within Romantic exploration history as Lady Hester Stanhope, John Galt and Johann Ludwig Burckhardt. However, the most influential travel descriptions of Malta were those written by English civil servants connected with the island in the first few years of the British occupation, in the context of a heated political debate regarding Malta's future and the security of the Empire.

Many of these travel accounts and histories written within the context of administrative service were essentially war propaganda. In 1802 and 1803, there were fears that Napoleon was planning a second campaign against Egypt via the Ionian islands, and although the Treaty of Amiens had restored Malta's sovereignty the British were reluctant to leave the island. Soon, the inevitable question arose: was Britain willing to go to war again over the possession of the island? Several well-placed administrative officials stationed in the Mediterranean argued strongly that it was – and they used the genres of travel writing in order to mount their campaign for public support.

William Eton, Inspector of Quarantine at Malta, was the central figure in this public campaign. Eton had established his reputation as a historian with his *Survey of the Turkish Empire* (1798). In 1803, as part of an effort to create support for war over the issue of Malta, he published the first two volumes of his *Authentic Materials for a History of the Principality of Malta*. Unsurprisingly, Eton argued against British evacuation from the island. As early as 1802, however, Eton had been sending to the radical agitator William Cobbett a series of provocative documents on 'the Maltese Question', intended for periodical publication in the *Political Register*. These articles had initiated a tense debate and the publication of Eton's history was rapidly followed by other similarly motivated accounts, most notably Sir John Barrow's *Account of Travels into South Africa* (1804) and Colonel Sir Mark Wood's *The Importance of Malta Considered*.

At stake in the issue of war over Malta was, finally, the question of Napoleon's intentions towards Egypt. While a consensus emerged that Malta must be retained as security against French invasion of Egypt, there was considerable debate over the extent of Napoleon's ambitions in the East. Barrow's account had suggested that colonisation of Egypt was an end in itself for the French and in 1804 Samuel Taylor Coleridge, in his capacity of secretary to the British Minister at Malta, was asked by Ball to prepare a memorandum in support of this view. In *Observations on Egypt*, Coleridge argued for Egypt's intrinsic value to the French as a colony and against fears that Napoleon intended to use Africa to undermine British control of India. Coleridge's primary sources in preparing this document were Henry Brougham's *Inquiry into the Colonial Policy of the European Powers* (1803) and Mark Wood's popular travel account of Malta and Egypt (see Donald Sultana, *Samuel Taylor Coleridge in Malta and Italy* (Oxford, 1969), p. 176).

Thus *The Importance of Malta Considered* is significant for several reasons. Addressed to Henry Dundas, the British Secretary of War, Wood's account consciously demonstrates the relationship between travel writing and the political administration of empire which is implicit in Romantic exploration writing as a genre. His publication played a distinct role in shaping early nineteenth-century policy toward Malta and Egypt. Wood also articulates clearly Malta's perceived importance for the security of the British Empire and, by extension, illuminates the British investment in the Middle East. Finally, Wood's text provides part of the context of imperial administration within which we might reconsider Coleridge's renewed investment in travel writing after 1805. The prefatory essay on 'The Importance of Malta', with which Wood introduces his travel account, is reproduced here in its entirety.

INTRODUCTION.

AS feveral members of both Houfes of Parliament had, during the late debates, expreffed fome doubts of the very great importance of Malta to this country, alleging that this ifland had only been called into notice by Bonaparte's expedition to Egypt, I have been induced to publifh the following letters, which fhow the fallacy of both affertions, and prove that the former adminiftration were apprized (at a much earlier period) of the high importance of Malta; nor is it to be fuppofed that men of their great talents and abilities could require any fuggeftion of mine to imprefs this truth on their minds. And if the prefent adminiftration agreed, by the treaty of Amiens, to give it up; they did not cede it to France from any idea of its infignificance,* but to obtain a much higher object, viz. the bleffing of peace.

Whoever for a moment cafts an eye on the map of Europe, muft be fatisfied, that the poffeffion of the ifland of Malta, from its fituation, harbour, and impregnable fortrefs (requiring only a fmall garrifon) muft be of the higheft importance to England, both in a commercial and political point of view. Whilft it ferves as a depôt, and protects our commerce in the Mediterranean and Ionian feas, it affords the only check we can have to reftrain the vaft plans and boundlefs ambition of the Firft Conful of France ; who confiders our

---

* About fix weeks before Bonaparte failed from Toulon, and whilft the public opinion was divided in refpect to the object of this great armament, in feveral converfations which I had with the prefent Chancellor of the Exchequer (at that time Speaker of the Houfe of Commons) upon this fubject, I had the fatisfaction to find, that his opinion refpecting the deftination of this armament, as well as of the importance of Malta, for the purpofe of defeating the prefent and all future attempts, exactly correfponded with my own.

ruin as a neceffary ftep to his own aggrandizement. It was therefore, perhaps, fortunate for this country, that by deftroying the
order of Malta, he put it out of the power of our government to
fulfil this article of the treaty of peace, and that he difplayed his
hoftile intentions before he was ready to carry them into complete
execution. The minifter who would now deliver up Malta into the
hands of France, would fign the death-warrant of his country, as we
fhould very foon be driven out of the Mediterranean, and our Eaft
India poffeffions rendered of little value, if not taken from us.

It was in the courfe of a journey from England to India, through
Egypt, that I was firft led to confider the great importance of Malta
to Great Britain, which fubfequent events have fully demonftrated.
Some of my friends, perhaps too partial, are of opinion, that there are
feveral of the remarks contained in my journal, that would be fer-
viceable to fuch of our countrymen as may be obliged to follow
this route. Influenced by this confideration alone, I have given it
to the Public, trufting to their candour and liberality to excufe any
errors or inaccuracies that may occur, it having been written on the
fpur of the occafion, and merely with a view to my own private
reference.

Portland-Place, November 14, 1796.

To the Right Hon. WILLIAM PITT and HENRY DUNDAS.

GENTLEMEN,

I TAKE the liberty to addreſs this letter to you jointly, wiſhing to take, what appears to me, a double chance of being heard upon a ſubjeĉt highly intereſting to our country.

In the ſtations you hold at this critical period, I am ſenſible, that with all poſſible diſpoſition on your parts to liſten to what every man may have to communicate, your time is too precious and too important to the public to allow of frequent intruſions from individuals.

It is to our ſituation in the Mediterranean particularly, that, at this time, I am deſirous of calling your attention. What I have to offer for your conſideration upon this ſubjeĉt is the reſult of long reflеĉtion, and not an opinion haſtily formed or influenced by the different events of the war. For at the time when we were in poſſeſſion of Toulon, and long before there could have been any apprehenſion of France becoming ſo formidable, my ſentiments, as to the neceſſity of Great Britain ſecuring ſome *tenable* port in the Mediterranean, were exaĉtly the ſame as at preſent.

It muſt certainly have been the events of the war, and not the premeditated policy of adminiſtration, which led them to take poſſeſſion of Corſica with a view of keeping it. Let any perſon of the moſt common judgment or reflеĉtion turn to the map of Europe; and conſider our ſituation, extent, and population, encumbered beſides with numerous and diſunited foreign poſſeſſions, and the utter impraĉticability of keeping Corſica by force muſt be ſelf-evident. Minorca, were it even in our power to retake it, is nearly as objectionable as Corfica, by reafon of its vicinity to France, and the very great eftablifhment required for its fecurity.

So long, however, as Great Britain is defirous of fupporting her naval pre-eminence amongft ftates, of protecting her commerce, and of curbing the ambition and aggrandizement of France, it is abfolutely neceffary for her, at any price, to fecure fome port in the Mediterranean, where her fleets may retire and refit, in times of danger; and from whence our enemies can be molefted.

Gibraltar, at the entrance of the Mediterranean, appears to have been placed there by nature, to enable this fmall ifland to refift the united powers of France and Spain.

Could another Gibraltar be found higher up the Mediterranean, which, exclufive of the ftrength of fituation, poffeffed a good harbour, the acquifition of fuch a place to this country would be invaluable.

There is a fmall rock fituated at the fouthern extremity of Italy, which, poffeffing both advantages, appears to me in conjunction with Gibraltar, to be eminently calculated for commanding the Mediterranean; and, the acquifition of which, as it forms a fmall independent eftablifhment of its own, unconnected with the continental powers, there is reafon to believe, would not prove a matter of much difficulty.

You muft immediately perceive that the place to which I allude is the ifland of Malta. There have been periods, I confefs, at which a negotiation for the poffeffion of this ifland might have been conducted with much greater probability of fuccefs than at prefent. At the time when our power in the Mediterranean was triumphant, and when the apprehenfion of French principles and fraternization carried with it greater horror and deteftation than it does at prefent, every thing was then at our devotion. Notwithftanding, however, that one opportunity has been loft, it is not improbable that, during the courfe of the prefent war, another may occur. Undoubtedly our power and confequence in the Mediterranean have lately fuffered a very fevere blow*; yet, poffibly,

* A little time after the evacuation of Toulon.

the powers of Italy may still see their danger, and, in place of that despondency and inaction which must render them an easy prey to the enemy, be at last roused to those exertions, which, when supported by the naval power of Britain, can alone secure their existence as independent states.

The Grand Master and Knights of Malta must doubtless see their own ruin involved in that of the Christian world, and, from a sense of danger, may be induced to unite with Britain and Ireland, which in return, can guarantee and secure to the knights, not merely their ancient privileges, but much more substantial advantages.

Half a million, or even a million sterling, would be well employed in securing to this country so valuable a port. In respect to the most advisable mode of negotiating such an arrangement, it would be presumption in me to say one word.

Whether Sir William Hamilton or Sir John Jervis might be serviceable in forwarding so desirable an acquisition, or who else may be best calculated for accomplishing so very important an object, His Majesty's ministers have the best means of judging. My only wish is to call the importance of this place to your attention, lest, amidst the hurry of other great and pressing concerns, this circumstance might escape your notice.

Were Providence to give us the power to place an impregnable fortress and harbour on any spot in the Mediterranean, most suitable to the views of our country, it would hardly be possible to select one preferable to Malta. It would give us completely the command of the Levant; not one ship from thence could sail to or from any port in Europe, unless by our permission, or under convoy of a superior fleet; the coasts of Spain, France, Italy, and Africa must be subject to our controul, and, whilst at war with this country, be kept under necessary subjection; from Africa and Sicily we could have ample supplies for our fleets and garrisons; and, by the Dardanelles, from the Euxine and Caspian Seas, inexhaustible supplies of various naval stores, which, if not secured to ourselves, must inevitably find their way to the arsenals of France.

Thefe, gentlemen, are furely fufficient advantages to induce you to ftrain every finew towards obtaining poffeffion of this invaluable fpot; but thofe advantages, great and important as they are, are ftill but a part of what may be ultimately expected. It is particularly to Mr. Dundas, as India minifter, that I addrefs the latter part of the prefent obfervations. It certainly muft have been often a fubject of your confideration, what the fituation of France was likely to be at the conclufion of a general peace ; fuppofing that we are fo fortunate as to fecure the independence of Holland and of the Netherlands; I will even go farther, and fuppofe that Great Britain is able to keep poffeffion of the Cape of Good Hope, and likewife of the harbour of Trincomale; acquifitions which, in the general received opinion, would effectually fecure our poffeffions in the Eaft, and prevent France from ever fending any dangerous armaments into that quarter.

Whoever, thinks and argues in this manner will be wonderfully deceived; as there is not only a much fhorter, but a much fafer route, by which armies may be fent to India, and one which, we may reft affured, fo foon as the new republic has a little time to look round her, will be greedily feized on by thofe vigilant and fharp-fighted republicans.

The rich province of Egypt may be faid to be contiguous to France, and remains an eafy and tempting bait to the republic, whenever fhe choofes to feize it.

Although a province of Turkey, yet it is fo remote, as well as fo independent of the Porte, that France will find it an eafy matter to obtain poffeffion of it. Moft likely fhe will ftir up a rebellion amongft the Beys; and, with the moft friendly profeffions toward the Porte, avail herfelf of this opportunity of feizing it for the republic.

I have paffed through that country, and can fpeak of it with confidence. It fwarms with Frenchmen; and the government is fo unftable, and the country fo defencelefs, that five thoufand republicans would make an eafy conqueft of one of the fineft and richeft provinces in the world, abounding with every thing defirable for the fupport of man.

When I fay that Egypt is contiguous to France, I wifh only to exprefs that its principal port, Alexandria, is within a few days fail of Toulon and of Marfeilles. The French republic having Spain and Italy at her devotion, (which muft undoubtedly be the cafe fhould we be expelled from the Mediterranean) will be capable not only of undertaking, but of carrying into effect, projects, which, during the monarchy, fhe durft not have thought of, much lefs have acted upon. Having poffeffion of Egypt, which unites the Mediterranean and Red Sea, the communication with India is expeditious and certain. In place of a traverfe of five or fix months round the Cape of Good-Hope, with the cafualties of fuch a voyage, the paffage from Suez to any part of the coaft of Malabar may be performed in lefs than one month, and to the coaft of Coromandel nearly in the fame time. Where then, gentlemen, will be the fecurity of India, when, for every man we can fend, the French will have the means of pouring in thoufands?

I know it may be argued, that there is fome difficulty of finding transports in the Red Sea, and that an Englifh fleet in the Straits of Babel Mandel will be a certain remedy for the apprehended evil. Whoever reafons in this manner, let me beg of him to reflect how many fuperior fleets we muft thus be obliged to keep, to be guarded at every point; and whether or not the enormous expenfe of fo many fleets and eftablifhments would not, in the courfe of a little time, prove fatal to our country.

It is better to forefee and prevent evils, than, by flumbering in a falfe fecurity, fuffer ourfelves to be furprifed. The poffeffion of Malta, whilft it would give us the complete command of the Mediterranean, and of the Levant, and prove the moft effectual curb that could be devifed to the ambitious projects of the new republic; would, at the fame time, be the moft likely means of protecting our eaftern empire, which otherwife muft be fubject to very imminent danger; and, although fuch an event may not happen immediately yet I will venture to predict, that it will take place within a very few years after the re-eſtabliſhment of a general peace.

I have the honour to be, with the greateſt reſpect,

Gentlemen,

Your moſt obedient

and moſt humble ſervant,

MARK WOOD.

London, April 25th, 1798.

The Right Hon. HENRY DUNDAS, &c. &c.

SIR,

It is now almoſt two years ſince I took the liberty of calling your attention to the infinite importance of ſecuring a ſmall *tenable* poſt in the Mediterranean, as well for the purpoſe of, checking the boundleſs ambition of the French republic as for the protection of our trade; and ſupporting that naval ſuperiority in every part of the world, ſo eſſential to our exiſtence as a free and independent ſtate.

At that time you ſtated, that for four years paſt, you had been aware of the importance of Malta; but although the acquiſition of it would be moſt deſirable for our country, you doubted its being ſo eaſily attainable as I ſeemed to imagine, and beſide, you ſeemed to think its ſituation rather too high up in the Mediterranean. Permit me, ſir, to call to your recollection, that it was this very ſituation, ſo high up the Mediterranean, which appeared to me to render Malta ſo very deſirable an acquiſition. My great object was the attainment of an impregnable poſt, which could be defended againſt all the world at a ſmall expenſe either of blood or treaſure; which would not only completely control the whole of the Mediterranean, Levant, and Adriatic, but ſecure us againſt any views which the French republic might have upon Egypt, the poſſeſſion of which would enable them more eaſily to diſpoſſeſs us of our eaſtern dominions than any meaſure in the power of man to deviſe.

I have long foreſeen, that ſo ſoon as the French government could diſengage itſelf from its more preſſing European concerns, their views would be directed to the poſſeſſion of Egypt, not only as a great and important national object to France, but one which, at the ſame time that it gratified the vanity of the people, would afford the means of providing for a large body of thofe officers and foldiers, whofe return to their own country is fo much dreaded; and, whilft it opened to their ambition the rich fpoils of Afia, held out to them the glory of driving from India their rivals, who alone dared prefcribe bounds to their rapine and infatiable ambition. But, fir, to return to my fubject, whether the prefent great armament fitting out at Toulon be deftined againft Ireland or Egypt, is to me immaterial, for I look upon it to be equally certain as if it had already happened, that in lefs than fix months from the prefent time the French republic will not only be completely in poffeffion of Lower Egypt, but that the conqueft of Upper Egypt will immediately follow, and that, in a fhort fpace of time they will have an army of twenty thoufand veteran infantry, a numerous artillery, and a body of the fineft cavalry in the world, within a Month's fail of our principal Afiatic fettlements.*.

Whoever knows any thing of Egypt, muft tell you, that the picture I now draw of the critical fituation of India is by no means exaggerated, and that every circumftance which I now record in this letter is not only practicable, but eafy.

I do not however, mean to excite your attention, without at the fame time pointing out to you the only means now in our power

* October 19th, 1797. Treaty of Campo Formio.
May 20th, 1798. Buonaparte failed from Toulon.
June 12. Takes poffeffion of Malta.
July 1ft. Lands at Alexandria; and by the middle of Auguft was in poffeffion of Upper and Lower Egypt.
June 28th. Court of Eaft India Directors direct two men of war to be ftationed in the Straits of Babel Mandel, and on the 26th of November order the ifland of Perim in the ftraits to be fortified.
March 1798. Tippoo Sultaun fends ambaffadors to the Mauritius; and governor Malartio publifhes an account of this embaffy, which ultimately led to the war with Tippoo.

N.B. From hence it is obvious, that had Buonaparte and the French government laid their plans judicioufly, had governor Malartic fent up the Red Sea a fufficient number of tranfports, of which there were great abundance at the Mauritius, by the 1ft of September Bonaparte might have landed ten thoufand chofen troops at Mangalore, without the fmalleft hindrance or moleftation. What effect this would have had on our fituation in India may be eafily conceived.

to counteract the prefent plans of France; but not a moment is to be loft, and nothing but the moft rapid and efficient meafures can poffibly protect India from the ftorm ready to burft upon her.

The poffeffion of Malta, is not at prefent within our reach; otherwife, in place of one million, at which, two years ago, I faid it would be a cheap purchafe to Great Britain, at the price of ten millions it would be a wife economy, as the expenfe of the great additional force neceffary for the protection of India, fuppofing it it could be faved (exclufive of other important political confiderations), would foon exceed that fum.

We are not therefore to confider how we can prevent France from poffeffing herfelf of Egypt, for that, I apprehend, we have not the means of doing; but we are to determine by what means we can beft prevent her from availing herfelf of the great refources and advantages which the poffeffion of that country muft afford her for quickly expelling us from India.

At all feafons of the year, excepting about forty days, the winds blow fair from Suez to India, fo that, as I have already ftated, the paffage may be made in a few weeks. Thank God, to counteract the numberlefs advantages which the French muft have in the poffeffion of Egypt, for expelling us from India, Nature has, in fome refpect, fet bounds to the facility by which otherwife this might be effected. On the one fide of the Red Sea, extenfive fandy deferts preclude the march of large armies, and although by Upper Egypt their approach towards the eaftern coaft of Africa and the Straits of Babel Mandel may be effected, yet by a judicious choice of fituation at the entrance of the Arabian Gulf or Red Sea, for the protection of our fhips of war, and where they could readily be watered and refitted, the danger to India may be averted.

Perhaps at this very time France may have ordered her tranfports and frigates at the Mauritius to rendezvous at Suez, or lower down the coaft towards Coffeir, to receive on board from eight to ten thoufand men, and which, if they have had the wifdom and forefight to arrange, fuch an army may be in India before any poffible meafures can be taken to prevent it. If they have laid their plans judicioufly, nothing could be more eafy; for, as there are plenty of tranfports at the Mauritius, (fhips captured from the Englifh) if, by the middle of June twenty tranfports and five frigates fhould have been ordered to rendezvous at Coffeir or at Suez, (as they can make their paffage) ten thoufand veteran French troops may be landed upon the Malabar coaft, and join Tippoo Sultaun, before there can be the fmalleft idea of any armament of the kind. Mauritius is fo fituated, and the paffage to the Arabian Gulf fo much out of the track of any of our fleets or cruizers, that thofe tranfports and frigates may be in the Red Sea, and have completed their bufinefs, without meeting with a fingle veffel, and before any of our fettlements in India, or our Cape fquadron can know any thing of the matter.

Let me therefore recommend, that this very important objeft be immediately communicated, not only to our admiral at the Cape, but to the Bombay government, and exprefs orders fent for cruizers to be kept conftantly at the Straits of Babel Mandel to watch the motions of the enemy; that they be alfo inftructed to fecure, without delay, fome ftrong fituation, fuch as can be rendered impregnable at a fmall expenfe, not only to give protection to our fhips of war, but to watch the motions of the enemy; and that in the felection of fuch a port they be guided, not only by its ftrength, but by its vicinity to the entrance of the Red Sea.

There is a fmall fteep rock and ifland at the entrance of the ftraits called Perim or Babel Mandel, the fituation of which is admirable for the above purpofe; but whether or not there be plenty of water, good anchorage, and other requifites, I am not fufficiently informed. I am however acquainted with a very able marine officer, who has furveyed and explored the whole of thofe parts, of whom I will make it my bufinefs to make farther enquiries, and take an early opportunity of acquainting you with his obfervations and opinions. In the mean time, let me intreat of you, as you value India, not to lofe a day in fending inftructions to our admirals and governors abroad, to be moft particularly watchful of the Straits of Babel Mandel, till fuch time at leaft as the French projects are further developed. Two line of battle fhips, and two or three fmall cruizers, ſtationed at Mocha, till there is leiſure to adopt ſome more regular ſyſtem of defence, will place India in ſecurity.

I have the honour to be,

Sir,

Your moſt obedient,

Humble ſervant,

MARK WOOD.

Piercefield, Auguft 16, 1798.

To the Right Honourable HENRY DUNDAS, &c. &c.

SIR,

In my laft letter I promifed to fubmit to you a few obfervations refpecting the very formidable armament which upwards of two months ago failed from Toulon, under General Bonaparte, and which, after capturing Malta, is faid to have proceeded in profecution of what is now generally believed to be the other object of the expedition, namely, the poffeffion of Egypt *, as a prelude to the project of ultimately expelling us from India.

This project I confider to be not only wifely planned, but of more eafy accomplifhment than what is generally fuppofed. About two years ago, I took the liberty of calling your attention to this moft important fubject, ftating, at that time, as my humble opinion, that fo foon as France could difengage herfelf from her European politics, fhe would turn her thoughts towards Egypt; and that we could not be too early nor too ftrenuous in our endeavours to counteract fo deftructive a fcheme; and likewife urging, as ftrongly as was becoming for me to do, that the poffeffion of Malta would be the moft effectual means of fecuring us againft fuch a project.

It was not from the perufal of Volney, or of other French travellers, that I was led to the confideration of this fubject; for my time has been too bufily occupied, to admit of fuch relaxation; but it naturally prefented itfelf to me about twenty years ago, during a journey to India, by this route, when the facility of the communica-

* The firft intelligence of Bonaparte having landed in Egypt was received in England in September 1798.

tion betwixt India and Europe, through Egypt, moſt forcibly ſtruck me; as alſo the great advantages France would derive from the poſſeſſion of that country.

Subſequent reflections confirmed me in my opinion, and induced me to draw your attention to the importance of Malta, as the beſt means of preventing this.

As the French had not, at that time, begun to develop any part of their plans, I only appreciated its value at a million ſterling; but I believe we are all very well convinced, that at ten times that ſum it would be an economical acquiſition. Although, at this early period, I received great ſatisfaction to be aſſured by you, that you had long attended to this grand object, yet I muſt confeſs, that it gave me conſiderable uneaſineſs to underſtand that you conſidered the acquiſition of it a more difficult matter than what I imagined.

When, however, I reflected that you had the aid of lord Minto, Sir William Hamilton, and other able men, and heard, from yourſelf, that you were fully awake to the importance of the acquiſition; I did not wiſh to preſs the buſineſs farther, left I might, unintentionally, give offence, when I had no view nor wiſh but to ſerve my country. Had not Bonaparte taken poſſeſſion of Malta, the communication with Egypt would have been completely intercepted; but, with it, the communication with France and Egypt has been ſecured, as there is no other commanding port where an enemy's fleet can be protected and re-fitted. Having no doubt, however, but that our government has, long ago, ſtationed a very powerful naval force in the Straits of Babel Mandel, as well as ſecured a ſtrong poſt at the entrance of the Red Sea, it will be totally impracticable for a French army to reach India by that Channel. The only probable route, therefore, by which Bonaparte can hope to reach India, will be by forming an army of ſuch magnitude and force as ſhall command itſelf a paſſage wherever it directs its courſe; and, notwithſtanding the route through ſome parts of Syria, particularly from Damaſcus to Palmyra, and from thence to the Euphrates, is acrofs deferts, yet, by proper arrangements, not only abundance of water, but of provifions, may be obtained. Egypt will be the grand depôt, from whence all fubordinate magazines will be fupplied; and, Bonaparte, previous to moving with the great body of his army, will fecure his left flank, by poffeffing himfelf of the fortreffes of Syria *, and afterwards eftablifh magazines and depôts at Damafcus, Palmyra, and other ftations.

As, exclufive of the grandeur and boldnefs of the expedition, (fo well calculated to flatter the vanity of the great nation) it may ftill be neceffary to amufe and deceive the mafs of the people; fcientific men, of whom fo much has been faid, are deftined to explore the ruins of Palmyra, and Babylon. The re-eftablifhment of the trade to Afia, through its original channels, before the difcovery of the Cape of Good Hope is held up to view, and Egypt and Syria are again to become the great marts for the produce of India.

Having no doubt that a French army in poffeffion of Egypt and Syria, would find no difficulty in getting to India, but what exertion and arrangement may overcome, permit me, for a moment, to draw your attention to the confideration of thofe means which we may ftill have in our power to defeat the chief object of this grand expedition; and thereby fave hundreds of millions, which muft be expended by our country in fo unequal a conteft—a conteft where we have every thing to lofe, and the enemy every thing to gain.

Is it, permit me to afk you, by increafing our European force in India, that we can expect to preferve that country? By no means; the attempt would be folly in the extreme; as, even were it practicable, this ifland could not bear that drain of men that would be neceffary to fupport fuch a force; and India, valuable as it is, would not be worth preferving at fuch an enormous expenfe.

It will probably be afked, by fome, are we not as able as the French to bear this expenfe? I would anfwer, by no means, even were we to regulate our conduct by the example of our neighbours.

---

* March 20th. Befieges Acre; and 21ft of May raifes the fiege.

A French army, of fifty to sixty thoufand men, would reach India without incurring a fingle livre of expenfe to France. The kingdoms through which they muft neceffarily pafs will furnifh them with every neceffary, and many luxuries; nor will they be more fcrupulous in their payments in Afia than what they have been in Europe: nor will the French feel that drain of men neceffary to fupport their Indian army; for, having once opened a paffage to that country, they will gladly difgorge into it thofe maffes of armed men, who, having already conquered Holland, Germany, Switzerland, and Italy, are now confidered as dangerous to their own government. Suppofing, therefore, that a French army, including auxiliaries, of 50 to 60,000 men fhould enter India, I will, in the firft place, briefly confider what meafures they are likely to adopt; and, fecondly, what ought to be done on our part, to counteract fuch a formidable invafion.

As Frenchmen of the prefent day have not many religious fcruples*, it would not furprife me fhould Bonaparte (fo foon as he is in poffeffion of Egypt and Syria) hoift the ftandard of Mahomet, and invite all the faithful to unite with him in the re-eftablifhment of the Mahometan government over Afia, and to reprefent its having been deftroyed by the faithlefs Englifh. To carry on the delufion, the French foldiery will affume the turban and light Afiatic drefs; and thus, by fineffe and dexterity, aided by the incredible bigotry of the Mahometans, Bonaparte will not only command the armies, but the treafures of the eaft.

By fuch means, occafionally ufing force, and making moft fevere examples† where he finds refiftance, I have no doubt that he may enter India with an army of any magnitude he wifhes.

The Mahrattas are the only native power in India, which united with the Englifh, would be likely to prefent any effectual oppofition to this mighty force; but, in the prefent divided ftate of that people, I fear it will be impoffible to convince them of their danger, till

* Auguft 1798, Bonaparte vifits the pyramids, and converfes with the mufti and imans. His confeffion of faith, &c. &c.

† March 6th, 1779. Takes Jaffa by affault, and puts the garrifon to the fword.

fuch time as effectual preparation is impracticable. Hence the French will be able to draw them into an infidious neutrality, fatal to our intereft, and effectually promoting their own.

As the ftorm approaches, our native corps of infantry and cavalry; as well as of European artillery, muft be confiderably increafed, and all the frontier fortifications completely repaired, provifioned, and garrifoned, fo as to ftop the progrefs of the enemy. No time ought to be loft in fetting on foot negotiations with every power, through whofe territories the French are likely to pafs; and no endeavour omitted to retard their progrefs towards Hindoftan. For this purpofe, a proper felection of ambaffadors will be of the greateft moment; a clever intelligent agent at Poonah, and another at Delhi, will be well fituated for conducting negotiations and alliances with all the neighbouring ftates, and to apprife them of their danger, in the event of a French army entering India. It would be moft defirable, could an alliance, offenfive and defenfive, be formed with Zemaun Shaw, and he be brought to act againft the French ; otherwife they will ufe his immenfe power and refources to advance their own intereft, under the pretext of efpoufing his. Above all, immediate and decifive meafures ought to be adopted to get rid of thofe French adventurers, at prefent in the fervice of the native powers in amity with the Englifh.

A monfieur Raymond, employed by the Nizam, commands fixteen battalions of infantry, a large body of cavalry and a well-ferved artillery ; and with Scindeah, a monfieur Perron, fucceffor to general De Boigne, has a well-difciplined force of nearly 20,000 men. Thefe adventurers muft, at all events, be got rid of; for, fhould the troops under their command unite with the French army, they will be infinitely more formidable than any other troops belonging to the native powers. Every thing muft, therefore, be rifked, rather than leave them as they are at prefent, ftationary upon our frontiers; and, fhould it be difficult to perfuade the Nizam and Mahrattas to difpenfe with their fervices, we muft endeavour to furprife and difband them *.

* October 22d, 1798. Colonel Roberts's detachment furrounds and difarms monfieur Raymond's corps in the fervice of the nizam, confifting of about 11,000 men.

Poffibly an offer to replace thofe French officers with Englifh, even were we to be at the expenfe of them, would be fucceſsful; by which means, we fhould have the double advantage of increafing our forces from 40 to 50,000 men, at no expenfe to ourfelves.

Befides thofe preparatory meafures abroad, others of a different nature fhould be adopted at home. A port in the Mediterranean muft be fecured, coft what it may, as a ftation for our fhips of war to victual and to re-fit. As the French have got the ftart of us by feizing Malta, it is very difficult to fay where a fit port is to be found; but, at all events, we muft cut off the communication betwixt France and Egypt. Meafures ought immediately to be taken to excite the Egyptian Beys and Arabs to give every poffible oppofition to the French; and, for this purpofe, money may be very advantageoufly diftributed amongft them. In this work a Mr. B. who has been long at Cairo, and muft, from his long refidence, have obtained a knowledge of the people and country of Egypt, would feem to be a ufeful perfon. In cafe of fuccefs, hold out to him competent rewards; for it will be a fervice of difficulty, as well as of danger, and eventually may be of great importance.

Not only the Arabian Gulf, but alfo the Perfian Gulf, muft be fecured, or elfe we fhall do our bufinefs imperfectly. For this purpofe, a ftation ought to be immediately occupied at the entrance of the Perfian Gulf, in the fame manner as I before recommended in the Straits of Babel Mandel. We formerly poffeffed the ifland of Ormus, at the mouth of the Perfian Gulf; and, on what account it was abandoned I do not know; but, if a more eligible fituation cannot be found, that ifland appears, in point of fituation, to be well calculated for the purpofe. You muft be perfectly aware that a poft cannot be fecured in one day. Preparations accordingly ought to be immediately fet about, otherwife our very active and enterprifing enemies will once more get the ftart of us.

I truft, fir, that, in the event of the French being able to effect their march toward India, not only all the precautions which I have thus haftily enumerated, but many which I have omitted, will be adopted, as the country has every thing to hope from your zeal and exertions.

After all, however, fhould a French army enter Hindoftan, a general war in India muft enfue, the event of which no man can forefee? But, even fhould we be ultimately fuccefsful, can we expect to incur a lefs expenfe than fifty millions; which will not only abforb the whole of the furplus revenue, but involve the Eaft India company in inevitable ruin? It therefore behoves us, fir, before we are reduced to fo unpleafant an alternative, wifely and maturely to confider, whether, even in the prefent advanced ftate of French preparation, we may not, by means of fome ftrenuous exertion, be yet enabled to avert the blow, and to refcue our country from fuch a calamity.

It appears to me, that, even fhould Bonaparte have difembarked his army, and have taken poffeffion of Egypt and of Syria, one chance ftill remains, not only of defeating the chief object of this expedition, but poffibly of converting it to the general benefit of Europe. It is evident that the Ottoman Porte has not the power, even had it the inclination, to arreft the progrefs of Bonaparte; and I have no doubt that they would fuffer Bonaparte to difpoffefs them, not only of Egypt and Syria, but alfo grant a free paffage to the French army, provided by thofe conceffions, they could efcape farther mifchief.

Ruffia * is the only power that can check Bonaparte's career; and I am convinced, that could we hold out any temptation to that wary nation, fo as to induce her to enter cordially into the war, we fhould not only deftroy the French projects towards the eaft, but fpeedily reftore peace to Europe. The force of the Ruffian empire is enormous, and the only difficulty is that of bringing this great power into action. Although difficult, this is not by any means impracticable;

---

* May 1799, the Ruffian fleet of twelve fail of the line and a number of tranfports pafs through the Dardanelles, and co-operate with the Britifh in the Mediterranean; and by the end of Auguft 1799, the French were expelled from Piedmont, Italy, and Switzerland, and a large Ruffian and Imperial force was prepared to enter the French territories.

and hence the neceffity of turning our attention fteadily and unremittingly to this great object. Were it not for the obftruction of the Dardanelles, the Ruffians could fend into the Mediterranean, in lefs than two months, twelve fhips of the line, and as many troops as could be wanted; and a force of this nature would be likely to anfwer our moft fanguine views. If any thing can operate upon Ruffia it will be the profpect of power, and the credit of deciding the fate of the Mediterranean. The poffeffion of Minorca may be held out to them, or of fome other port, the inftant it can be procured. If money be required, two or three millions could not be better employed. The Porte muft firft be called on to defend her neutrality, and not merely to affemble an army to prevent the French from paffing through Syria on their route to India, but alfo to difpoffefs them of Egypt. In cafe of a refufal, which is likely to happen, and for which the Porte will plead inability, we muft demand a paffage through the Dardanelles for the Ruffian fleet and army, for the purpofes of defending that neutrality which the Turks have acknowledged themfelves unable to do. This, if refufed, we muft be prepared to compel, and which, in conjunction with the Ruffians, will not be difficult. Should threats of fetting fire to Conftantinople, and to all the Turkifh veffels in the Levant, be ftill infufficient to induce the Porte to liften to reafon, I think we fhall be juftified in compelling her to accede to a propofition, which involves not only the fecurity of the moft valuable part of the Britifh empire, but the peace and good order of Europe.

I have the honour to be,

Sir,

Your moft obedient fervant,

MARK WOOD.

Pouqueville:
Travels through the Ottoman Empire

· F. C. H. L. Pouqueville, *Travels through the Morea, Albania, and Several Other Parts of the Ottoman Empire to Constantinople During the Years 1798, 1799, 1800, and 1801. Comprising a Description of those Countries, of the Manners and Customs of the Inhabitants, &c. &c.* (London: Richard Phillips, 1806), pp. iii–vi, 101–5, 112–37.

The French traveller, physician and diplomat François Charles Hugues Laurent Pouqueville (1770–1838) wrote several descriptions of his extended residence in the European Levant. His first publication, *Travels through the Ottoman Empire*, provides a particularly interesting account of Constantinople and of European relations with the Ottoman Empire at the height of the Napoleonic Wars. Meanwhile, his subsequent narratives – particularly *Travels in Southern Epirus, Acarnania, Aetolia, Attica, and Pelopenesus* (1822) – record important information about the development of Romantic philhellenism and attitudes toward the renegade Ali Pasha Tepelene.

Pouqueville set out for the East in 1798, intending to explore Egypt as part of Napoleon's recently established Commission of Arts and Sciences. Upon his arrival, ill health required his almost immediate return to Europe, and Pouqueville's travels might have ended there. However, on the return voyage, his convoy was captured off the coast of Sicily and, as Pouqueville explains, 'In short, I was reduced to slavery by a Tripoline corsair, and unfortunately separated from my friend Bessieres' (see below, p. 121). *Travels through the Ottoman Empire* describes his subsequent removal from Italy to Constantinople, his imprisonment in the Sultan's fortress, his release and his further travels.

Despite the romance of Pouqueville's early adventures, his subsequent travel account offers an entirely typical Romantic description of Constantinople. As Byron was to complain, few foreign landscapes were so well known as the Sultan's capital, and Pouqueville's narrative is representative of this genre of travel writing. Indeed, the ready familiarity which characterises Pouqueville's own first encounter with the city testifies to Constantinople's power as an imaginative locus for Europeans – both as the final destination of the Romantic Grand Tour and as the originary site of all things Oriental. This first encounter is described in the selection from the text reproduced below.

While Pouqueville's initial travels in the Ottoman East were involuntary, he later served as the French ambassador at Janina from 1806 to 1816, appointed by Napoleon to the court of the renegade Ali Pasha Tepelene. From this position Pouqueville witnessed and, as a diplomat, guided some of the Romantic period's most delicate Ottoman relations, as Europe began to negotiate foreign policy in the region independent of the Sultan or Constantinople. His account, along with Hobhouse's *Journey through Albania* (1813) and Bessières's *Mémoire sur la vie et la puissance d'Ali Pacha, visir de Janina* (1820), should be considered as important historical records of the diplomatic tensions surrounding Romantic travel in the European Levant.

AUTHOR's PREFACE.

THE state of modern Greece is but little known. The two travellers who have given us most information on the subject, are Messrs. Choiseuil Gouffier, and Felix Beaujour; the former of whom viewed the country only as an antiquarian, while the latter investigated its commercial advantages. Tournefort and Olivier describe merely its isles; and every other traveller, without exception, has made statements which are either false or incomplete.

Having been left in that country by the chance of war, and during my stay there surveyed the most interesting parts of ancient Greece, I flatter myself that my work will be found to contain much novelty in the description of the Morea and Albania, as well as in the account of Constantinople.

That the reader may be enabled to judge of the truth of my statements, and to conceive the situation to which I was reduced, I shall in a few words give an outline of the voyage which succeeded my captivity. I left France in the character of physician attached to the Commission of Arts and Sciences, which was destined to the East. Shortly after arriving in Egypt, the bad state of my health obliged me to quit the country with a view of returning to

Italy.   I therefore embarked with my colleague Bessieres, also a member of the Commission, in a Leghorn tartane.   We were joined on board by Colonel Poitivin of the Engineers, who had just recovered from a long sickness; Colonel Charbonnel of the Artillery; the Commissary Fornier; Beauvais, Commanding adjutant; Girard, a member of the commission; Joie and Bouvier Officers of the Marines; Guerini, Inquisitor of Malta; and a guide named Mathieu, belonging to the General in Chief. Some domestics, and an Egyptian cahouas or courier belonging to the Beys, formed the remainder of the passengers.

Colonel Charbonnel was conveyed on board some days before our departure. This officer was afflicted with a violent ophthalmia, accompanied with a dreadful dysentery; but not wishing to quit the army, he had received permission to repair to Malta, where he was to serve after his recovery. According to the instructions which he had received from the Commandant of Marines at Alexandria, who was ordered to furnish him the means of reaching his destination, he was to quit us at Messina, and proceed to Malta in a *speronare** : but our unpropitious stars, together with the ignorance of the sailors, caused our frail bark to run to leeward of the Pharos of Messina, and thus we were carried towards the eastern extremity of Calabria; a circumstance which I shall explain in the course of the work.

* A *speronare* is a boat which conveys provisions from Sicily to Malta, and is employed in the general navigation of the channel.

In short, I was reduced to slavery by a Tripoline corsair, and unfortunately separated from my friend Bessieres; but it will be seen how much I profited by his observations, and those of Charbonnel, relative to Albania.

In what relates to the Morea and Constantinople, I have not inserted many events which occurred to me; but have sacrificed my journal and a detail of my personal adventures, to make room for matter of more importance. In speaking of Constantinople, so often described by travellers, I have avoided the repetition of former accounts: and I can confidently assert that my information is new, particularly that which relates to the imperial castle of the Seven Towers, in which I was imprisoned twenty-five months; to the gardens, and the harem of the Sultan, both of which I saw; and to the misfortunes of the French prisoners in Turkey.

The maps given with this work, have been prepared by the geographer of Anacharsis, M. Barbie du Bocage; who has considered the details which I have furnished of the Morea worthy of insertion in a fine map of that country, which he has drawn out by order of the Marshal of the Empire.

Such is the result of my labours, which were often interrupted during an unfortunate captivity of three years. If it be favourably received, I shall not regret the fatigue which I have undergone; but shall banish from my memory the dangers to which I was frequently exposed by my eagerness to acquire information.

★　　★　　★　　★　　★

I now respired, for the first time in my life, the odoriferous emanations of the territory of Asia. At break of day our boat returned to the town; and thanks to the capidgi-bachi, who this time was not drunk, the captain was let off on paying a few dollars for the guns that had been fired, though he was liable to be hanged for attempting to pass in the night, and creating alarm. All being, however, settled, we skimmed the surface of the currents, which pour into the Ægean sea the waters of the Palus-Meotides, the Pontus Euxinus, and the Propontide.

A spectacle entirely new to us, now attracted our attention. A numerous herd of dolphins playing on the waves appeared to escort us. Confined between Europe and Asia, we saw a variety of towns and hamlets succeed each other; and as some were lost in the distance, others continually arose to excite our curiosity. Indeed, I saw so many beauties this day, that I thought myself in a new world, and forgot the punishment with which I had been threatened. In the course of the day, we cast anchor off the village of St. Etienne, and in the night experienced a dreadful storm, accompanied by thunder and torrents of rain, which wetted us to the skin. Here some of the passengers left us to proceed by land to Constantinople; and the next day we sailed with a light south wind for that city.

It is impossible to express the surprise and astonishment that are felt on first beholding this pompous city, which is worthy of the title of "Queen of the World." Its seven hills, crowned by as many imperial mosques; its amphitheatres, covered with a multitude of houses, painted with various colours; its shining domes, pyramidal cypresses, and elegant steeples, together with its port, arsenal, hotels of Pera, and the palaces of the "Great King," the title of sultan Padischa, all conspire to entrance the mind.

We saw, at the pavilion where the sultan comes out to embark, his caik covered with an awning of purple, embellished with fringe and gold lace; twenty-four sailors of an athletic stature were sitting on the benches, with their silk sleeves turned up, and their gilt oars in their hands, waiting for the sultan to enter the barge; while the artillerymen of Tophana, with lighted matches, were watching his appearance to salute him with a discharge of their guns. We passed this spot, and anchored at Galata: the master of the ship immediately went to the lieutenant of the grand vizier with the letter of the pacha of the Morea, announcing our translation to Constantinople; and the capidgi-bachi, with his suite, set off for the city.

While we were in the port, we were visited by a clerk of the drogman, who took down our names; and at five in the evening we were separated from the soldiers, who were thrown into the Bagne, or common dungeon, while we were conducted to the castle of the Seven Towers.

CHAP. XI.

ENTRY IN THE SEVEN TOWERS.—NAMES OF THE PRI-SONERS WHOM WE FOUND THERE, INCLUDING OUR TWO COMRADES.—PARTICULARS OF THE ARREST OF M.-RUFFIN.—EXPULSION OF THE FRENCH FROM THE PALACE OF THEIR AMBASSADOR.—ACCOUNT OF THE ADVENTURES OF MESSRS. BEAUVAIS AND GERARD, INCLUDING THEIR ITINERARY FROM PAXOUS TO CON-STANTINOPLE.

WE thanked our kind stars when we found that we were to be conducted to the castle of the Seven Towers. This Bastile, the idea of which would at any other time have been sufficient to ter-rify us, now appeared merely as a relief to our misfortunes; and we passed through its massy gates without alarm. The janissa-aries who escorted us from the port, and whose mildness and frank behaviour had agreeably surprised us, shewed the order for our imprisonment to the commandant; they then held out their hands, and solicited some reward for their trouble, when the guards of the Seven Towers drove them roughly from the outer gate, and compelled us to enter the court-yard without mak-ing them any recompense. Our astonishment may easily be conceived, when, on passing the first inclosure, we heard our names called from a window by Messrs. Gerard and Beauvais, who had been six months at this place: they pressed us to their bosom. It is necessary to experience misfortune, and to incur the dangers from which we had escaped, to judge of our feelings on being united, even in captivity.

The first person to whom we were introduced, was M. Ruf-fin, the French chargé d'affaires: his misfortunes, the mildness of his physiognomy, and the white hair which covered his head, prepossessed us in his favour, and his frankness soon gained our affections: there were with him the secretary of legation, M. Kieffer, and M. Dantan, his interpreter. We afterwards paid our respects to General Lasalsette, M. Richemont, whose wounds, which he received at Prevesa, were scarcely healed; the Adju-tant-General Rose, who laboured under a disease which termi-nated his existence; and M. Hotte, a chief of brigade. I was then called to the outer gate to assist in the examination of a few trunks, which had not been taken from us, and one of which was filled with books. As the Turks were suspicious of every thing in the form of paper or print, they detained my copies of

Livy, Tacitus, Virgil, Horace, Ovid, and other classical works, which had been respected by the pirates of Barbary, and which had afforded me much agreeable recreation in the former part of my captivity. I fortunately took the precaution of tearing up my journal, and of stuffing it in my pockets, as if it were waste paper, by which I was enabled to continue and complete it, by writing it in an enigmatic style, which would have rendered it unintelligible to any future spoliator.

They now began to provide us with lodging; and a few planks placed upon two tressels, with a miserable mattrass, formed our temporary bed, on which we lay without undressing.

The kiaya, or lieutenant of the castle, who was called Zadig Aga, the next day presented the prize which he had made, to the drogman of the Porte; and Virgil, Horace, Lucan, &c. being suspected authors, were ordered before the interpreter to the sultan. As his excellency did not understand latin, I trembled lest he should take those *chef d'œuvres* for conjuring books, and that I might lose them; but they contented themselves with sealing the trunk which contained them, and at the end of six months they were given me again.

The kiaya, on returning from court, where he had received orders relative to our confinement, put us the next day in a room which was occupied by the domestics of the chargé d'affaires, who had been turned out for our accommodation; and this time I had the satisfaction of being joined to my friend Fornier. But though we were inseparably attached by misfortune, we received the melancholy information, that we should not be long together: our room was dark and unwholesome; but it was supportable, considering what we had endured, though we apprehended that we should not long possess it, as it was intimated to us, that we should be conducted to the Black Sea. Our propensity for travelling, however, was rather diminished by the disgust which we had imbibed from our last voyage.

They mentioned to us several of our countrymen who had preceded us in the Seven Towers, and who, from an inveterate hatred towards the French, had been sent by the government to the fortresses on the Black Sea. We thus learnt the names of several highly respectable persons who had been tyrannically sent to distant prisons by the fanatical Turks; but by an unexampled pusilanimity they took care not to inform us of the miseries they experienced in the prison of Cavak, on the Bosphorus. By the influence of the ministers of the combined powers, the mufti was deposed, and the Porte issued secret orders for watching the conduct of every Frenchman who resided in the empire.

In short, the most arbitrary conduct was now displayed towards every person in the interest of France; and on the 10th o

September, a dreadful system of tyranny was displayed towards the French who resided in the Levant. The principal drogman for France was ordered to court; and the reis effendi, after having overwhelmed him with protestations of friendship, said, that he wished to have an interview with M. Ruffin, and the whole legation. The chargé d'affaires, on receiving this news, which many of his suite thought to be indicative of the most fortunate consequences, foresaw what would take place. He repaired to court at the time appointed, and the reis effendi paid him, as well as the whole legation, the utmost respect: he invited them to sit down, and ordered them to be served with coffee; after which, without any preliminary conversation, he read the declaration of war, and concluded by sending them all to the Seven Towers; after which the chargé d'affaires found at the door, for himself and his suite, an escort of eight hundred janissaries, who conducted them all to prison.

The sultan was sitting in a keosk to enjoy the sight of his ancient allies riding to captivity: they experienced on their route, the silent pity of all whom they met; and a woman having presumed to speak in their favour, was severely chastised by the regiment of janissaries who formed the escort.

Ten months had passed since this event occurred, and the rage of the enemies of the French was still far from being satisfied: for Spencer Smith expelled from the national palace the Frenchmen to whom that place had been granted as a prison. I could say much on the fanatical and ungrateful conduct of this minister, but I shall prefer passing to my companions in misfortune, and shall proceed to state the events which befel Messrs. Beauvais and Gerard, who were separated from us, as I have already related, and whom we found in the castle of the Seven Towers.

The passengers of the tartan the Madona di Monti Negro, who parted from us on the 26th November, remained on board the corsair, which was pursued by a Neapolitan frigate; and they expected to be landed at Corfu, according to the promise which was made them by Orouchs, the captain. At nightfall the Neapolitan ship hoisted its colours, and fired over the corsair to bring her to: the vessels were so near that our prisoners could distinguish the dress of the Neapolitans; but darkness having come on rather suddenly, the Tripolitan changed her course, and by this artifice effected his escape. The next day they found themselves on the coast of Italy, near Otranto, and so near to land, that the Calabrian fishermen, fearful of being taken, took refuge with their barks in the creeks under the protection of the batteries.

Towards noon the captain of the corsair perceived two vessels at a distance; and as he suspected that they were fishing smacks, he proposed, to attack them. All his crew, with the telescope in hand, examined them minutely, and unanimously determined to run them down: they made all sail with this intent; but what was their surprise, when the supposed fishing smacks proved to be two Neapolitan frigates, one of which was the ship they had escaped from the evening before! They discovered and pursued the pirate, who became thunderstruck, and saw nothing before him but the Bagne, the only place worthy of receiving such wretches, while the Frenchmen were gladdened with the hope of a deliverance, which they conceived to be beyond a doubt. The frigates gained, and began to fire on the corsairs, who, prostrating themselves on deck, invoked God and the Prophet, shed tears, and finally returned the fire of the frigates.

Notwithstanding this audacity, every thing announced that the author of our misfortune would be taken in his turn, and that he could only escape by some event bordering upon a miracle : this event, however, took place : a calm came on, which caused the two frigates to remain stationary, when the corsairs resorting to their sweeps, soon got out of reach ; they then left the coast of Calabria, where slavery stared them in the face ; but in crossing the gulph of Otranto or Tarranto, they found themselves in the wake of the French packet le Vif, which left Egypt at the same time as ourselves; but they dared not attack this vessel, as it carried cannon. The next day, which was the third of our capture, the pirate came to anchor off the little isle of Paxous, opposite to Parga, in Albania.

By the report of the artillery of Corfu, which was at that time besieged, together with the information gathered from the inhabitants of the isle, the pirates learned of the war between France and Turkey. The fear of being obliged to make restitution, had long rendered the corsair uncertain as to the conduct he should adopt toward his French prisoners ; but as soon as he learned the state of affairs, he testified the greatest satisfaction ; and his crew, partaking of his sentiments, became overjoyed. They landed to purchase provisions, which they did not give themselves the trouble to cheapen ; they regaled all whom they met from morning to night, and were incessantly firing off their guns. The most insignificant fisherman who came on board, was dignified with the title of captain, and they saluted him with their whole artillery, as if he had been an admiral; nothing was heard but songs and the firing of pistols ; and Ibrahim Tchiaoux, one of the important personages of the Tripolitan vessel, drank brandy instead of water. In short, they all dissipated with the most ridiculous prodigality, what they had so easily acquired.

CHAP. XII.

ACCOUNT OF THE IMPERIAL CASTLE OF THE SEVEN TOWERS, ITS INTERNAL REGULATIONS, TOPOGRAPHY, &c.—GENERAL MODE OF LIFE AMONGST THE PRISONERS.—VISIT OF THE AGA.—PRINCIPAL DROGMAN OF THE TURKS.—DEATH OF ADJUTANT-GENERAL ROSE.—VISIT OF THE ISTAMBOL EFFENDI.—ATTACK ON THE SEVEN TOWERS BY THE LAZZARONI, OR INHABITANTS OF CHOLCIS.—EVENTS WHICH HAPPENED IN THE OTTOMAN EMPIRE DURING THE FIST YEAR OF OUR DETENTION.—SOME ACCOUNT OF CONSTANTINOPLE.

AFTER the above account of the adventures of Messrs. Beauvais and Gerard, I shall proceed to a description of the castle of the Seven Towers, and its antiquities. This building, which the Turks call Hiedicouler, and the Greeks, Eftacoulades, is mentioned in the history of the Roman empire as early as the sixth century of the Christian era, as a spot which contributed to the defence of Constantinople ; the embrasures of some of the towers, and of those which flank the rampart of the town, from the southern angle of the castle to the sea, shew that this place was the principal bulwark of the town on the coast of the Propontis, in the latter periods of the empire.

In 1453, Mahomed II. after an obstinate siege, entered Constantinople, and gained possession of the Seven Towers, the gates of which were opened to him through terror; though the Turks maintain that he sacrificed 12,000 men to gain this important post. But the conqueror, foreseeing that the Greek empire was his own, thought so little of the Seven Towers, that he would not allow the breaches to be repaired.

Since that period this place, which is said to have contained the treasures of the different sultans, has been celebrated by great events; the principal of which is the death of one of the most virtuous descendants of the sultan, Osman II. This unfortunate prince was killed by a janissary, his slave; and every week the Mussulmans solemnly curse, in the barracks of the janissaries, the name of the assassin. I shall briefly describe the misfortunes of this monarch.

Osman II. had marched at the head of his armies: six times, in a battle against the Polanders, he ordered a charge to be made, and each time the janissaries refused to obey him. From this moment he despised a corps which was only terrible in sedition. In consequence of this reverse of fortune he became melancholy, and devoted his attention to magic, when the appearance of a comet in the year 1618, afflicted both him and the empire: his preceptor, Codja-Omer Effendi, advised him, in order to allay the irritation of the Gods, to undertake a journey to Mecca; but his ministers, as well as all the spahis and janissaries, opposed this pilgrimage; the sultan wavered in his determination, and a dream decided his conduct.

He thought he saw himself covered with his armour, sitting on his throne, and employed in reading the koran, when Mahomet appeared to him, snatched the book from his hand, struck him on the face, and threw him to the ground. New terrors now arose: his perfidious enemies, who wished to overthrow him, again advised him to undertake the pilgrimage, for which he at last gave orders in spite of the remonstrance of his friends. A sudden alarm immediately became general, which produced an insurrection. Mustapha, who was deposed for his weakness, was taken from his prison, and pressed by the populace to resume the throne; while a thousand voices demanded the death of Osman. Far, however, from being intimidated, he quitted the seraglio, and proceeded to the barracks of the janissaries, exclaiming, "let us go to the spot on which kings are made." But here he was overwhelmed with insults, and soon dragged to the Seven Towers, in the way to which a janissary struck him with a stick. At length, on entering the first gate of the castle, the fatal cord was suddenly thrown over his head; but before they could tighten it, he had the presence of mind to slip it with his hand, and knock down the principal executioner; on which his grand vizier seized him by the most sensible part of his body, when Osman fainted with pain, and was strangled.

Since the death of this monarch, the Seven Towers have been the theatre of the most sanguinary executions, of which each step gives a melancholy proof. On one side is the tomb of a vizier, who, for his services in conquering the isle of Candia, was put to death. On the walls are numerous dull sentences, written and signed by Turks and Greek princes who were murdered at different times ; while the towers are filled with chains, ancient arms, tombs, and ruins : the " Well of Blood," frightful dungeons, and damp vaults, in which are many passages from the koran, and other inscriptions, added to the dismal croakings of vultures and ravens, and the beating of the waves, fill up the melancholy picture.

I shall now give some account of the external form, extent, and signs of the antiquity of this castle, which no other traveller has described.

Besides what I have above related, the Seven Towers are particularly known in Europe as the prison in which the Turks shut up the ambassadors and ministers of the powers with whom they are at war. At the time of which I am speaking, the place contained the French legation and a number of officers, amongst whom I was comprised. The persons detained in this prison are distinguished from all other prisoners of war by having a taim, or boarding table, allowed them by the sultan, as well as by the name of hostages, of which the Turks are accustomed to speak very high ; according to them it is a special favour to be the moussafirs or hostages of the sultan ; and indeed, though they are closely guarded, their detention may be considered as a favour, when compared with the situation of the other prisoners of war, whom the barbarians condemn to public labours in the Bagne, or prison for slaves.

The Seven Towers are called in the state papers by the title of the Imperial Fortress, and are governed by an aga, who has a guard, with a band of music, under his orders. This appointment is generally an honourable retirement, with a salary of 6000 piastres, equal to about 10,000 French francs, arising from certain lands in the environs of Rodosto. The aga who commanded during my captivity, was called Abdul Hamid ; he was a venerable old man, of Tartar origin, who had been employed in the seraglio in the quality of muzzim or sexton. On becoming sixty years of age, and being no longer able to sing in a mosque, or summon the people from a minaret, he was appointed to the place in question. On the whole, he was a brave and virtuous man, and had none of the fanaticism of those who only make an outward show of religion. If the fear of being calumniated by

those who surrounded him, rendered him sometimes severe towards us, we had no right to accuse him of the vexations we experienced. Though possessing the natural avarice of a Turk,
he was not insensible to any little attention that was shewn him ;
and more than once I surprised him familiarly drinking coffee
with our scullion, who was a Greek papas from Cerigo. Thus,
a difference of condition in life goes for nothing in Turkey, where
a porter may become a vizier or general in twenty-four hours ;
and a Turk who is sure of not being observed, voluntarily treats
as his equal a raia, whom he oppresses in public.

This aga had under his orders a kiaya or lieutenant, and a garrison of fifty-four disdarlis, divided into ten sections, each commanded by a beluk-bachi or corporal. Without mentioning the
names of those illustrious personages, I shall merely say, that the
lieutenant of the castle was a designer in a manufactory of oil
cloth ; and that amongst the corporals were the imaun or curate
of the Seven Towers, a waterman, a pipe-maker, and others of
equal consequence. As to the soldiers, they were a set of miserable creatures, who received a pay of six aspers * per day, and
who nevertheless bore the envy of other men for the place they
enjoyed. The aga, who is appointed by the Porte, chuses his
lieutenant from the beluk-bachis, and generally fixes on the
oldest for promotion ; he also appoints the beluk-bachis, who
are obliged to give him a security of 100 piastres, which he returns to them in case they resign or are deposed.

The advantage resulting to the Turks who form the garrison of
the Seven Towers is, first, a certain degree of respect in their
district ; and secondly, that they are exempt from actual service,
a duty from which no Mussulman can be excused when circumstances require it. The beluk-bachis also have a pay of twelve
piastres per day for their board ; and the aga gives them two meals
in the time of the Ramazan or great fast, which lasts twenty-eight
days. They form a sort of council, of which he is the president,
and in which they consult on the division of the spoil made from
the prisoners in their power. At these meetings they enter into
arguments about discipline ; and their disputes often run so high,
that the commandant, who sits at the corner of a sofa, is obliged
to reconcile them by chastising them all with a stick, or expelling
them from his presence, after holding a sort of juridical inquest on
their conduct.

The castle of the Seven Towers is situated at the eastern extremity of the Propontis or Sea of Marmora, and its form is a
tolerably regular pentagon, each angle of which is flanked by a
tower. Its largest face, which is to the west, has, besides the

* The asper is equal to nine French deniers.

two towers which close its angles, two others that form the two sides of the ancient triumphal arch of Constantine, which led to the golden gate. The gate which affords entrance to the castle, opens on the east side of the town; and the surface of the whole building is about 5,500 square fathoms; the largest side, which runs from north to south, formerly had four towers, but at present there are only three. The first forms one of the sides of the first gate of Constantinople; it is round and covered with lead; the wall which joins it, with the first marble tower of the arch of Constantine, is sixty feet high: it has a parapet, and contains six pieces of iron ordnance, which command the road of St. Stephen. The first marble tower that is observed on leaving the one just mentioned, is an enormous mass from ninety to a hundred feet high, and has a platform; it is built of polished marble from the base to the top, on the field side, where it forms an angle which runs more than forty feet in the second circumvallation; and the marble is rough on the internal side of this circumvallation. This tower, though much damaged by the shocks of earthquakes, is still in a tolerable state. The frise which forms its finishing, is in a good state; and there may be seen at its northern and southern angles, two Roman eagles, sculptured in a bad style. The wall which runs from its eastern angle to the arch of Constantine, is of an equal height, and retains the frise with which it is finished. There may be seen on it the marks of cannon shot, the breaches made by which are repaired with brick. The eastern face of this tower, which is in the circumference of the Seven Towers, has the aperture of a large gate, but affords on the inside nothing worthy of particular notice.

The triumphal arch of Constantine, which occupies the middle space between the two marble towers, led to the gate made in the wall of the second external circumvallation of the Seven Towers. One can no longer form an idea of the ornaments of that arch, which was upwards of ninety feet high, as they have been pulverized by the artillery; but, on the inside of the first circumvallation, they still present a vast and entire escutcheon, surrounded by a wreath of laurel, with representations of Jupiter's lightning at the bottom, and inclosing the chrysilon. On both sides of this arch there were two lateral doors of a round form, which are now stopped up by masonry; and the arch itself is obstructed by two ranges of dungeons, built by the Turks upon brick vaults. The small lateral aperture to the left, which has been blocked up, has been converted into a powder-magazine; but as it is lower than the surface of the ground, the water drains into it, and renders it a nest of toads and salamanders. From hence to the second marble tower, the rampart exhibits a continuation of the frise, though partly destroyed by an enormous breach repaired with bricks; and on the inside the wall is covered, as far as the second marble tower, with the kitchen of the prisoners. This tower is in no manner like the first, as it contains nothing but damp and horrible dungeons, in which thousands of prisoners devoted to death have made their lamentations: the principal of these caves is known by the name of the "Dungeon of Blood," and deserves a particular description. The first door which leads to it, is of wood, and opens into a corridor twelve feet long by four wide; at the end of which, is an ascent of two steps, by which you reach another door of wrought iron, that opens into a semi-circular gallery, which is likewise terminated by a wrought-iron door. At length, ten feet farther you arrive at a door composed of enormous beams, which opens into the dungeon, and into which I think no one can enter without being seized with an involuntary shuddering. Into this place of misery, the light of heaven never penetrates, nor was the voice of a friend ever heard in it, to console the victim whom despotism had condemned to death.

The sombre glare of flambeaux cast a deadly light round this dungeon, so much was the air deprived of its vivifying particles; by its reflections, however, we were able to read a few inscriptions, that had been cut on the humid marble; but the eye could not reach to the roof of this noisome vault, which was buried in darkness. In the middle of this sarcophagus is a well on a level with the ground, which is half-closed by two flag-stones that have been conveyed to its mouth: the Turks give it the name of the "*Well of Blood*," because they used to throw into it the heads of those who were decapitated in the dungeon, from which circumstance it acquired its name. Thus are buried in oblivion the names of many of the greatest men in the empire, whom a mere look of the sultan can cause to be destroyed at his pleasure.

In the tower which contains the Cavern of Blood, there is a flight of steps leading to several other cells, the height of which being greater than that of the ramparts, admits of the prisoners seeing Constantinople through narrow loop holes. Here the persons detained as hostages were formerly shut up; but they are now allowed to hire a lodging, as I shall speedily explain. The same flight of stairs leads to the platform of this tower, and to the triumphal arch, as well as to the second tower; but the entrance to the latter is closed at top by a portcullis, covered with shrubs and ruins, which proves that this spot has been unfrequented for many years.

From the marble tower just mentioned to the southern angle of the castle, the rampart affords nothing remarkable; nor does it contain any artillery. The tower which flanked this angle has fallen to ruins, and its foundation forms in the second external circumvallation a sort of cistern, or rather inclosure, in which trees have sprung up. The whole of the rampart to the south is without artillery.

The third angle of the pentagon, or the southern angle, is defended by a round tower formed of two parts; the first is seventy feet high, and is pierced with embrasures, that make a gallery round another tower, which seems to rise from the midst of the former. The whole of the roof rests upon the embrasures of the inner tower; and the height of this singular building is altogether at least one hundred and twenty feet. In the space which separates it from another tower, which flanks the eastern angle, the rampart, which is lower than that of the south and west, is furnished with four pieces of cannon, which command the town side, and a part of the sea-shore. The tower of the eastern angle only differs from that just mentioned in its form, which is a kind of dodecagon. Near this is the gate by which you enter the castle; it is made in a small square tower, and in this the prisoners are occasionally kept in irons. It contains nothing remarkable, except its doors, which were formerly of wood, but which are now made of iron, in consequence of a prisoner having effected his escape by burning them down.

From this gate to the last tower that remains to be mentioned, the rampart contains ten pieces of cannon, which command the town. This last tower has fallen to decay, and will soon be entirely in ruins; for the Turks do not know how to repair an old building, as they daily see large fragments of the interior walls fall down, without paying the least attention to the circumstance.

From this description of the ramparts and fortifications, I shall proceed to give an account of the inside of the castle. The gate by which you enter, is painted red, coated with bars of iron, and crowned by a portcullis, which is let down in cases of danger. To the right of this gate, at the spot where the sultan Osman was strangled, is an armoury filled with old shields, chains, and ancient arms; and to the left is a small cabin, which is the station of the kiaya. To reach the second circumvallation, you pass along a paved causeway, and near a small mosque: this space is filled with about forty houses and gardens, some heaps of stones, and several lines of trees, which have grown spontaneously on the ruins. This spot formerly contained some elegant houses, but they were destroyed by an accidental fire about twenty years ago; since which, the Turks have not rebuilt them.

The second space contains the house of the aga, and that of the prisoners who are kept as hostages: it is closed by a length of wall about eighteen feet high, and is entered by a large red gate: to the left is the guard-house of the soldiers, which is a sort of chamber furnished with a miserable sofa, and not capa ble of containing more than ten men. No military attributes or arms are to be seen in it, nor any thing but about a dozen sopes or sticks, with which only the guards are armed. Opposite to the end of this pavillion is a wing of a building, which runs about six fathoms from the arch of Constantine: this is the residence of the aga, of which we occupied a part.

The Porte, in its firmans, sentences its state prisoners to con finement in the dungeons, but leaves the aga the privilege of letting out to them a part of his own residence. The divi sion which we occupied, consisted of a ground floor, which we did not use, and of a first and second floor. The pavillion that joined to ours was inhabited by the commandant and his women; there were behind it a small garden, and the opening that led to the first marble tower. With respect to this tower, I ought to state, that our chargé d'affaires having, towards the close of our captivity, hired the pavillion of the aga, for himself and his wife, I had an opportunity of seeing the inside of the tower: notwith standing its darkness, I could distinguish a wooden coffin; and my curiosity tempting me to take off the lid, on which was sculp tured an Egyptian figure with very long ears, I perceived a mum my broken in three pieces, and the head of which I contrived to carry off. I afterwards found, by consulting the Turkish an nals, some passages of which M. Ruffin translated for me, that it was a present from the king of France to Charles XII. king of Sweden, when he retired to Bender about ninety-four years ago. The mummy was conveyed from Egypt, but was stopped by the Janissaries who guarded the gate of Adrianople. The caimacan immediately put his seal upon it, and it was deposited in the castle of the Seven Towers, as the relics of a saint. I never heard, what lady Montague has asserted, that the Turks consider it as a palladium, on which depends the preservation of the empire; but this is one of the many pleasant fictions in her work. Ac cording to her hypothesis, I have broken the charm, and accele rated the downfall of a great empire.

A small paved street which leads from the gate of the second inclosure to the triumphal arch, separates the house of the aga from the garden, which on this side is bounded by palisades; this garden is partly of a square form, and one of its sides, which is pa rallel to the second marble tower, is ten fathoms four feet long, by three fathoms wide, while the other which is parallel to the house of the aga, is ten fathoms long, by an equal width. In the first part of it, is the cemetry of the martyrs; which occupies a square surface of two fathoms; it contains the tombs of the Turkish chiefs who fell in the assault on the Seven Towers. They still keep the fosses around the stones, which are of a gigantic size, in order that they may excite a higher opinion of their valiant ancestors. This spot is surrounded by a small wall about two feet high; and every night a lantern is lighted in it, which the meuzzin is obliged to keep burning. The inside of this garden was well planted by the Moscovites, who formed it into landscapes, and built in it two keosks or pavillions; but as every thing goes to ruin in the hands of the Turks, we found nothing but the remains of these embellishments. Our situation was too irksome, on account of a restriction of implements, to allow us to make similar improvements. We therefore contented ourselves with forming grass plats; and one of our comrades engraved on a marble slab in the second tower, the following inscription:

" *To the memory of the French who expired in the chains of the Ottomans,* 1801.

The interior of the Seven Towers affords nothing worthy of observation. I know not why the authors of the Encyclopedie say, that there may be seen in one of the courts the mortar employed for pounding the oulemas; for most of the Turks told me that it was in the seraglio; but the most reasonable amongst them were of opinion, that this instrument was only an ideal object of terror, and that it has not existed for several centuries. In fact, there is nothing in those courts, but heaps of enormous marble balls for loading pieces of a much larger calibre than the artillery of the ramparts; hence I know not by what fatality preceding travellers have been induced to relate in their publications so much of the marvellous.

The Seven Towers are inhabited within the first circumvallation by some poor Turks, who live in the houses with their families: they belong to the guard of the castle; and to make out a subsistence, they are obliged to exercise several professions. The imaun of the little mosque which it contains, lives there; but his jurisdiction extends to the environs, where he performs the funereal service, and other duties of his religion, from which he derives some emolument. The person who filled this office at the time of our residence, bought it for 150 piastres of one of the soldiers, who preferred the condition of a labouring bricklayer to that of imaun, the former profession having been transmitted from father to son, ever since the capture of Constantinople. The imaun who succeeded him, was besides, a belouk-bachi, or corporal of one of the sections of the garrison, and took his turn in mounting guard over us; he read his language tolerably well, and knew the koran by heart without understanding a word of Arabic, on which account he bore the surname of Hafiz, which is given to all who know the holy book by heart; and notwithstanding this qualification he did not possess two ideas.

I shall now give a description of the external circumvallation, which will be found more interesting.

On going out from the triumphal arch of Constantine, you formerly passed under the golden gate, which is now blocked up; but this outlet from the Seven Towers now only leads to the second circumvallation, or external inclosure of the fortifications, which is formed by the space comprised between the first and second rampart: the soil is mostly occupied by a half-cultivated garden. About thirty paces from the triumphal arch, are four cypresses and some sycamores formed in groupes, which present a picturesque appearance, when observed from the village of St. Stephen.

The Turks have filled up the golden gate with solid brickwork, with a view to make it into a cistern; and the commandant has built two paviliions amongst the mass of ruins which still remains there. A fountain has also been formed which empties itself into a square reservoir in a garden before one of those pavillions, and here they repair to smoke. This is also the chief place of repose for the aga, whose perspective is limited by the marble towers.

The sides of the triumphal arch contain a number of Greek inscriptions, written with a red colour, which express the name and glory of God; they are cut on different parts of the marble, and, as well as some Greek crosses, appear to have been the work of some pious soldier while on guard.

Opposite to the first marble tower, on a half moon of the rampart of the second external space, a keosk or belvidere has been built, in which every week they permitted us, for a small remuneration, to enter, and respire the fresh air. The ascent to it is by six small steps: it is divided into two apartments; and that which we were allowed to enter, contained nine windows, and was furnished with a sofa. From this building, the view extends over an infinity of cemetries and gardens, and towards the fertile fields of Thrace; while to the left we could see a village containing a number of manufactories of candles, catgut, &c. Beyond this we could even distinguish the distant isles of Marmara. In the wall of the second rampart, on the outside, are the remains of the golden gate, and there may be seen two columns of white marble, the shaft of which is of a single piece, and from its diameter, gives reason to suppose that they are from thirty to thirty-five feet high; they are, as well as their capitals, in a perfect state of preservation. There are twelve other columns that sustain the entablatures, which formerly contained bas-reliefs; but there do not appear to be any inscriptions.

In this same space appears a melancholy subject for meditation; it is the tomb of the grand vizier who conquered Candia;

with those of his son and wife. Covered with glory, and ennobled for his services, envy drew upon him the disgrace of his sovereign. He was precipitated from the summit of grandeur, and thrown into the Cavern of Blood, where he was strangled. His son and wife obtained permission to unite their ashes with his: their tombs are carefully preserved, and the Turks have even decorated them with a gilt rail-work, which serves for the support of high jessamins and other odoriferous plants. A flaming sword and a simple inscription, keep alive the remembrance of the services of the father, the virtues of the wife, and the premature end of a son of extraordinary promise.

By the aid of chance, time, and bribery, we were enabled to examine the space comprised between the first and second rampart, which continues to extend to the sea-shore, and to which we entered by a door in the wall which cut the space transversely: this space we called the great garden. As soon as we entered, we came to the excavation of the base of one of the towers, which, I have already observed, has fallen down. To the right was the wall, perforated with embrasures, together with bastions; and on the left was the rampart of the city, sixty feet high. This rampart is flanked by seven large, though mean towers, all of an ancient form, and built antecedent to the use of cannon. The embrasures of the towers are black; and the Greeks assured me that this was caused by the Grecian fire which was thrown amongst the barbarian armies. In the interval between the first and second of these towers, is a small column of white marble, indicating the tomb of a tchor-bachi, or colonel of janissaries, who fell at the taking of Constantinople: the Turks revere him like a saint, and chance has placed round his tomb a high laurel. a walnut, a pomegranate, and a fig-tree, which form a kind of arch; indeed it seems as if nature wished to distinguish this resting place of a warrior by the beauty of its vegetation.

The fourth tower is of a square form, and has suffered much by earthquakes; it bears the following inscription, which I give just as it exists, though Procopius has quoted it in a manner which implies a different sense; even Spon and Tournefort have given it in a different manner from me; but though their quotation have the same meaning, neither of these travellers had an opportunity of copying it on the spot, which I had, in consequence of my captivity. It is

ΠΑCΙ·ΡΩΜΑΙΩΙC ΜΕΓΑΛΕΠCΗΟΕ Ο ΘΩΜΑΝΟC ΝΕΟΝ Ο ΠΑ ΙΜΕΓΙC·
TOC TON ΔΕ ΠΡΓΟΝ ΕΚ ΒΑΘΡΟΝ.

which signifies "the great, the most great Roman has built for the Greeks, a temple and a tower from the foundation."

The fifth tower is split from the battlements to the foundation. I passed between the cleft in the wall, and found that it led to the neighbouring gardens: this would have been a good place to escape from, if we could have hoped to find an asylum; but a Frenchman had no friend at Byzantium, where every one was set against him.

The base of the seventh tower stands in the sea; it contains nothing inside, but on its finishing is the following inscription .

ΠΥΡΓΟΣ ΒΑΣΙΛΕΩΝ
ΚΑΙ ΚΟΝΣΤΑΝΤΙΝΟΠΟΛΙΤΑΝΩΝ

which is, " The tower of the kings, and of the Constantinopolitans." A monogramic cross terminates this legend.

The air of the Seven Towers is in general unwholesome, and may give rise to the scurvy; indeed the north wind only can render the city wholesome; for when the south wind blows, it conveys fogs and stenches from the manufactories and neighbouring slaughter-houses, which would be fatal if this temperature were of long duration.   To these inconveniences may be added, that of the insects of hot countries, and a number of yellowish scorpions, which crept even into our beds.   The apartments which we occupied, and particularly those on the first story, were constantly damp, and swarmed with reptiles, while in winter they were extremely cold; nevertheless, Providence supported us in this difficult crisis, and our gaiety was scarcely ever diminished, as we lived in constant hope of a better fate.   But to give a more complete idea of our situation, I shall briefly relate our manner of living in this prison.

I have said that each of us took to useful occupations; we even had some good books, through the interest of M. Suzzo, the drogman of the Porte; and we contrived means of corresponding with our unfortunate fellow citizens who were confined in the Bagne.   We adopted various means to prevent a discovery of this secret correspondence.   Sometimes we made use of the minister of the drogman, who took our letters according to their addresses, without having any doubt as to what they contained, he having read, or pretended to read them from beginning to end; but as this method might be discovered, our industry suggested several others, which would be more safe.   In order to obtain news-papers, &c. we procured a little trunk, which took entirely to pieces, and contained a number of secret drawers, which none could find out unless acquainted with its principle.   We afterwards gradually extended our correspondence, and some of us even committed dispatches to the extremities of Asia Minor, whither several Frenchmen had been transported.   But if our days passed away amidst various plans of instruction and amusement, we had our periods of affliction, one of which was the death of a companion of our captivity.

I have already observed, that the adjutant-general Rose was attacked by a disease which led him to the tomb: in fact, in November, 1799, he finished his career. After his death, M. Ruffin in vain addressed the Porte, praying that this officer might be allowed an honourable interment; his corpse, however, was left amongst us: and the Christian churches were not even satisfied with imitating the Turks. The clergyman of St. Matthias not only refused to perform the funereal service, but even to allow a bier to carry the corpse, asserting that he would sooner suffer death, than interfere in the burial of a Frenchman. At length, after we had despaired of obtaining a tomb for our comrade, a decree was transmitted from the caimacan to the aga of the Seven Towers; its substance was a permission to inter the body of a *Caffre,* who had died in the imperial castle of the Seven Towers. One of the clerks of the drogman came at the same time with four Armenian porters, who carried off the body, and buried it in a neighbouring field, by the road leading to St. Stephen's. Thus so much were the bonds of social intercourse dissolved, that not a Christian minister could be found liberal enough to pay the last duties to a member of that benevolent religion, which only commands charity.

A short time after this event, the istambol-effendi, who is the lieutenant-general of the police of Constantinople, visited the aga of the Seven Towers. This was a great honour conferred upon so low an officer as a disdar; and our commandant therefore received him in his best manner, being at the head of his guards, who were under arms; that is, with their sticks in their hands. After being conducted to the keosk, where he was presented with a pipe and coffee, and paid the customary compliments, the istambol-effendi ordered a dozen piastres to be distributed to the soldiers of the Seven Towers, and then took his leave. Every Turk is avaricious, and the istambol was a Turkish minister. On his way home, he stopped at the shop of a poor grocer, where, pretending to find short weights, he had him nailed by the ear to the door of his shop, and fined him fifty piastres, with which he indemnified himself for his present to the soldiers.

A catastrophe of a serious nature, occurred soon after the visit of the lieutenant of police. A laze, or inhabitant of Colchis, was imprisoned in the Seven Towers by order of the bostangi-bachi, for the crime of assassination, which is considered as a trifling sin by the people in this country. His comrades, who were on board two vessels at anchor under the Seven Towers, learned that their companion was to be strangled the next night, and resolved to save him. They in consequence landed, and repaired to the castle. The aga in vain endeavoured to treat with them; they paid no attention to his threats of firing upon them with the artillery. In short, they forced the gates: the guard was beaten, and the rebels entered the castle, when some one cried out that there were French infidels confined in it: instead, however, of falling upon us, they thought only of their companion, whom they found and carried off; but scarcely were they outside the gates, before they announced their victory by a general discharge of their fire-arms. They afterwards returned on board, and immediately sailed for Syria.

The aga, who thought his character compromised by this affair, went the next day to the caimacan, and informed him of what had happened; but that officer only laughed at the circumstance, and said that the fellows had acted right. It is thus that, in Turkey, success renders legitimate, actions most contrary to order; while in affairs of greater importance the Porte itself concludes by taking a rebel into its service, against whom it had fought and failed.

After this accident, the aga and his guard never failed to barricade themselves on the slightest report of any seditious movement: they then strengthened the gates by placing against them large beams; and though the commandant was responsible for our persons, he trembled much more for his piastres, of which, if he were to be robbed, his superiors would only laugh at him, as they did on the elopement of the laze. Nevertheless he shewed a slight degree of courage on a critical occasion, which happened some months afterwards. The Haiducks, or banditti of Romelia, descended from the mountains of Macedonia and Thrace in great numbers; their army increased daily, and at length amounted to sixty thousand men. Each little division which the Turks sent against them went over to their ranks, because, in the first place, resistance to so great a force would have been useless; and in the next, there was more profit to be derived as a Haiduck than as a soldier of the sultan.

The Porte justly alarmed, came to the resolution of sending a strong army against the vagabonds, whose object was nothing but plunder. According to the custom, which consists in sending European soldiers if the theatre of war be in Asia, and if in Europe ordering troops from Asia, the legions of Georgia were sent against the banditti: they were commanded by Betal-Pacha; and the greatest success was expected from his operations.

The pacha of Nicomedia was to join the chief of the Georgians with a considerable body of troops; and as he had landed in Europe to the east of Constantinople, he wanted to lodge in the castle of the Seven Towers, but the aga refused to let him, under the pretence that he had mussafirs or hostages in his possession. At length the affair became serious, when the Porte interfered, and prevailed upon the pacha to fix himself outside the walls of the city.

To follow the events of this memorable year I must add, that the pacha of Nicomedia having taken the field before forming a junction with Betal-Pacha, was attacked and completely defeated by the rebels, who took his artillery and baggage; on which his troops abandoned him, and went over to the enemy. Attributing, however, his want of success to fate, he thought he might shew himself at Constantinople. His first reception by the vizier was of a consolatory nature; he covered him with a fine pelisse, called him by the title of brother, and invited him to prostrate himself before the sultan. The pacha of Nicomedia, transported with joy, took his advice, and followed him to court. They had already passed the first yard, and were entering the second gate, when two executioners, concealed for the purpose, rushed upon him, strangled him, and cut off his head, which was stuck upon the very door he had a minute previously entered full of joy and expectations. The vizier fell at the feet of his master, and was loaded with praises for ensnaring a pacha whom the sultan wished to get rid of.

In this year also a treaty was concluded, which gave a sort of political existence to the Republic of the Seven Islands, by placing them under the protection of the Ottoman Porte.

I shall now give a brief account of modern Constantinople. This city, which, if it were inhabited by a civilized people, would be the glory of the world, is so well known as not to require any details on its topography, or the luxury of its perspective. Many travellers have spoken of its monuments, and the manners of its inhabitants; but I believe no one has described the general appearance of the town itself.

At first the mind of the observer is astonished at the beauty of Constantinople, and the magnificence of its ports; but other sentiments arise on penetrating within its walls. Fatigued by the inequality of the soil of its amphitheatres, which look so finely in perspective, he finds only narrow and unpaved streets filled with dust or mud; and every where closed gates meet his eye, while a wonderful silence prevails, which is not interrupted by the voice of the people or their pursuits of industry. In the parts devoted to commerce one can, on the contrary, scarcely breathe. Here the multitude meet and jostle each other, but without any of that noise which is inseparable from the markets of our own country, and other places of assembly in Europe. If the traveller enter the bezestins, his eye is struck by an immense quantity of rich merchandize spread without order: here, however, the usual carelessness of the Turks seems to be abandoned; for they have taken precautions against fire: high walls, iron gates, and solid vaults have transformed public warehouses into little towns; but these places are greatly inconvenient at the time of a plague.

The Turk, who here displays for sale the precious shawls of India, arms, jewels, and the finest diamonds, does not appear as if in an obscure shop; he does not seem anxious, or as if caring, to sell his goods: incapable of overcharging, he takes away, without saying a word, the merchandize for which any one offers him a price beneath its value, and he seems to sit behind his counter rather to oblige than to enrich himself, while he may often be seen to quit his shop without leaving any one in care of it. In this bezestin, where every thing excites curiosity, there may be seen, by the side of the phlegmatic Turk, the industrious and active Greek, the deep and reflecting Armenian, and the avaricious Jew, who exert their respective talents and ingenuity. But in the time when the plague afflicts this vast city, every one should avoid those receptacles of commerce: for there the pestilence not only exerts its greatest ravages, but it may be said to issue thence, when the weather favours its developement; because the miasma remains in the pelisses and furs of persons who have died of the epidemy, and which the dealers here heap together without thinking of the consequences.

If from those places we visit another mart, where man does not blush to sell the handsomest and most interesting of the female sex, a singular spectacle affords subjects for meditation. Let the reader conceive the idea of a large square building surrounded by porticos, or rather of a range of stabling with a yard in the middle, and he will thus be acquainted with the plan of the woman-market of Constantinople. Beneath the porticos which lead to the apartments of the slaves, runs a bench along the wall, and here in rainy weather they are exposed for sale.

The day on which I visited this place being very fine, I saw the slaves in the middle of the yard, sitting cross-legged upon mats, in parties of fifteen together: the clothing of white cloth which covered them, bespoke their miserable condition; but they were far from being affected by it, as they laughed, chattered, and made so much noise that one could scarcely hear one's self speak. Some of them who were sitting under the portico to avoid the rays of the sun, were particularly cheerful, and amused themselves with singing. In general I did not consider them as handsome; and though they were between three and four hundred in number, I did not observe one who could merit the high reputation which the Georgian and Circassian women have obtained: they were mostly fat women, of a pale complexion; and I distinguished some who had blue eyes and light hair. The Turks who came to cheapen them, roamed about from group to group, made them open their mouths, inspected their hands, and examined them as we do animals. I was inclined to follow them, and was already in the middle of the court, when one of the guardians, with a poignard in his hand, came up, and swearing at me for an infidel, ordered me to get out: to such an attack there was no reply; and I obeyed. I afterwards learnt that no person could enter this market without a special firman from the Porte; but my imprudence was of use to me on many subsequent occasions.

From this bazar the traveller naturally proceeds to the church of St. Sophie, to pay the tribute of admiration which every stranger owes to a monument that has been so well described by every traveller, as to leave nothing new to be said of it. On paying an imaun you are admitted without difficulty to the galleries of St. Sophie, and may contemplate with leisure that stately edifice, whose greatest merit is the beautiful marble of which it is composed. The Greeks, however, speak of it with a sort of admiration, which proves that they consider it far superior to either of the seven wonders of the world; and they have transmitted in a common song an account of the riches which it formerly contained. The poet, who was doubtless some good priest that lived about the time of the capture of Constantinople by Mahomet II., has informed us that St. Sophie had eighteen steeples, and fifteen bells to call the faithful to devotion; and that the duty was performed by fifty-two head priests, or archbishops, three hundred and two priests, twenty-four deacons, fifty chaunters, and forty-two confessors. He afterwards enters into a detail of the fine candelabras, censors, and gold crosses, which are kept secure; but he does not speak of the luxurious decorations or the beauty of the architecture, the remains of which are still worthy of admiration. He might also have specified the great revenues of this church, which are derived from twelve hundred shops that were given on its foundation by Constantine and Anastacius, and which now form the income of the imauns.

After visiting the mosque of St. Sophie, the traveller will see with pleasure those of Sultan Achmet and the Sulimania, monuments of which the most minute descriptions have been given, and which have been dispersed throughout Europe by the efforts of the pencil.

CHAP. XIII.

ACCOUNT OF CONSTANTINOPLE CONTINUED.—COFFEE-
HOUSES.—TERIAKIS, OR TAKERS OF OPIUM.—ANEC-
DOTE OF A TURK WHO DAILY SWALLOWED CORROSIVE
SUBLIMATE.—KEBADGIS OR ROASTERS.—COSTUME.—
RECREATIONS OF THE TURKS.--DANCERS.--PRIVILEGED
DRUNKARDS.—MIDNIGHT GUNS.—FIRES.

To continue the same subject would be to fatigue the reader; I shall therefore break the thread of my narrative in order to re-capitulate the principal dishes in use at Constantinople, which, considered in a dietetic view, must possess no small interest. I shall begin with the regimen of a Mussulman's kitchen.

In the house of every Turk in easy circumstances there are three separate tables, namely, that of the master of the family, who in general takes his meals alone; the table of the children, who, out of respect to their father, never eat with him; and that of the mother, who lives secluded in her apartment. In the ha-rems, in which there are several women, each has her particular cover.

The Turk divides his food into two meals, and the rich man, who lives in luxury, has, besides, a slight luncheon. As they are all accustomed to rise at break of day, the rich Turk care-lessly throwing himself upon a sopha, after a short prayer, claps his hands as a signal for the slave to bring him his pipe. Nothing can exceed the delight which he receives from smoking; he burns aloes with the tobacco, and thus sits absorbed in a profound reverie; he is at length disturbed by being presented with a slight infusion of Mocha coffee; in which the grounds remain suspend-ed*, and he drinks it gently from the edge of the cup; his crossed legs on which he sits are almost useless, and he is obliged to be lifted up by two domestics. His abundant clothes, the cushion on which he sits, the voluptuousness of the harem, and other ex-cesses, completely enervate his frame.

The morning of the opulent man is always passed in the way here described, or in mechanically rolling between his hands the tchespi, a sort of chaplet which the Mussulmans play with for pastime. Towards noon they bring his dinner, and on this occa-sion the greatest simplicity prevails: the table contains neither cloth, forks, plates, or knives; a salt-cellar, some wooden, shell,

* It will be a novelty to many of our readers, to learn that the Turkish method of making coffee has lately been introduced into the metropolis. It is effected by digestion, which supersedes the necessity of boiling, in a machine which contains a muslin bag, filled with coffee, through which the water is poured into the pot, and the grounds remain suspended. ED.

or copper spoons, and a large dish, which is handed round to the guests, form the whole of the apparatus; and instead of a cloth being laid upon the table, the latter is placed upon cloth. The bread is distributed cut into mouthfuls, and the dish is garnished with five or six parcels of sallad, gerkins, celery, and other pickles. Afterwards the sauces and ragouts are brought, which will be subsequently described, and the meal concludes with the pilau, which has been already mentioned. On no occasion do they ever make use of desserts: the fruits of the different seasons supply the place of bye-dishes; and each person eats of them, as much as he pleases during dinner. A quarter of an hour is sufficient for the whole ceremony; and the indolent Turk seems to consider it a labour to supply the wants of nature.

The drinks, which, however, they do not use till they have finished their meals, are water and sherbet, which are handed round in a crystal glass that serves all the guests: wine, which is apparently proscribed, is only drunk in the taverns. The Turkish history mentions several sultans who have given public examples of this violation of the Koran; but since the several edicts of Murad IV. his successors have endeavoured to save appearances. It is only the dervises, monks, soldiers, sailors, and the lower order who bear the scandal of drunkenness.

In the the afternoon the rich Turk passes his time in an airy keosk. Those who reside on the banks of the Bosphorus, delight in looking towards the agreeable scites of Asia, where the remains of their fathers are interred, it being customary for the families of the opulent Turks of Constantinople to be buried in Asia; they therefore contemplate that country as the one which is to be an asylum for the Mussulmans when, according to an old prophecy, *a nation of fair men shall have driven them from Europe!!* A Turk in the situation just alluded to, becomes intoxicated with the vapours of the pipe, and refreshes himself with sherbet perfumed with musk, which the slaves pour out for him. Being distanced from all society, he orders his women to be sent for, and without in the least discomposing his gravity, he commands them to dance before him.

The supper, which is served upon the tables at sunset, is composed with more attention than the dinner; but it is dispatched with equal celerity: the pipe terminates the day, whose monotonous round admits of no variety, nor of any of those accessary amusements which constitute the pleasure of life.

The people of the east are far from enjoying a pleasant existence; their aliments are gross, and in general unwholesome. In summer they almost renounce the use of bread, and feed upon scarcely any thing but gourds, melons, and other aqueous fruits. This season also constantly produces epidemic diseases of the most terrible kind ; it is then that the plague extends its ravages on bodies weakened by abundant perspiration, and which are not restored by proper nutriment. This remark, simple as it may appear, will shew the cause of the return of the epidemic fever, which superficial observers represent, as continually exerting its ravages in Constantinople. It is a fact, that in a year when fruit is abundant and corn is scarce, the climate is fatal to the people, as the hot and moist temperature favours the developement of pestilential effluvia.

Coffee is not to be classed amongst the privations which these people experience : this drink is, like tobacco, in general use ; the Turks smoke to excess, and the custom, though it was not known in the east till the year 1605, is now a want even of infancy. Such of the women as are not addicted to smoking, amuse themselves with chewing mastich-root from Chio, which imparts to the breath a smell like that of violets ; but the considerable excretion of saliva which the mastication excites, is detrimental to the digestive functions.

Such is a summary of the manner of living amongst the Orientals, whose sobriety affords a striking contrast to the sumptuous repasts of the energetic people of the north. The table of an European, for instance, who resides at Constantinople, is totally different from that of a Turk : the Frank will have at his meals the red wine of Tenedos and those of Asia, and he can vary, according to the season, the rare and delicious fruits that abound in the markets.

The principal species of game which come amongst their animal food, are partridges, pheasants and hares, which are found in the forests of Belgrade ; with the woodcocks, wild boar, and rabbits from the isles of the Princes. In the autumn the markets are filled with quails and all species of poultry, alive ; but the Turks, instead of taking the trouble to fatten them, merely blow them, and swell the cellular membrane, which makes them appear fat, and thus the buyer is imposed on. The Thracian ox begins to come into general use ; and the sheep of Caramania, with a triangular tail, affords a faintish kind of mutton ; but the herds which graze on the hills of Macedonia beyond Thessaly, yield a succulent and much-admired nutriment. Fish is likewise abundant ; but the Turks prefer the salted carp of the Don, which the Russians sell them in a prepared state. Shell-fish are likewise obtained in profusion ; the Franks and Greeks, however, are the only persons who eat them, as the Turks, eject all those species from their culinary system. These wretched people are also unacquainted with the art of the dairy ; and though they might make excellent cheese, yet it always has an acrid flavour. It is true that the wants of life are not so great with an inhabitant of the east, who is naturally abstemious, as with a person from the north, which is proved from a view of the city, in which you only find a few biscuit-bakers, while the cooks are simple kebadgis, or roasters. These are unacquainted with the art of roasting mutton by the spit, but do it by means of an economical oven, which dresses slices in a few minutes. Travellers nevertheless conceive meat so dressed to be the most delicious in the country; and they are right.

A few of the dervises, and other indolent men who abhor activity or labour, seem to measure their appetite by the property they possess; and hence they may be seen passing half a day together over a cup of coffee, and a few pipes of tobacco. The coffee-houses are, in consequence, the resort of lazy people, who smoke, talk about politics, and relate stories, while some of the coffee-house-keepers, in order to draw custom, adopt the profession of barbers, and shave the head and beard.

There are other men who live even cheaper than those just mentioned: being strangers to the luxury of the table, a pill of opium satisfies their hunger, makes them drunk, and throws them into the most pleasing extacy. These men are more decried than real drunkards.

The dervises, oulimas, and lazy fellows in general, are those who make most use of opium: they begin by using half a grain of that substance, and continue to increase the dose till they find it does not produce the desired effect. They take care not to drink water after it, which would give them the most violent colic: but the man who at the age of twenty takes to opium, seldom attains an age beyond thirty or thirty-six years. In the course of a few years the dose is increased to upwards of a drachm, or sixty grains. At this time a pallid countenance and extreme leanness announce a state of cachexia, which is only the prelude to a general marasmus, that can only be compared to itself. The infatuation is so great, that the certainty of death and all the infirmities which lead to it, is incapable of correcting a theriaki, or person addicted to the use of opium; he coldly answers any one who apprizes him of his danger, that *his happiness is incomparable when he has absorbed his pill of opium.* If he be asked to define this supernatural felicity, he only says, that it is impossible to describe it, as it is a pleasure not to be explained. These miserable beings, however, towards the close of their life, or rather of that state of stupefaction into which they are plunged, experience the most severe pains, and a continual hunger; they are tormented by a desperate satyriasis, without the capability of satisfying their desires; in short, they experience pains, which even their delicious paregoric cannot assuage; and having become hideous, deformed by numerous periostoses, deprived of their teeth, their eyes sunk into their head, and afflicted with an incessant trembling, they cease to exist a long time before their life is at an end.

Such are the effects of opium amongst those unfortunate people, who may be seen collected together daily in one quarter of Constantinople: it would be curious to ascertain the internal state of men who have died of this excess; and the cadaveric autopsia would doubtless disclose some important circumstances. I fear, however, that, in this respect, curiosity cannot be satisfied; for the ideas of the Mussulmans are very different from our own. Woe be to that man who might be surprised stealing a corpse! I really think that, on such an occasion, the whole city would rise, as the Turks would consider it a greater catastrophe than the loss of a province.

There might, however, be mentioned amongst the theriakis a phenomenon of longevity, which forms an exception to the common rule, and which I should be cautious of relating if the fact were not attested by the most reputable persons who are still alive, and some of whom are even now at Paris. I allude to a theriaki, who as late as the year 1800, was known throughout Constantinople by the name of *Suleyman Yeyen,* or *Suleyman, the taker of the corrosive Sublimate.* At the time when I resided in that city, this man was stated to be nearly a hundred years old: he had seen the reigns of sultans Achmet III. who ascended the throne in 1703, Osman, Mahmoud, Mustapha III. Abdul Hamid, and Selim III. In his youth he accustomed himself to take opium, and though he progressively augmented the doses, he could not obtain the pleasure he wished for, which induced him to adopt the use of sublimate, the effects of which he had heard boasted of. This old man had therefore taken it daily for upwards of thirty years, and in 1797, his daily dose exceeded a drachm or sixty grains! I was told that at this period he went into the shop of a Turkish Jew, and asked for a drachm of sublimate, which he diluted in a glass of water, and swallowed in an instant. The apothecary being horribly alarmed lest he should be accused of poisoning the Turk, shut up his shop, and became greatly afflicted at what had taken place; but his surprise may be conceived when the next day the Turk came, and asked for a similar dose of sublimate!!! I intended to find out this man when I regained my liberty; but a variety of important circumstances prevented me from ascertaining a fact, of which, however, I can have no doubt, when it is asserted by every body, and particularly as I have been many times assured of it by Messrs. Ruffin and Dantan.

I shall add another remark which I have no where met with, and which relates to the thickness of the heads of the people of

Constantinople : though a fact, it was mentioned to me in a way of ridicule by M. Ruffin. I mean the hardness of the skull independent of the turban, which varies according to the profession or religion. If a man be pursued by the guard, he is stopped by their adroitly throwing a stick at him, which stops between his legs and causes him to fall ; and the janissaries on coming up with him never fail to strike him violently on the head with their sope or stick. After stunning him by this means, they pass their sticks through his waistband, and thus carry him to prison on their shoulders, where without any care or assistance they leave him to recover, and he generally gets well in two or three days. This remark confirms an observation that has often been made relative to the rapid cure of wounds on the head in southern climates.

I shall now return to my view of Constantinople.—An European who has not seen that city, cannot form any idea of a place where the grave and serious people have neither walks, shews, dances, nor any of those amusements which give variety and pleasure to existence, excepting the fêtes of the Bairam, at which the Mussulmans suspend their labour, and take the pleasure of sitting on some elevated spots to smoke and enjoy an agreeable landscape. It cannot be said that they have any shews or dramatic spectacles : for we ought not to give that name to the indecent scenes of the puppet-shew kind, which those men, so jealous of their wives, cause to be represented in their families. "The hero of the piece," said M. Sevin, whose words I quote, " is an infamous wretch whom they call *Caragueuse*, and who appears on the stage with all the attributes of the famous god of Lampsacus. In the first act he gets married, and consummates the ceremony in the presence of the honest assembly : in the second act his wife lies in, and the child immediately begins a very filthy dialogue with its father. In the third act Caragueuse assumes the habit of a dervise, and immediately after taking the sacred oath, comes a terrible dragon, which swallows him up and all his company ; but the monster not finding them very digestible, vomits up the monks one after the other. They then sweep the stage, and the audience withdraws."

Caragueuse is always accompanied by a simpleton, called Codja Haivat, who is the jack-pudding of the English, or something like our Giles : he receives the blows intended for his master, and is ridiculed by him for his blunders and stupidity. I witnessed several of these farces, in which I did not observe that the rules of Aristotle were more respected than his morals. Between the acts they often give the representation of a Jewish funeral, the procession of which is closed by a pieman announcing his commodities in the Portuguese language, which is that spoken by the Jews of Constantinople.

Hence the Turks have neither fêtes nor dramatic amusements; but their places of resort are filled with jugglers, who make serpents dance to the sound of the drum, players on glasses, and leaders of bears: there may also be seen bodies of Bohemians or Tchinguenets, who perform the most lascivious and disgusting dances to the sound of gentle music. These miserable wretches, though professing Islamism, are reproved and excommunicated by the Turks, who make them pay the caratch, like the other vassals of the empire; justly refusing to consider them as Mussulmans.

In the taverns, which amount to several thousands in the capital of the faithful, there is a kind of female dancers called jamakis, who are Greeks from the isles of the Archipelago: they are elegantly dressed, and wear valuable shawls, bracelets, necklaces, and long hair; they perfume themselves, use rouge, and affect all the revolting manners of prostitutes. The indolent Turks are continually feasting them, giving them money, and sometimes are so enraptured, that they fall foul of each other for the honour of their society. The guard, who then runs to the aid of the combatants, separates them by rolling between them the full or empty hogsheads which stand in the place, for here the casks and the drinkers are together; the tavern is then shut up, and the owner cannot get leave to re-open it till he has paid a fine of some dollars. The grand vizier, in order to fill his coffers, commands, during the festival of the Bairam, and in times of calamity, that the taverns, which are licensed like the gaming-houses in Europe, shall be shut; and soon afterwards he receives a petition from the Greeks accompanied with a present, which settles all difficulties.

The news of the opening of the taverns spreads joy amongst the drinkers, who form a numerous class, though they are often chastised for their breach of decorum. A Turk found drunk in the streets by the guard is condemned to the bastinado, which punishment is inflicted three times if he as often commit the offence; after this he is considered incorrigible, and receives the title of an imperial or privileged drunkard. The next time he is arrested and in danger of receiving punishment, he has only to tell his name and prove his privilege in order to be released.

This singular manner of branding a drunkard is not the only one employed. If a man, from any cause whatever, acquire the hatred of his neighbours, ten or twelve of them go to the cadi, and state that they have a complaint against him; if the cadi insist on farther explanation, they merely say that he is a good sort of man, but that they cannot consent to have him for a neighbour : they then mention his name, and the judge is, according to custom, obliged to make him change his quarters. The punishment does not end, however, with this expulsion, for the culprit carries with him a sort of scandalous certificate ; and if fresh complaints be three times made from the place of his new residence, the government then interferes, and the individual is banished. Such a censure renders the Turks and all the inhabitants of Constantinople extremely circumspect, and excites an emulation in every quarter of the town to support its own reputation.

When justice adopts its forms for the punishment of condemned criminals, it always assumes a horrid character peculiar to barbarous people ; but it is never so terrific and dreadful as on the execution of the decrees of the vizier in the middle of the night. I never recollect an occurrence of this kind which took place during my captivity, without feeling my hair stand on end. It was after the autumnal equinox when I went out during the night to respire the fresh air which circulated through the garden within the walls of the Seven Towers ; the moon shone uncommonly bright, the Bosphorus was calm, and all was buried in death-like silence : I could not refrain from giving way to melancholy ideas ; at times I anticipated the happiness I should enjoy by returning to the bosom of my family, when I was roused from my reverie by the report of the artillery of Hissar, which resounded across the canal in tremendous echoes. I at first thought that it was a signal from some shipping in distress ; but being alarmed by a second report, I asked our guards what it meant, when they informed me, that it announced to the vizier who was asleep in his harem, the execution of his orders. Some janissaries who had been capitally convicted, had just suffered death, and their bodies been thrown into the sea; the number of cannon fired was equal to that of the persons executed.

But though this signal of death be dreadful, the rolling of the drum to give notice of a fire is not less so, as it is heard from the ramparts of the Seven Towers, where it is beaten to alarm the inhabitants of the environs: this signal, however, does not commence till the janissary aga has began his tour; when a thousand confused voices are heard, and particularly that of the watchman, who strikes the ground with his feruled stick, and announces the event by crying in a lamentable tone, " Yangun war, there is a fire:" the janissaries then repair in crowds to the spot under pretence of preventing its ravages; but their general object is plunder.

The inhabitants of Constantinople, who are so often the victims of conflagration, never attempt to save their goods; they even consider the calamity to be necessary to the city they inhabit. Each family is in the habit of keeping its most valuable articles in a certain box, which is placed every evening on a table, in order in case of accidents to enable them to carry it off. When they go to take a walk, or when the whole family goes out, they carry it with them, and nobody would leave it in a house for four and twenty hours. There may, however, be seen speculators offering to purchase a building when the fire is approaching towards it; and it is not rare to find an owner so infatuated, as to prefer losing his property, rather than make such a bargain. From this circumstance we may conceive how dear rent must be in a city which changes its appearance every fifteen years in consequence of fires, and where the progress of the flames is so rapid, that the inhabitants often have scarcely time to jump out of window. For this reason the people are obliged to be always on the alert; most of them sleep in part of their clothes, as do the women with their bracelets, jewels, &c. on their persons; nevertheless, many of these unfortunates, and great numbers of children, perish in the flames, or are buried in the ruins.

When these accidents happen, the sultan does not fail to repair to the place of danger, where he distributes money to encourage the people to exert themselves, and punishes those who plunder, by causing them to be thrown into the fire; but all their care and assistance are unavailing, as they know not how to subdue the fire, which makes dreadful ravages in a city built of wood, and painted with oil of spikenard. The pumpers use their pumps more frequently to souse those who are present, than to stop the progress of the flames. Every person makes a point of offering his house to the Grand Seignior; but he takes up his residence in that which is most secure from danger.

Such is a rapid view of this city, inhabited by a people, who belong in no respect to Europe, except by the spot which they occupy in it; a city in which there is no post-office, where the streets have no particular denomination, the inhabitants no family name, but are only distinguished by equivocal sirnames; and lastly, where nobody knows his own age, as there are no registers to prove the civilized state of the people. There reign oppression, licentiousness, despotism, and equality; a system of laws, and another of terror; there the assassin is punished, and applauded; there may be found an assemblage of virtue and vice, of civilization and barbarism: nothing, in short, seems at Constantinople in its place. The observer who goes there for meditation, will find incessant food for his curiosity; for much remains to be known and published relative to the Turks, whom a modern writer has described to be a people of *antithesis*.

Morier:
Journey through Persia

James Justinian Morier, *A Journey through Persia, Armenia, and Asia Minor, to Con-stantinople, in the Years 1808 and 1809* (London, 1812), pp. 292–319.

James Justinian Morier (1780–1849), traveller, ambassador and renowned novelist, wrote several popular accounts of Persia, all drawn from his diplomatic experience in the East during the Napoleonic Wars. While Morier's career in the foreign service made him a prominent figure within government circles, his public reputation rested upon the success of his travel narratives and his orientalist novels. These works, documenting the intricacies of early nineteenth-century Anglo-Persian imperial relations, helped to construct popular ideas of Persian culture for the Romantic reading audience.

A naturalised British subject, Morier came from a Swiss family with a history of diplomatic appointments. His own career in the foreign service began in 1808, when he accompanied the new British ambassador, Harford Jones, to Persia. Anglo-Persian relations in 1808 were at a point of considerable tension following the recent failure of Malcolm's mission to the Shah, with Tehran openly courting Napoleon. Jones had been appointed to resolve matters more advantageously and Morier was attached to his embassy, first as treasurer and later as public secretary.

By 1809, Jones had successfully secured a preliminary treaty between Britain and Persia's Fath Ali Shah, and Morier was charged with escorting Mirza Abul Hasan, the Persian ambassador, to London. In addition to undertaking an extensive journey in the company of the amiable Hasan, Morier also acted as host to the envoy during the next year in London. While diplomatic negotiations proceeded slowly, Hasan was lionised by English society and Morier came to a position of social prominence by extension. Partly as a result of this popularity, Morier was encouraged to publish his Persian journals and his first travel account, *A Journey through Persia*, appeared in 1812.

In 1811, however, Morier had returned to Persia with Mirza Abul Hasan and with the newly appointed British ambassador, Sir Gore Ouseley, who was to relieve Harford Jones. When Ouseley resigned his appointment in 1814, Morier subsequently became ambassador to Persia himself. By 1815, however, the war with France had ended and Anglo-Persian relations became less important for the security of British colonial possessions. When the embassy was downgraded in 1816, Morier returned to England.

Meanwhile, Morier's first travel book had been well reviewed in England and, as he enthusiastically reported to his brother, '[I] have set myself on the road to authorship' (quoted in Henry McKenzie Johnston, *Ottoman and Persian Odysseys: James Morier, Creator of Hajji Baba of Ispahan, and his Brothers* (London, 1998), p. 173). Part of the narrative's popularity stemmed from the romanticised exoticism with which Morier had imbued the account. For, as one of Morier's colleagues in Tehran observed, 'from the motives of policy ... [he has] painted this country in warmer colours than it deserves' (quoted in Johnston, *Ottoman and Persian Odysseys*, p. 173). In short, the descriptions were intended to flatter the Persian court and to advance British diplomatic objectives in the region. While many Romantic travel narratives participated in the project of imperial expansion and consolidation, Morier's account is a particularly overt instance of the intimate relationship between Romantic rhetoric and empire building.

Although Morier published a second well-received travel account in 1818, under the title *A Second Journey through Persia, Armenia and Asia Minor to Constantinople between the Years 1810 and 1816*, his renown as both author and orientalist stemmed from the wildly popular response to his first novel, *Adventures of Hajji Baba of Ispahan*, published in 1824. As a late Romantic oriental tale, Morier's novel incorporates travel materials into both its descriptions and its narrative framework, while developing a fantastic – and often satirical – representation of 'real life' within Persian court culture. Morier's success was followed by a sequel, *Adventures of Hajji Baba in England* (1828), and by several other popular oriental novels, including *Zohrab the Hostage* (1832) and *Ayesha, the Maid of Kars* (1834).

CHAP. XVI.

TABRIZ TO ARZ-ROUM.

PERSIAN. TRAVELLING—DEPARTURE FROM TABRIZ—BEAUTY OF
THE COUNTRY—LAKE OF SHAHEE—STATION OF RAHDARS—
KHOI; TOWN; GARDENS; PLAIN—AGRICULTURE—ELAUTS—
CONVENIENCE OF TENTS—COURDISTAN ROBBERS—HERDS OF
MARES—FRONTIERS OF PERSIA AND TURKEY—BAYAZID—
MOUNT ARARAT—RECEPTION IN THE TENTS OF THE ELAUTS
—DIADIN; THE EUPHRATES—IBRAHIM PACHA; VISIT TO HIS
ENEMY TIMUR BEG; RECEPTION AT THE CASTLE OF TURPA
CALEH—DEPOPULATION OF THE COUNTRY—OMEN—RIVER
ARAXES—CONDUCT OF THE AGA OF ALWAR.

THE mode of travelling in Persia is easy and commodious. In winter they generally begin their journey at sun-rise. The baggage proceeds, and then the master. He breakfasts either before he sets off, or in in a more pleasant spot on the road, (regarding in each case the advantage of a stream of running water as the motive of preference;) and thus he allows time for his luggage to reach the stage before him, and his people to prepare every thing for his reception, spread his carpets, and get the necessary articles for cooking his dinner. On his arrival he eats his *choshtá*, or intermediate meal, and then sleeps. At sun-set he takes another repast (his *noshtá*); and his servants then pack up every thing ready for his departure the next morning. He proceeds by easy stages, generally from five to six leagues a-day, which, as he always rides his own horses, is a good day's journey at the common rate of travelling. If he has a *Mehmandar* with him, he is fed and lodged and travels entirely at the public expence. When the *Mehmandar* arrives at the village, he produces his *firman*, (in which the kind and quantity of the articles to be provided are specified;) and demands a correspondent supply from the inhabitants.

1st June, 1809. We left the *Khoi* gate of *Tabriz* at seven o'clock, and in six hours and a half reached *Ali Shah*, a distance called by the people of the country six *fursungs*, and which I reckoned at twenty-four miles. From the top of our lodging at *Ali Shah*, I could see the mountain near which *Tabriz* is situated, I can therefore place exactly the bearing of our route, at N. 75 W. We kept to the Eastward of the plain in consequence of the difficulties along the road through the centre, which was then in many places overflowed

Near *Tabriz* on the left, are some gardens and houses, called *Hucknavar;* then the village of *Mayan.* To the Eastward of the city itself, is a conspicuous hill called the *Bahalil Tapé*, which abounds in every kind of game. Having travelled three miles from *Tabriz* on a bearing nearly N. we came to a bridge of nine large and three small arches, thrown over the river *Agi*, which, flowing from E. to W. falls at length into the lake of *Shahee*. The river rises near *Ardebil;* and is fordable by mules where we crossed it, though we prefered the bridge, which happened indeed to be in better repair than those between *Teheran* and *Tabriz.* At about four miles from the city, we passed a village called *Alwar;* and three miles further another of the same name, each surrounded with a cultivated territory, intersected by a thousand dikes and *kanauts.* The greatest part of the plain is of a soil strongly impregnated with salt; and as in every other district of the same quality, we witnessed the curious effects of the vapour, (called *Ser Aub*) which overspread the plain. About four miles before we reached *Ali Shah*, we crossed a bridge of four arches, over a pool of standing salt water. The industry of agriculture was visible, and the crops of barley and corn were luxuriant and promising.

The plain of *Tabriz* extends far to the W. and S.; the mountains which border it on those directions being just designed in very light tints in the horizon. To the Northward and Eastward it is bounded by hard-featured lands of an inferior elevation, indicating on their surfaces the minerals below. There are several pretty villages situated to the North, on the declivity of the mountain about three or four miles from *Ali Shah*, and which, together with it and others to the W. are in the *Mahalé* or district of *Ghunéh*.

The lake of *Shahee* is about seven *fursungs* from *Ali Shah*, and the middle of the long mountain (which extends into the centre of the lake, and which now appeared isolated on the horizon of the plain) bore S. 50 W. of our station.

In my progress to *Constantinople*, I traversed a country in its conformation most picturesque, and in its productions most luxuriant. No traveller in any season, or in any direction, could have passed these scenes without admiration; but I saw them in all the richness of spring, contrasted with a winter in Persia; and after the leafless and barren region which I had passed, I enjoyed doubly the wild prodigality of vegetation, which in the early part of the year is displayed through Asia Minor. The impression therefore of delight which I experienced, was strongest at the first point of contrast; and the first verdure and foliage which I saw near *Tabriz*, appeared to me to constitute the very perfection of landscape.

2d June. If a writer of romance would describe beautiful scenery, he might select our departure from *Ali Shah*. We began our journey by a most charming moonlight; and the sky was delightfully serene. Just as the sun was rising we reached an orchard, (full of every species of fruit, particularly almonds, and) skirting the town of *Shebester;* which, embosomed in trees of every hue, was situated on the declivity of the mountains on our right.

Shebester is a large town, surrounded by several villages, and by more wood and cultivation, than any spot I had yet seen in Persia. Hitherto indeed the want of trees, either as a shade to the road, or as a relief to the inequalities of the heights, had been constant and uniform. We admired therefore doubly the beauties of our present course. Streams of running water were meandering in every direction amid the numerous willows, poplars, almonds, and other trees, which bordered our road: and at intervals the artificial dikes were opened to admit water into the beds of rice. The greater part of the country was covered with verdure, for the new corn was already well advanced both in maturity and plenty. Peasantry enlivened the fields by the labours of the spade or the plough.

After quitting *Shebester* we came in full view of the delightful lake of *Shahee.* It derives its name from the surrounding *Mahalé,* which may contain twenty villages. I was told that its waters are as salt as the sea, and that the sand over which they flow, produces the salt used at *Tabriz.* It extended itself N. W. and S. E. before us, and its Western extremities were terminated by a stupendous chain of mountains, whose snowy summits, softened by the haze, contrasted admirably with the light azure of the lake. As we proceeded, the long mountain (which I mentioned in the route of yesterday, extending itself and forming a peninsula in the lake) appeared to have no connection whatever with the surrounding lands; and, by a stranger to the real topography, would have been pronounced an island. Its termination (to the south as seen from our road) was in the form of a sugar-loaf.

Near *Shebester* we passed the village of *Misholéh,* and, lower down in the plain, those of *Arsaléh* and *Halee,* on the left of the road. Others indeed are seen at every turn, situated at small intervals on either side alternately, all in the *Mahalé* of *Ghunéh.* Among them are *Besh-kefelout,* on the left; *Khomyéh,* prettily surrounded with verdure, on the right; *Shinwar*, on the left again; *Kuzec-dunar*, on the right, three *fursungs* before we reached our stage at *Tasouj*; and on the left, about two miles from the borders of the lake, *Alibanglou*, the first place in the *Bolouk* of *Aeenzaub*. In this line we stopt and fed our cattle and ourselves; while a refreshing breeze from the Westward just curled up the waters of the lake, and waved the corn fields which extended themselves on all sides of us.

Our bread and *moss* was shared by a stranger who was going to *Oroumi*, a large town, distant thirty *fursungs* from *Tabriz*; and situated, by the pointing of his hand, S. 50 W. from us, on the left or West side of the lake, which the road continues to skirt through its whole course. On the East of the lake is *Saouk Bolag*, the site of the ancient city of *Sheherivan*. The country, through which we passed in the day, was interesting and picturesque; in every turn of the view enriched by the lake and its surrounding capes and mountains.

From all that I could learn in this region, (and I inquired of many who had travelled repeatedly over this part of *Aderbigian*), there appeared to exist no other lake than this of *Shahee*. And I have as regularly made direct inquiries about the situation of the city of *Van* and its lake, without obtaining any thing like a satisfactory answer. On the contrary, the very existence of such a place, and such a lake, was always denied; I mention this, when the position of *Van* has been clearly ascertained, to shew how general was the ignorance of the people on every subject which was not immediately within their own circumscribed district. Nor was I more successful in my inquiries on the real extent of the lake before them: every one said that it was very large, and that it reached further, than from its appearance we might suppose.

At about five miles from *Tasouj*, there is a village on the left called *Rahdar Khoné*; and then a station of *Rahdars*, or custom-house officers. As we passed it, one of them, a man of a much more respectable appearance than any of the class whom we had seen on other occasions, told us that a driver with seven loaded mules had gone forwards, and refused to pay the duties, alleging that his beasts were carrying part of our baggage ; and were therefore in the King's service, and as such exempt from the impost.   In fact, however, my *Charwardar* (or conductor of the mules or caravan) had added to my charge this number, above those that were necessary for my purposes ; and, having already received a part of their hire from me, was now employing them still more to his own profit, by conveying upon them, duty-free, in my name, the goods of some *Tabriz* merchants.   On discovering the fraud, I resigned him into the hands of the officer, with full liberty to exact his dues ; a licence, under which he begun immediately to cudgel the shoulders of the defaulter.   The duties here are high, being five *reals* on each load.

Some miles before we reached *Tasouj*, the lake begins to make an elliptical termination, and the road to turn off on a more Northern angle.   We were eight hours in travelling the whole distance from *Ali Shah*, which we reckoned at thirty-two miles, on a bearing of N. 60 W.   *Tasouj*, from the great extent of the ruined walls about it, appears once to have been a large place, but it is now reduced, by earthquakes, to the denomination of a village.   There are remains of domed bazars and mosques, spread in every part of the place.

June 3.   The distance from *Tasouj* to *Khoi* is called eight *fursungs* ; we were however nine hours on the road, and calculated the journey at thirty-six miles.   The general direction was N. 30 W.   Our course for the first ten miles, to the foot of the range, (which encloses the plain and lake of *Shahee*) bore nearly West ; when we suddenly turned to the North through the mountains ; and, for ten miles more, wound among them through some very narrow defiles, and by some sharp ascents and descents, till we reached on the opposite side the plain of *Khoi*.   Towards the lake the mountains are mostly of an argillaceous soil, but change into fine earth as they approach the plain of *Khoi*.   In this direction they are green to their very summits, and their intervening vallies are covered with the finest pastures.

We had left *Tasouj* by moon-light : we could not therefore discover with any accuracy the nature of the country, which we traversed in the first part of our route; though we discerned indistinctly groves of trees, and heard the falling cascade in the recesses of the vallies. The first view of the plain of *Khoi*, from the summit of the pass in the mountains, is sublime. The city and its more immediate territory are seen on the N. but separated from the rest of the plain by a border of green hills, which seem to divide the expanse into two parts. At the distance of two *fursungs* from *Khoi*, we passed on the right the village of *Disajiz*, surrounded by fields of wheat and barley. On the left of the plain are some more villages; and one curious mound of red soil, crowned by a hillock of salt, besides several other white mounds, which are described as entirely of the same substance. We passed the small range of hills, and came all at once upon the more circumscribed plain of *Khoi*, which is opened by a seven-arched bridge, bordered on each side by rocks, and forming with the fine stream below a complete picture. The river is called the *Otour*, and flows from W. to E. falling into the *Arras* or *Araxes*, about twelve *fursungs* further to the Eastward.

The plain of *Khoi* (in breadth from N. to S. five miles, and in length ten) was the richest tract that we had seen. It was covered with corn, broken only here and there by the foliage of enclosed gardens. Of these gardens we ventured to enter one, which was renowned all over the country for its beauty and fruitfulness. It stands on the left of the road about two miles from the walls of *Khoi*, and was made by HOSSEIN KHAN, Governor of the city in the time of AGA MOHAMED KHAN; but it has now become the property of the government. It consists of a fine alley of *chenar* trees, which leads up to a pleasure-house, now falling into decay, built on the elevation of six terraces, from each of which falls a beautiful cascade, conducted by *kanauts* from the neighbouring mountains. On the right and left is a wood of fruit trees of every sort and description, with a fine crop of grass at their roots. From the pleasure-house is seen, through the alleys of *chenars*, the whole territory of *Khoi*, one of the most lively landscapes that we found in Persia. The *chenar* is really a delightful tree; its bole is of a fine white and smooth bark, and its foliage, which grows in a tuft at the summit, is of a bright green. Those in the garden had not attained their full growth. Their trunks are every where carved with the invocation of "*Ya Ali*;" proceeding probably from the ecstacies of those, who visit this little Persian paradise.

Khoi is surrounded with a wall, and with towers of a different construction to any which we had remarked in other fortified towns of Persia. They are triangular in front, with a species of connecting work behind them. There are four gates, which are of stone, and very superior to most of those that I had noticed elsewhere. Within the walls are twenty mosques and six baths. There are said to be ten thousand houses, and a population of fifty thousand persons, of which the larger proportion are Armenians. The Mussulmans live in a parish or *Mahalé* of their own. The territory is so extremely fertile, that *Khoi*, with the surrounding villages, pays annually to the public treasure the sum of one hundred thousand *tomauns*. *Khoi* is much warmer, from its local situation, than *Tabriz*. Roses here were in full flower, whereas a little opening bud was reckoned a rarity at *Tabriz*; and probably in twenty days from the date of our visit, the plain lost its verdure, and assumed the beautiful gilding of a ripe corn-field.

Six *fursungs* South from *Khoi* is an equally large and populous town called *Salmas*; where, as I afterwards learnt at *Arz-roum*, are "sculp-" tured rocks and many ruins." My informer added, that one of the subjects represented two men, of whom one, looking over his left shoulder, pointed with his hand to a spot which the people of the neighbourhood affirm to contain a hidden treasure, though they admit that the deposit has escaped all research.

4th of June, 1809. The Prince had ordered four men to attend us into the Turkish territories; and as they did not reach us at *Khoi*, we should probably have awaited their arrival there, if I had not resisted such an arrangement, declaring that it would be better to advance one mile, than in our circumstances to remain idle for one single day.   Accordingly, notwithstanding the pressing invitation of Nejef Kooli Khan, the Governor, to stay the day with him, we departed for *Péréh*, a village two *fursungs* from *Khoi*, which I call six miles, and in a bearing of N. 60 W.   The morning was one of the loveliest in Spring, lightly covered with clouds, with a softness in the air which seemed to soothe every varied work of nature into tacit enjoyment of the bounty and munificence of their Almighty Creator.   I shall ever recollect with thankfulness the delightful sensations which I experienced in passing the beautiful plain of *Khoi;* where every innocent sense received its gratification, and ripened into thoughts teeming with love and gratitude to their divine Maker.

Every thing was rich and beautiful : the mountains were green to their very summits; and their inequalites were here and there enriched by beds of wild flowers of the most lively and luxuriant hues.   Scarcely two miles from *Khoi* is a very large collection of houses and gardens, which is a *Mahalé* or parish of the town, and is well inhabited.   A stream from the mountains runs through it; and on the skirts to the N. are two pillars of brick, which are described either as the tomb or the cenotaph of a famous poet and learned *Mollah* of *Tabriz*, called *Shemsé*. *Péréh* is a pretty village, situated on the declivity of the hills, which gradually form the bases of the adjoining mountains; on the summit of one of these hills is an old square fort, now in ruins : and in its neighhood are two other villages called *Pesé* and *Zaidé*.   There are walnut-trees, willows, poplars, elms, and fruit-trees of every description in the highest perfection, with a great profusion of grass.

On this as well as on the other side of *Tabriz*, the peasants convey their loads on the backs of oxen, on which indeed they frequently ride themselves.   At *Péréh* I saw the first wheeled-carriage (excepting gun-carriages) that I had noticed in Persia.   It was exactly similar to the Turkish *Araba*.   Besides their plough, which I have already described, the Persians have the large rake, which serves as a harrow, and is fastened to a pole and drawn like a plough by yoked oxen: they have another implement of agriculture, which is certainly capable of much improvement. It is a pole fixt transversely on another to which the oxen are yoked ; on each of these is a small wooden cylinder about half a foot long: and these insignificant things are dragged as a roller over the ground.

June the 5th. We went from *Péréh* to *Zauviéh* in six hours and a half, on a bearing of N. 50 W. which may be twenty-four miles. During the whole of the preceding evening it had rained, accompanied by thunder and lightning. Our ride, therefore, was rendered muddy. From *Péréh* we entered some mountains of easy access ; which, about ten miles before we reached *Zauviéh*, opened into a plain surrounded like a basin by mountains, on all sides gradually inclining to the centre. On entering the plain, high on the right on the declivity of the mountain, is the village of *Selawan ;* and on the left a small village called *Khoré ;* and on the turn of the road towards it, are two stone lions among some rude and ancient tomb-stones. The greater part of the population of the plain is composed of Armenians. To the West are very high mountains, the tops of which were covered with snow, and their roots, when we passed by, were nearly concealed by the heavy clouds that rested upon them.

The snow was melting, and frequently streams were pouring from the mountains. Yet the difference of the temperature of the air here, and that which we had experienced within a few days, was very sensible ; and before sun-rise it was piercingly cold. The plain was cultivated in all parts. The whole of the soil, over which we passed, was of the finest brown mould; so that, excepting some summits of the mountains, the country was one universal carpet of verdure.

We met a large party of the *Elauts* or wandering tribes, composed mostly of women and children, who were travelling to a fresh encampment. One of the women, who had the care of two children, had dismounted ; and the extreme agility with which she got on her horse again, without any other aid than her own hands and feet, shewed how much she was accustomed to this sort of life.

We sent forwards our *Mehmandar* to desire that tents might be pitched for us, because we had been advised to avoid the village on account of the plague, which sometimes visits these parts. Accordingly we found four tents pitched for us, two of horse-hair, (the real *Kara Khader* of the *Eels*), and two white tents, rude enough indeed, but so delightfully situated in the plain, surrounded by corn fields, that we quite revelled in the exchange.

We had not long taken possession of our humble encampment, when a storm of thunder, lightning and hail overwhelmed us, in a manner which completely destroyed all the comfort of our interior arrangements. Hail-stones fell in numbers which entirely filled every corner of our tent, and so large, that measuring one I found it to be an inch in diameter, and so strongly congealed that they lay on the ground undiminished in size, until the sun once more broke out and dissolved them. The hills near us received a new covering of snow, shewing their summits as the storm rolled away, in sublime grandeur. The peasants told us, that this weather was very common to them. Although this was but an ungracious beginning to a pastoral life, yet I must own that to me it still had so many delights compared with the confinement of houses, that with all the present disadvantages I would willingly prefer it to a residence in the towns of Persia. Among its enjoyments is that of its freedom from vermin, from which (particularly fleas) we had hitherto suffered so much; not that the people are singularly dirty, but the creatures are the usual productions of the place and season. A Persian who was conversing with us in our tent, on seeing my servant beating a coat with a cane to clean it of the vermin which it had collected at the former stage, very gravely asked, " Pray what crime has that " coat committed, that makes the *Frangee* beat it so?"

June the 6th. The quantity of rain that had fallen during the course of the day had completely saturated the greatest part of our clothes and baggage, and materially increased the weight of the lading of our mules. Thanks to God, it did not rain in the night ; and we slept soundly till about an hour before the break of day, when we quitted our black tents for the village of *Cara-ainéh.* The distance, on a bearing of N. 20 W. is called five *fursungs;* but though we were nearly six hours on the road, I shall not reckon it at more than eighteen miles, because we were delayed in our progress by the mud, which the rain and hail had created. We took a turn to the Eastward from our encampment, and came to a village called *Iekaftee,* on the borders of a mountain torrent swoln and rendered so rapid by the late storms, that two or three of our mules had nearly been carried away by its violence. On the right of the road (at the distance of five miles from our last station) is a spring dammed up, except at an aperture in one of its corners, through which a small quantity of water is permitted to ooze out, called in Turkish, *Ak-bolagh,* or " white spring :" and three miles further, and distant from the road two miles, on the left, is a collection of a few wretched hovels called *Kurkendéh,* surrounded by cultivated fields. About this spot the road was formerly so infested with the *Curdistan* robbers, that it was never passed without danger : but since Prince ABBAS MIRZA has had the government of *Aderbigian* in his hands, he has so completely expelled the freebooters from their haunts, that no district is now so safe. We traversed a pass formed by the gradual meeting of the roots of the mountains, and then entered an oval plain, extending, on a rough calculation, in length eight miles from N. to S. and three in breadth. The village of *Cara-ainéh,* our *Menzil,* is here immediately seen, and is easily marked by a square fort, which, rising from the midst of its miserable huts, appears a palace in comparison. This village is the chief of a *Mahalé* of the same name, composed of about twenty-one villages, the principal of which are *Hiderlou, Nabekandi, Gelish Acha, Sedel, Zaiveh,* and *Ak-dezeh.* From *Cara-ainéh* there is a road to *Van,* a distance of fifty miles, on a bearing of S. W.

We had now reached the dregs of Persia. Beyond *Khoi* and *Pérék* both the habitations and the people bore an appearance of misery, indicative of a neglected country. This deterioration is probably inseparable from the borders of two states, which are ill-defined as to territory and actual property. None but the *Ket Khoda* had a decent coat, and all the rest were in tatters and beggary.

The *Thaubet* of *Cara-ainéh* had been appointed to his government only the day before our arrival, an excuse which he alleged for his inability to satisfy us in several of our inquiries. His appearance, indeed, bespoke the truth of his apology; for he was dressed from head to foot in new clothes, new cap, new coat, new slippers; doubtless to impress his peasantry with a sense of his superiority. We had rain all the day, and almost incessant thunder and lightning. The tract over which we passed, though generally of admirable soil, was for the greater part waste. We saw, however, immense flocks, some perhaps of one thousand sheep, grazing in the fat pastures on the declivities and in the recesses of the mountains; and large herds also of mares with their foals. These were the property of the *Elauts*: the mares belonging to the King are kept in *Mazanderan*, which is said to afford the finest pasture of his dominions. Their foals are thence distributed to the troops as they may be wanted. The Guardian or Controller of these Royal herds is an officer of considerable consequence, and is selected always from men of rank and importance in the state. He is called *Ełkhee-chee* or Master of the Mares, and resides at *Asterabad*, where he holds his office, registering every foal as it falls. He has subordinate agents, entrusted severally with the charge of twenty mares, and with the choice of their pastures, besides the inferior grooms who tend the animals daily. The foals are not backed until they have completed their third year.

7th. The morning was darkened by clouds which covered the whole sky; the thickest resting on the tops of the mountains, and extending themselves in some parts nearly to the bases. We quitted our wretched habitation at *Cara-ainéh*, to pace a miserable road; the bottom of which, always wet and deep, was rendered still more impracticable by a shower of rain that overtook us, soon after we had quitted the village. Almost at the extremity of the plain is a swamp; on the surface of the waters of which were innumerable flocks of ducks and other wild-fowl. We noticed two cranes stepping away before us at a great pace, and hiding their legs from us by letting fall their tails. The soil was rich almost beyond calculation, and afforded the finest pastures. We crossed the village of *Ak-dezeh*, and then leaving the plain, wound through the vallies which were formed by the Western mountains. The whole country was watered by numerous torrents; or. the borders of one we spread as our breakfast, the scanty remains of our yesterday's meal; which, in such a spot however, would have been a real treat to the lovers of romance. The scene indeed, alone, consoled us for our bad fare at *Cara-ainéh*. A stupendous mass of rock rose perpendicularly over our heads; and at our feet foamed and roared the torrent, while the whole view was enriched by the verdure of the distant landscape, and enlivened by the chirping of innumerable birds. About twelve miles from *Cara-ainéh* are several hills; the declivities of which are strewed with large masses of black rock, evidently from their weight and their calcined appearance, full of metal. The whole seems to be volcanic matter.

After quitting these hills we came into the plain, at the extremity of which is situated *Agajik*, a miserable Armenian village, about the same size as our former stage. We were six hours and a half in travelling the distance, twenty-two miles, on a bearing of N. 20 W. In the centre of the plain a caravan, from *Oroumi*, was grazing its mules: the driver of it told us, that he had been eight days on the journey, at the rate of four *agatch* a day, making a total of about one hundred miles. Here the distances are measured by the *agatch*, which corresponds exactly to the *sahat* or hour. The village consisted of huts, surrounding an old square fort on a hill: Our lodging was a covered building, in the roof of which were two small holes to admit light; and in the interior of which a square of twenty feet was parted off by a wall three feet high, for the residence of the master, while the remainder was reserved for his cattle. The costume of the people was changing fast; and the black sheep-skin cap of Persia was scarcely seen.

The day was overspread with clouds till near sun-set, when it cleared away a little to the Northward, and shewed us the sublime and venerable mountain of *Ararat*. It bore N. 10 E. of our station, and presented a stupendous mass to our view. The Persians told me that it was eight hours distance from us; and added many a story of its wonders. Such as—that no one, who attempted to ascend it, ever returned; and that one hundred men who had been sent from *Arzroum* by the *Pacha*, to effect the undertaking, all died. The Armenian priest assured me, with a very grave face, that the ark was still there. There is a smaller mountain on the same range, bearing N. 30 E. which is called by the Turks, *Cochuk Agri-dagh*, as the larger *Ararat* is called *Agri-dagh*. *Ararat* is the *Macis* of the Armenians. The sources of the *Euphrates* are twelve hours from *Agajik*, in a direction of N. 50 W. by the peasant's pointing. The Armenians told me that they had a *Zeeauret*, or place of devotion, at the sources called *Wes Kionk*.

8th. We left *Agajik* with five men, who, according to the custom, accompanied us out of their frontier into the Turkish territory. At about two miles and a half from *Agajik* is another Armenian village, called *Kilsé*, from the ruins of a church *(Ecclesia)*, which forms a conspicuous object among its mean huts, being well-built with a fine white stone, with arched doors and windows. Even in its ruins, however, the present poor inhabitants still contrive to keep up a place of worship within the interior.

About three miles and a half N. 30 W. from *Agajik*, are the boundaries of the Persian and Turkish territories marked by a ruined tower, situated in the centre of a valley.

As we were feeding our horses, the person whom we had sent to *Bayazid* (to intimate our approach to the locum-tenens of IBRAHIM

PACHA, who was himself on an excursion against the *Courds)* returned, and told us that the Acting-governor would not receive us into the city, nor give us a passage near it; alleging as a reason, that his master the *Pacha* had left strict orders, that during his absence no strangers, and particularly no Persians, should be admitted. This unexpected news staggered us at first, but at length we determined to send one of the *Mirza's* own men to exert the influence of his master's station in our favour. We proceeded, following our messenger: the road took a turn to N. 30 E. and shewed us once again in a much larger exposure than before the stupendous *Ararat*. It is indeed a sublime and almost terrific object. It rises from an immense variety of lands; and is covered with snow, and almost always surrounded with clouds.

We stopt at a small Armenian village called *Kerdek*, (on the left of the road, one *fursung* from *Bayazid*,) to await the return of our second messenger. We did not tarry long, when he appeared, though only to confirm the report of his predecessor. The Turks would not suffer him even alone to enter the city: for as soon as he approached, they fired a musket or two, to convince him that their resistance would not be confined to threats; and when he endeavoured to come to a parley, they answered him only with ill language and abuse. We determined therefore immediately upon taking a circuit to avoid *Bayazid*, and seeking IBRAHIM PACHA himself, from whom we expected a handsome reception; as the Persians represented him to me as a vassal of their Prince ABBAS MIRZA, fearing Him rather than his own sovereign. Our road to day averaged N. 10 W. a distance of ten miles; the same bearing indeed: may be extended to *Bayazid*, on a further distance of four miles. *Bayazid,* as I learned in its neighbourhood, is situated close at the foot of Mount *Ararat* : it is peopled principally by Armenians. On a hill about it, is a castle, which by its defenders is said to be strong.; they are very jealous however of the curiosity of a Persian.

9th. Three men, whom we anxiously expected from Prince ABBAS MIRZA to accompany us to *Constantinople*, joined us on the evening of the 8th; and so far therefore our delay at this miserable village was convenient. We gave them just time to feed their horses; and then, about an hour before sun-set, resumed our march to take up our quarters for the night on the bank of a little running stream; the rich pastures, through which the waters flowed, refreshed our cattle, but we ourselves were obliged to pass the night in the open field with a heavy dew falling, yet, thank God, with a fine clear sky. During the course of the night a Turk arrived from *Bayazid* to say, that he was sent by the *Kiayah* to be our *Mehmandar* to the presence of his master; adding, indeed, that the Vice-Governor regretted the misunderstanding on which he had acted, for he had been told that we were followed by a large body of horsemen. On further questioning the Turk we found, that the wife of IBRAHIM PACHA (hearing that there was an *Elchee*, an Embassador, without the town, and that admittance had been refused to him) made loud remonstrances to the *Kiayah* on the impropriety of his conduct, and interceded so far in our behalf that he sent us these excuses. Though we were ill satisfied with the conduct of this person, we thought it better not to reject the attendance of the officer whom he had deputed to escort us, as we were among a wild and unmanageable people.

We travelled an hour and a half, in one of the clearest and most beautiful mornings that the heavens ever produced; and passing on our left the two villages of *Dizzéh* and *Kizzil Dizzéh*, we came to an opening of a small plain covered with the black tents and cattle of the *Elauts*. Here also we had a view of Mount *Ararat*; the clouds no longer rested on its summit, but circled round it below. We went to the largest tent in the plain, and there enjoyed an opportunity of learning that the hospitality of these people is not exaggerated. As soon as it was announced at the tent that strangers were coming, every thing was in motion: some carried our horses to the best pastures, others spread carpets for us, one was dispatched to the flock to bring a fat lamb, the women immediately made preparation for cooking, and we had not sat long before two large dishes of stewed lamb, with several basins of *yaourt*, were placed before us. The senior of the tribe, an old man (by his own account indeed more than eighty-five years of age) dressed in his best clothes, came out to us, and welcomed us to his tent with such kindness, yet with such respect, that his sincerity could not be mistaken. He was still full of activity and fire, although he had lost all his teeth, and his beard was as white as the snow on the venerable mountain near his tent. The simplicity of his manners and the interesting scenery around reminded me, in the strongest colours of the life of the patriarchs: and more immediately of Him whose history is inseparable from the mountains of *Ararat*. Nothing indeed could accord better with the spot than the figure of our ancient host. His people were a part of the tribe of *Jelalee*, and their principal seat was *Erivan*; but they ranged through the country:

> And pastured on from verdant stage to stage,
> Where fields and fountains fresh could best engage.
> Toil was not then: of nothing took they heed
> But with wild beasts the sylvan war to wage,
> And o'er vast plains their herds and flocks to feed;
> Blest sons of nature they! true golden age indeed.
> *Castle of Indolence*, xxxvii.

We quitted our hospitable friends, (who appeared to be almost more grateful for our visit than we for their kindness), and passed along the plain. Mount *Ararat* bore N. 40 E. and extended itself completely to our view. Its N. W. ascent is not so rapid as its S. E. and I should conceive that in this quarter it might be possible to ascend it. In six hours and a half, after leaving our last encampment, we reached *Diadin*. It is a large village with a fort and towers; under which, in a deep channel of perpendicular rock, runs the eastern *Euphrates*, there a shallow stream about twenty feet in breadth. It rises about four *agatch* or twelve miles from *Diadin*, on a bearing of S. 50 W. by the direction of a man's hand; and in the country is called the *Frat*; the name assumed at *Arz-roum*, by the Western stream.

At *Diadin* we were not permitted to go near their miserable castle. The houses of the place are built of mud and stones, and the rooms are calculated to lodge the animals as well as the family. A small compartment only is reserved for the master; and in general the rest of the space is left for his cattle. We did not, indeed, enter their habitations, for every door was shut against us; and when, by great management, we had secured shelter for ourselves, our people, and our cattle, we found equal difficulty in procuring food. ABDULLA PACHA, a rebel Courd, with whom IBRAHIM PACHA was at open war, had in fact carried away all the flocks, and destroyed all the crops of this village. We could not therefore expect an easy supply of corn for our horses; but after much intreaty a little was produced, for which indeed we paid an amazing price. A piece of barley bread was delivered to each man; and the masters, by a very marked favour, were supplied with a mess of eggs and a basin of *yaourt*.

The houses for the *Conaks* or reception of strangers, here as in all other places in Turkey were regularly defined; but when the *Mirza* and I were entering that appropriated to ourselves, we were received at the door by a woman, who, with her face totally uncovered, boldly bad defiance to the *Conak-chee*, and (with the most threatening looks, and with all the volubility of her sex,) swore that nobody should enter her dwelling. However, by a little negociation we pacified our hostess, and were at length admitted into her stable, where we spread our carpets and composed ourselves to sleep. The women here barely cover their faces; and, as we afterwards learnt, are notorious for depravity: they appear very healthy. The men are as wild as savages; and seem to be under no law. Independently of their own immediate distresses, one of the reasons for their inhospitality to Persians is very natural; several Embassadors had been sent to *Constantinople*, and since that time every traveller, who had two or three attendants, assumed the same dignity. The discovery of the fraud has necessarily roused the caution of the Turks.

10th. We were nine hours on the road to *Youngali*, called nine *agatch*, and which I calculated at thirty-two miles on a bearing of N. 65 W. The *Euphrates* accompanied us all the way through a country of grass, but of little cultivation. Four miles after leaving *Diadin* we passed the village of *Jugan*, about a mile and a half on our left: then four miles further, still on the left and on the other bank of the *Euphrates*, *Utch Klissé*. Here a high and snow-covered mountain called *Kussá Dagh* appears in view; and (extending to the S. and W.) the range of *Ala-Dagh*. In the village is an Armenian Church, a very respectable looking building, much resembling an European structure. It has two wings with a shelving roof, and is covered by a small dome built of stone, apparently not in much decay.

At the termination of that branch of the mountain near which *Utch Klissé* stands, there is a stone bridge thrown over the *Euphrates*. We continued by the bank of the river, which winds from E. to W. creating verdure on each side as it flows. We passed through a village now in ruins called *Alakou*; and on the slope of the hill (three miles on the left of the road) that of *Comoulja*; another called *Belasou*, is close on the banks of the river; and, about eight miles further, having passed the miserable huts at *Cadi Kieu*, we reached after a very sultry ride, our *Conak* at *Youngali*. All these villages are in the *Mahalé* of *Alashgerd*.

When we had been about an hour on our road, I missed a small carpet from my baggage, and sent back therefore my servant to reclaim it from our host at *Diadin*. From the looks which he cast at our goods, I had frequently suspected his honesty, but I might have spared my suspicions and my trouble; for I received nothing but oaths. Near to *Utch Klissé*, we met the battering train of IBRAHIM PACHA, which consisted of two field pieces, returning from the siege of *Turpa Caléh*, the castle of TIMUR BEG, who had revolted from his authority.

We learned that after a siege of five months, in which the *Pacha* had fired his guns one hundred and fifty times at the town and castle, he had succeeded in killing one fowl and one dog.

IBRAHIM PACHA, who was at another village three miles from *Youngali*, sent his *Haznadar* or treasurer to escort us to our lodging. The misery here was even greater than that of the preceding day. No corn for our horses, nor even grass without hard blows. The whole of the country was in a state of absolute devastation from the incursions of the *Courds*; and our course presented nothing but difficulties, for IBRAHIM PACHA was at war with all the country round. He professed indeed to respect the *firman* of ABBAS MIRZA, and when we sent him that with which we had been furnished, he immediately carried it to his head; saying that he was the Prince's servant in all things; and that there was nothing which he would not willingly do to serve him. We never fared worse, however, than at this village. The people that surrounded us bore the looks of savages, and their general behaviour corresponded with their appearance.

To the South of *Youngali*, as I was told at the place, lies *Van*; and to the S. W. the large *Mahalé* of *Kensus*.

11th. We left *Youngali*, dissatisfied with our host: the Persians indeed were miserable with the scanty hospitality which they received at his village. When we were left by the two officers, who escorted us to their master's frontier, we were advised not to go near *Turpa Caléh*, as we should undoubtedly be molested. Yet the situation, in which this war of the rival chiefs had placed us, was so difficult, that we incurred equal hazard either in passing the castle of TIMUR BEG, without offering our respects, or in venturing near it after coming from the domains of his enemy. We determined, therefore, to state our story simply, and throw ourselves on his hospitality. We crossed a most beautiful plain, covered with villages, and watered by numerous streams. We forded three considerable torrents, which poured from the N. mountains, and, swoln by the melting snows, threw themselves into the *Euphrates*, which was flowing at the Southern extremity of the plain from E. to W. Three miles from *Youngali* we came to *Cara-Klissé*, a large village peopled by *Courds* and *Armenians;* and then made a circuit to the N. to avoid a swampy road in the centre of the plain. We passed through several villages, the inhabitants of which seeing the numbers of our company mistook us for one of the fighting parties, and crowded on the tops of their houses at our approach. Of these places, the principal were named *Datté Tapé, Kesick;* and *Arnat.*

Turpa Caléh is situated N. 60 W. from *Youngali*, on a distance of about fifteen miles or four hours. It is a larger place than any that we had seen since *Khoi.* The town is scattered on the slope of a conical hill, on the top of which is a castle. This the Turks deem impregnable, and with justice, if the failure of the late siege be a criterion, though the fort seems in every part accessible to cannon. The high mountain of *Kussé Dagh* overlooks the town and attracts continual clouds over it. We proceeded warily; and, about a mile before we reached the place, halted and sent forwards a man to reconnoitre the appearance and dispositions of the people, and to report on the expediency of our advance. He returned with the intelligence that we had nothing to fear; and we directed our course therefore to the *Conac* or dwelling of the *Kiayah*, the chief officer of Timur Beg. Here we dismounted, and were introduced immediately into a dark room, where twenty torpid Turks were indulging themselves in the quiet delights of smoking. The *Kiayah* sat in the corner, but rose when the *Mirza* entered; and, having said the usual " *Khosh gueldin*" (you are welcome,) closed his lips and left his guest to display the compliments and insinuative flattery so natural to his nation. The loquaciousness and vivacity of the Persian formed an inimitable contrast with the dull and heavy laconism of the Turk.

When we had smoked and drunk coffee, a man came to inform us that Timur Beg was ready to receive us. The *Mirza* and I immediately proceeded, leaving the rest of our party with the *Kiayah.* We ascended to the castle by a steep and difficult path, and entered it by a large iron door. We were introduced into a spacious room at the summit. The Chief (attended by all his principal warriors gravely seated around) occupied a window commanding an extensive view of the country over which we had travelled, and more particularly the district of his rival, the *Pacha*. When we also were seated, and the usual compliments had passed, the *Mirza* begun a prepared speech unfolding our condition, announcing that we threw ourselves at his mercy, asking the rights of hospitality from him, and intermixing throughout some very severe invective against his enemy the *Pacha*. The mode succeeded: and TIMUR BEG instantly replied, that we had nothing to fear; that under his protection we were safe; that our necessities should be supplied, and that his officers should receive orders to treat us with distinction and kindness at a neighbouring village; for he hoped, as the only favour that he required of us, that we would not sojourn in his castle for that night.

When these preliminaries were settled, I had time to observe that there was much to admire in our host. He was about forty years of age, with a singularly open and manly countenance, and with manners the most graceful and dignified. He related his own history and his differences with IBRAHIM PACHA in language so simple, yet so expressive, that we acquired a deep interest in his fate; particularly, when he expatiated on the *Pacha's* tyranny and inordinate rapaciousness, and on the misery in which his exactions had involved all the peasantry of the district. During the course however of his conversation with the *Mirza*, I remarked one of his observations which was very characteristic of a semi-barbarous society. He inquired who I was? and being informed that I was of the *Sect of Isau* (JESUS), or, in other words, a Christian, he continued (with a look of pity, having observed that I had refused a pipe), "These fellows, I hear, have neither pipes nor tobacco in "their country: *haivan dar*, they are beasts:" as if to say, assuming that we did not possess the knowledge or the means of their favourite enjoyment, "how far inferior to us must those be who cannot "smoke."

Our host kept strictly to his word: we were sent forwards four miles further to the promised village of *Molah Suleiman,* escorted by two of his officers; and supplied with all that the place could afford, a sheep, fowls, and rice for ourselves, and corn for our horses.

12th.   We passed over a mountainous tract of country from *Molah Suleiman* to *Deli-baba,* a distance which we travelled in ten hours, and which I reckoned at thirty-five miles, on a bearing of N. 30 W. as well as the intricacies of the turns would permit me to observe.   Before we entered the mountains, (when we had travelled about three miles, and just above the little village of *Zadiéh,)* I had the parting view of Mount *Ararat,* which bore from us N. 80 E.   We were told that the road was much infested by the *Courds,* particularly at a pass in the mountains called *Gerdina,* and we placed ourselves therefore in a posture of defence.   But we traversed the whole extent without seeing a human being, till we reached *Dahar,* a village of *Courds* in the mountains twenty miles from *Molah Suleiman.*   We then proceeded winding in a variety of directions, with a scorching sun over our heads, to the entrance of a pass which, through two stupendous rocks, leads into the plain of *Deli-baba.*   This pass might be made an admirable military position, and in its present state is a most picturesque object.   A stream from the mountains runs through it: on the left is a rock three hundred feet perpendicular, and on the other side is another of less height, but pierced with three holes, as if it were by the hand of man.

On entering the plain we saw numbers of peasants with their *arabahs* or carts.   They told us they had fled from their village in the fear of ABDULLA AGA, who, from his station near *Erivan,* makes predatory excursions all over the country.   They added that *Deli-baba* was totally depopulated; however we did not believe them, and proceeded. We found indeed a very bad reception, for the inhabitants mistook us for enemies, collected together at our approach, refused us admittance, and fired several muskets at us.   At length the chief of the village came out to meet us, and we agreed to establish ourselves at a distance, feed our cattle, and depart. The fear of ABDULLA AGA created such a distrust, that we were avoided by every one whom we met; and even when any permitted us to approach, all our assurances were insufficient to inspire them with confidence. Although we offered great prices for the necessaries of our supply, the people would hardly sell a single article; and the few pieces of bread and eggs which formed our meal at *Deli-baba* were not procured without the greatest difficulty.

Although the country is in a terrible state of disturbance, caravans travel freely on the road. We met a large one which had been eight days from *Arz-roum*. Our mule-driver happened to kill a serpent; he cut it immediately in two pieces, and threw the parts on different sides, saying, " It is a lucky sign, our enemies will not overcome us."

The soil over which we passed was admirably rich, and the most delightful spring reigned on the tops of the mountains, where we culled nosegays of a thousand hues; yet the snow lay in several places, and covered the fetlocks of our horses, while close to it rose every flower.

13th. We quitted the village of *Deli-baba* early in the morning, having passed a night full of anxiety and watchfulness in the open fields; as we were told that we were not safe, and might probably be attacked, though nothing, thank God, disturbed us. We proceeded on a bearing of West to *Amra Kieu*, a village prettily situated at the utmost extremity of a plain, and surrounded by some trees, (in our later course a very scarce object) the willow and the plane. We crossed a beautiful country cultivated in most parts, and considering the extreme misery of the inhabitants themselves, looking very prosperous. The spring was here in its first burst, and the corn was scarcely a span high: the fields were no longer watered by dikes as in Persia, for the nature of the seasons and of the country render unnecessary any artificial means of irrigation. The hills to the Northward of the plain, through which we passed, rise in a gentle acclivity, and to our view displayed habitations and culture; but as we met no person on the

road, I could not learn the names of the villages in various parts. At
two hours, (seven miles,) from *Deli-baba*, and about a mile from the
road, is *Batman Kieu*, situated in the bosom of a valley delightfully
watered and cultivated. The houses of *Amra Kieu*, our resting place,
are built with the fir tree, and their roofs are formed by rafters of
wood, geometrically placed, which are afterwards covered with earth,
and constitute a strong dome. This is a better construction than any
that we had lately observed. Small two-wheeled carts, to which oxen
are yoked, are used here by the peasantry. The sheep are very fine,
with large tails and good wool.

14th. We went from *Amra Kieu*, due West towards *Alwar*, ten miles.
Three miles after quitting *Amra Kieu*, we came to the banks of the
Araxes; which enters the plain from the mountains near *Yaghan*, a large
village situated about three miles from the road. The stream flows
here from N. 65 E. to S. 30 W. It takes its rise in the *Mahalé* of
Khunus; and where it issues from the ground is called *Bin Gieul*, or
a thousand springs. In its course it closely follows the mountains which
we had left at the extremity of the plain. Little irrigation is drawn
from it through the neighbouring territory. We crossed it over a very
well-built stone bridge of seven arches; by the measurement of which
the river was about one hundred and sixty paces in breadth. Just
at this point a stream flows into it from the Westward, taking its
course close to *Hassan Caléh*. Immediately on passing the bridge
we came to a village called *Kupré Kieu*, and then continued on a
fine road, and through a delightful plain strewed with villages, distant
in general two or three miles from each other. The principal of these
are *Arsunjéh*, on the left, and *Gumec* and *Miagen*, on the right of the
road. All the plain was well cultivated; and the peasants were here
sowing their corn. We passed by *Hassan Caléh*, a large town situated
around a hill; on the summit is an old fortification, the curious walls of
which are chequered with the embrasures of former times. We crossed
the stream by the town, over a bridge of two arches. Close to the

bridge is a bath built over a spring, the heat of which is almost that of scalding water: yet when we looked in, several men were up to their chins in it. The basin is about thirty feet in diameter, and is enclosed by an old structure. Several other springs of the same temperature adjoin it.

We had procured a man from the Governor *(Cazi)* of *Hassan Caléh*, to conduct us to *Alwar*, but the *Aga* of that place positively refused to admit us or to lodge us, and added in direct terms that he did not care for *Cazi*, *Pacha*, or any one else, and that we might go any where we chose; if at least we did not disturb Him. After vollies of abuse on both sides, we were content as before to take up our quarters in the open fields, under the shade of a tree, that luckily was situated near the village, and saved us from an ardent sun. Here we saw geese for the first time.

Whilst seated under the tree, vowing vengeance on the *Aga* of *Alwar*, (having dispatched a man to the Governor of *Arz-roum* to state our case), we were visited by a respectable, yet sly-looking Turk, who came quietly and settled himself on our carpet. He begun by telling us that he was a *yoljee* (a traveller) like ourselves ; and inquired what made us so angry. We broke out into every species of invective against the *Aga* of the village, who had obliged us to remain like our horses and mules, under a tree, refusing us the most common offices of hospitality; and added, that we had in consequence sent a messenger to the Governor of *Arz-roum* to complain of the affront, hoping at the same time that the inhospitable *Aga* would either lose his head, or at least get a severe bastinado. We had some suspicion that the personage to whom we were talking was the very *Aga* himself, and were therefore less scrupulous in our abuse. This suspicion proved true: our visitor begun by taking the *Aga's* part, saying that the country was in a great state of alarm, and that the people feared to receive into their towns so many strangers, and particularly Persians, and finished in his own person by intreating us not to write to the Governor of *Arz-roum*. He went away accordingly in some fright, and allowed us to get provisions from his village, a permission which he had not granted before.

We spent the night, however, in the open air, and in the fear of rain: much, indeed, was falling on all sides of us with thunder and lightning.

Hobhouse:
Journey through Albania

John Cam Hobhouse, *A Journey through Albania, and Other Provinces of Turkey in Europe and Asia, to Constantinople, During the Years 1809 and 1810*, 2 vols (second edn London: James Cawthorn, 1813), vol. I, pp. 142–58, vol. II, pp. 912–34.

During his life, John Cam Hobhouse (1786–1869), Baron Broughton de Gyfford, published three travel narratives: *A Journey through Albania and Other Provinces of Turkey* (1813); *Historical Illustrations to the Fourth Canto of Childe Harold* (1818); and *Italy: Remarks Made in Several Visits, from the Years 1816–1854* (1859). In one way or another, each account recorded details of his friendship with Lord Byron, whose own travel journal in verse, *Childe Harold's Pilgrimage*, was unquestionably the period's most prominent exploration account of the Ottoman Morea. Meanwhile, Hobhouse's descriptions in *A Journey through Albania* provide valuable insights into Romantic representations of the Islamic East.

Hobhouse and Byron met at Cambridge, and in 1809 and 1810 they travelled the East on a wartime version of the gentleman's Grand Tour, primarily visiting Greece, Albania and Constantinople. While the tour certainly had a sexual dimension, these various explorations may also have been accompanied by some diplomatic service in Albania, where Hobhouse and Byron visited the renegade governor Ali Pasha. Dubbed by Byron the 'Muslim Bonaparte', Ali Pasha Tepelene in many respects symbolised European stereotypes of the Islamic oriental and, as K. E. Fleming has recently argued, his 'prominent role in the cultivation of European romanticist, philhellene, and Orientalist sensibilities of the eighteenth century has long been overlooked' (see Fleming, *The Muslim Bonaparte: Diplomacy and Orientalism in Ali Pasha's Greece* (Princeton, 1999), p. 5). Certainly, both Byron's poem and Hobhouse's narrative descriptions contributed to popular perceptions of Ali Pasha as an embodiment of Eastern 'character' – licentious, brutal and perverse.

One of the rhetorical objectives of Hobhouse's tour was to create public personae for himself and for Byron. Indeed, Hobhouse's correspondence with Byron indicates the degree to which this work, like *Historical Illustrations* later, was imagined as a collaborative effort and was focused on public reputation. In 1811, he wrote to Byron:

The *Travels* are going on swimmingly, plain prose is to be my fate. You shall be immortalised you rogue you shall. Your arrival will give me a great push forward. I promise myself that you will let me have all your drawings engraved for the work, which shall, as you are come, be a splendid thing. Clarke's *Greece* will not be out for 9 months – if I can but cut in before him!! (quoted in Michael Joyce, *My Friend H: John Cam Hobhouse, Baron Broughton de Gyfford* (London, 1948), p. 28).

Hobhouse suggests here that *A Journey through Albania* was more about Byron, literary prominence and their rakish public images than about Albania or Greece. Indeed, when it appeared, Hobhouse's travel account did help to immortalise Byron, seeming to confirm through historical documentation elements of the poet's own exaggerated and roguish self-representation. And while Hobhouse's own public reputation would be in politics and not prose, the first edition of his travel volume sold out within a matter of days and reviews of the publication consistently praised the work – at a time when travel literature was a subject of frequent derision and scorn. Indeed, one review, written by prominent fellow traveller Sir John Barrow, predicted that 'the work itself will have a standard place in all collections of voyages and travels' (quoted in Joyce, *My Friend H*, p. 42), and Hobhouse's account was, in fact, a prominent account of the Levant throughout the Romantic period. It remains an important reflection of early nineteenth-century orientalism and an early record of the project of building 'Byronism'.

LETTER XIII.

Continuation of the Manners of the Albanians—Expression of their Meaning by Signs—their Liveliness—Passionate Temper —their Education—their Language—their Morals—Religion—their Nationality—their love of Arms—The Albanian Robbers—their Way of Life—and Mode of Attack—their Surgeons—The Albanian Dances—Albanians in Foreign Service—in Egypt—Italy—the Morea—under Mustapha Bairactar—Albanian Settlers—in different Parts of the Levant —and in Calabria.

THE same distaste of trouble, of which mention has been made in my last Letter, seems to be apparent in a singular habit, prevalent with the Albanians, of expressing their meaning by short signs instead of words. Take one or two instances :—If one of them is asked, whether there is any fear of robbers in such a road, and he means to say that there is no cause for alarm, he pushes his little red cap over his eyes, as much as to say, a man might walk there blindfolded. Sometimes, instead of saying, " No, *not at all; not the least in the world;"* he puts the nail of his thumb under his upper fore-teeth, and draws it out smartly, making the same kind of sound as we employ in place of the interjection, alas ! It is not very easy to know when they mean to answer in the affirmative, and when in the negative, as a shake of the head serves both for *no* and *yes.*

But the sluggishness, or rather the hatred of work, observable in this nation, by no means carries with it that grave and torpid air which is seen in the generality of the Turks. On the contrary, they are lively, and even playful; and though their home sports are not of the active kind, yet they show their delight at their Turkish draughts and other sedentary games, by loud bursts of laughter, and other signs of childish joy. They are very furious also in their expressions of like and dislike; and as they have but little command of their temper, and prefer at all times open force to fraud, they make no study of the concealment of their passions. We once saw one of them offer to run a dirk into his arm, upon the mention of the name of a Greek girl, with whom he was deeply smitten; for he drew his weapon, and, turning up his sleeve, exclaimed, " Shall I do it? shall I do it ?"—What satisfaction he could suppose this cutting himself could give to his mistress, it is not easy to conjecture. But this is a practice also of the Greeks, who perform the sacrifice, not with the amorous transport of the Albanian, but out of mere gallantry, in the presence of their dulcineas, serenading them and drinking to their healths.

There is nothing more sanguinary in the character of the Albanians, than in that of the other inhabitants of the Levant; though, as they live under no laws, and each individual is the redresser of his own wrongs, bloodshed cannot but frequently occur. A blow is revenged, by the meanest amongst them, with the instant death of the offender : their military discipline admits of no such punishment, and their soldiers are hanged and beheaded, but never beaten. The custom of wearing arms openly, which has been considered as one of the certain signs of barbarity, instead of increasing, diminishes the instances of murder, for it is

of no such punishment, and their soldiers are hanged and beheaded, but never beaten. ' The custom of wearing arms openly,
which has been considered as one of the certain signs of barbarity,
instead of increasing, diminishes the instances of murder, for it is
not probable that a man will often hazard an offence, for which
he may instantly lose his life. They are not of a malignant disposition, and when cruel, with the exception of some tribes, it is
more from sudden passion than from a principle of revenge.
Treachery is a vice hardly to be found amongst them; such as
have experienced your favour, or, as their saying is, have eaten
your bread, and even those who are hired into your service, are
entirely to be depended upon; and are capable often of the
warmest and most devoted attachment. Take, by the way, that
this fond fidelity is more observable in the Mahometan, than in
the Christian Albanians.

There are very few of them who cannot speak Greek, and, as
their own is not a written language, a great many write and read
that tongue. These are very proud of their acquirements, and so
far from thinking it necessary to conceal their education, display
their learning as ostentatiously as their valour. Were an Albanian to sit for his picture, he would wish to be drawn, like the
admirable Creichton, with a sword in one hand and a book in the
other.

The Turkish language is known but to very few, even of the
Mahometans amongst them. Of the Albanian language, there is
collected for your inspection, almost the first specimen ever put
to paper. The basis of it is said to be Sclavonian, mixed with a
variety of other tongues, of which the Turkish is most predominant, though the modern Greek, the Italian, the French, and

even words that sound like English, have a share in the composition of this strange medley. The infinitive seems to be formed by the syllable *ti*.

I feel no great inclination to speak of the morals of the Albanians. Their women, who are almost all of them without education, and speak no other than their native tongue, are considered as their cattle, and are used as such, being, except the very superior sort, obliged to labour, and often punished with blows. They have, in truth, rather a contempt, and even aversion for their females, and there is nothing in any of their occasional inclinations, which can be said to partake of what we call the tender passion. Yet all of them get married who can, as it is a sign of wealth, and as they wish to have a domestic slave. Besides, as in most parts of the country the females are not nearly so numerous as the other sex, the bride often does not bring a portion to her husband, but the man to his wife; and he is obliged to get together about a thousand piasters, before he can expect to be married.

A young fellow, being asked by us if he was going to get a wife, shook his head, and said he was not rich enough. Some time afterwards he came to us in great glee, with a letter in his hand from his father, part of which he read to us, couched in these very words: " *I wish you to come home—I have got a wife for you.*" Just as if he had said, I have got a cow for you.

Though the Mahometans amongst them veil their women, and conceal them in their harems, they are said to be less jealous than other Turks, and they seldom have more than one wife. In short, their habit of life, which forms almost all of them into bands of soldiers or outlaws, appears to render them quite independent of the other sex, whom they never mention, nor seem to miss in their usual concerns or amusements.

The same habit is productive of a system, which is carried by them to an extent of which no nation, perhaps, either modern or ancient, unless we reluctantly except the Thebans, can furnish a similar instance. Not even the Gothic Taifali (I must refer to Gibbon for their depraved institution *) could be quoted against this assertion, and sufficient proof should be given of its truth, were I not aware of the propriety of the maxim approved, or probably invented by the great Latin historian. " Scelera ostendi oporteat (dum puniuntur) flagitia abscondi †." After this information, it may be considered very singular that the Albanians are exceedingly decent in their outward manners and behaviour, never admitting an immodest word or gesture in their conversation, nor indulging in that kind of talk, which is the delight of some, even above the lower orders, in more civilized parts of the world. But this is a part of Mahometan discipline, and though it may appear a necessary concomitant of their strange system which destroys the natural equality of the sexes, is surely to be admired and imitated.

From what has been before said, it may be implied, that the Christian religion, if the degrading superstition of the Greek church can deserve such a title, has been far from extirpated by the Mahometan conquerors of Albania. Even in the upper country, where the Turks are most predominant, several villages of Christians are to be found. On the coast nearly all the people are of that persuasion, some of them being of the Latin church.

* Decline and Fall, cap. 26.
† Tacit. De Morib. German, cap. 12.

The Turks are not strict in the observance of the Mahometan law, though I never heard any of them swear by Christ*. The Christians adhere pretty closely to the tenets, but pay no sort of reverence to the ministers of their church, whom they abuse openly and despise, because they are not soldiers, and are considered to be slaves, being usually Greeks by nation.

Lady M. W. Montague, whose book is so commonly read that I shall scarcely be pardoned for quoting rather than referring to it, talking of the Arnoots, says, in her agreeable manner— " These people, living between Christians and Mahometans, and not being skilled in controversy, declare that they are utterly unable to judge which religion is best, but to be certain of not entirely rejecting the truth, they very prudently follow both. They go to the moscks on Fridays, and to the church on Sundays, saying, for their excuse, that they are sure of protection from the true Prophet; but which that is, they are not able to determine in this world."

This may have been true in the days of our accomplished countrywoman, but I could not learn that there is now to be found an instance of so philosophical an indifference, or rather of so wise a precaution. However, it is certain that the Christians, who can fairly be called Albanians, are scarcely, if at all, to be distinguished from the Mahometans. They carry arms, and many of them are enrolled in the service of Ali, and differ in no respect from his other soldiers. There is a spirit of independence and a love of their country, in the whole people, which, in a great measure, does away the vast distinction, observable in other

* Voyage en Albanie, 149.

parts of Turkey, between the followers of the two religions. For when the natives of other provinces, upon being asked who they are, will say, " we are Turks," or, " we are Christians," a man of this country answers, " I am an Albanian." The salute also, and the shaking of hands, is as much observed between a Turk and Christian, as between two Turks or two Christians.

Nationality, a passion at all times stronger in mountaineers than in inhabitants of the plains, is most conspicuous in their character. If one of them is travelling from home, and hears of a countryman resident near any place which he may pass, though he has never seen or heard of the man before, he will go out of his way to visit him. I have several times witnessed the delight they manifest at an accidental meeting of this kind, and have observed that it is much more apparent than the emotion of two English friends on such an occasion. Their whole manner is indeed very affectionate, and when, after a short absence, an Albanian happens to light upon an acquaintance, he gives him his right hand and kisses him on the cheek, which is also repeated at parting; when, if they have passed upon the road, each, after they have got to a little distance, fires off his pistols and his gun.

No foreign country, nor any new sights, can take away from them the remembrance and the love of their mountains, their friends, and their own villages. They are perpetually recurring to them, and making invidious comparisons between their native place, and every thing about them in other countries. They consider that all other men, whether Turks or Christians, are cowards if opposed to their countrymen; and, in fact, as they have long been accounted the best soldiers in the Turkish empire, they have some reason for the pride which can be discerned in their poorest peasants. The strut of one of them, and the air of defiance which he puts on, with his hand on his sabre and his red cap a little on one side over his forehead, are such, as no one who has once seen them, would ever forget.

All of them are warriors, and equally capable of using the sword and the long gun; the latter weapon, when slung across their right shoulders, they carry without any apparent effort, running up their hills with great ease and agility. As all of them bear arms, it is not easy to distinguish a soldier in service from a peasant; though perhaps the surest distinction is the sabre, which, as has been said, is seldom worn publicly, except by those in the employment of their Pasha. However, most of their cottages are furnished both with this weapon and with pistols. Nor are their arms for show; for, until very lately, (and in some parts it is the case even now), every district was either upon the defensive against the bands of robbers, or was in alliance with them, and in rebellion against the Pashas of the Porte. Some of almost every village have belonged to these bands, and as no disgrace is attached to plundering upon so large a scale, it is very common to hear a man say, " when I was a robber."

It is early in the summer that these banditti, in bodies of two, five, and seven hundred, and sometimes even of a thousand, assemble under some formidable chief, and leaving the towns and villages where they have separately passed the winter, retire to the summits of the most lofty mountains. The recesses of Metzovo, and of the hills now called Agrapha, at the bottom of the Gulf of Arta, which command, as it were, the passes from Greece and Thessaly into Albania, are amongst their most favourite haunts. They live some in caves, but many of them in the open air, under no other covering than their capotes. The flocks of the shepherds, who are in concert with them, supply them with meat, and in the night-time they steal down singly into the villages in their alliance, and procure bread. No violence is used on this occasion; the messenger taps gently at the door of the cottages, and whispering the words, " Bread, bread," (psomè, psomè) is immediately understood by the peasant, and provided with what he wants. A traveller has some chance of being awakened in his humble lodging by one of these midnight visitants; but would hardly guess what sort of character, or whose purveyor, the intruder really was. Their drink is water only, and they are very particular in the choice of their springs. They have spies throughout the country, to give them notice of the approach of an enemy, or of any whom they may plunder; and, as they are always on the alert, they move instantly, on such intelligence, from the tops of the hills, and occupy the passes in the woods.

In their mode of attack they are extremely cautious. They lie patiently, and in dead silence, perhaps for hours, covered with leaves, behind stones, in the water-courses, or in the thickets, on each side of the road. They suffer their prey to get into the midst of them, when, if the party be armed or numerous, they fire upon them suddenly without rising, and continue to do so, unless beaten, until they have made their adversaries throw down their arms, and ask for quarter. In that case, the prisoners are then gagged, and bound, and plundered; and if there is amongst them a man of consequence, the robbers make him write to his friends for a ransom of so many thousand piasters, and, if the money arrives, they release him; if it does not, they cut off his head, or keep him amongst them until they disperse.

If there is no probability of their being resisted, they start up at once, without firing, and seize their plunder. Resistance is often made with success, and with very little bloodshed; for, on the first shot being fired, the attacked run different ways, get behind stones and trees, and return the fire upon the robbers, who, unless they are very superior in number, do not attempt to dislodge them with the sabre, but continue under cover, or re- treat.

An English gentleman travelling in the country, had the op- portunity of seeing one of these skirmishes: he told me the story at Ioannina. He was escorted by thirty soldiers of Ali's. In passing a road, with a rocky hill on one side and a wood on the other, thirty-five Albanians suddenly made their appearance: the guard instantly began to climb up the hill, and get under cover of the rocks: firing from behind the stones, and striving with their adversaries, which should get the most elevated station to defend. They continued jumping from crag to crag, dropping down, and firing at each other for twenty minutes, leaving the Englishman in the road, till, at last, the two parties discovered that each of them belonged to the Pasha, and that they had mu- tually mistaken each other for robbers. During the whole con- test, not one of either side had been even wounded. However, it is not owing to cowardice, but custom, that they always fight in this manner, as well in open warfare as in these petty battles in their own mountains, except where they have any cavalry em- ployed, or where, as in the affair of Prevesa, there is a great disproportion between the numbers of the enemy and their own force. But their fights are not always bloodless: whatever was effected against the Russians during the last campaign, was done by Mouctar Pasha and his Albanian troops.

The life they lead in the course of their profession as plunderers, enables them to support every hardship, and to take the field, when in regular service, without baggage or tents of any kind. If badly wounded, they leave their corps, and retire to their homes until they are cured, when they return to the field. Many amongst them know how, in their rude manner, to heal a wound, and set a bone, and they even attempt the more delicate operations of surgery.—The French Consul at Athens was persuaded to trust a very valuable life in the hands of one of them, and was so fortunate as to be relieved by the complete reduction and cure of a hernia, under which he had long laboured.

After the tops of the mountains become untenable from the snow and rain of autumn, these bands of outlaws leave their haunts, and usually separate; many of them going into the towns of Livadia, Thebes, Athens, the Negroponte, and also over to Corfu, and to Santa Maura, where they live upon their plunder, or go into some employment, which they always quit on a stated day in the spring.

Robbing and stealing are reckoned two entirely different things. Very few amongst them are ever guilty of the latter vice; not so many, perhaps, as of the lower orders in many other nations. Not only the youth of the Albanians is exercised in arms, but their manhood, and even their advanced age; and it is not till years and infirmities have made them decrepid, that they become the constant tenants of their cottages.

Although lazy in the intervals of peace, there is one amusement of which (as it reminds them of their wars, and is, in itself, a sort of friendly contest) they partake with the most persevering energy and outrageous glee. I allude to their dances, which, though principally resorted to after the fatigues of a march, and during their nights on the mountains, are yet occasionally their diversion on the green of their own villages.

There is in them only one variety: either the hands of the party (a dozen, or more, in number) are locked in each other behind their backs; or every man has a handkerchief in his hand, which is held by the next to him, and so on through a long string of them. The first is a slow dance. The party stand in a semicircle; and their musicians in the middle, a fiddler, and a man with a lute, continue walking from side to side, accompanying with their music the movements, which are nothing but the bending and unbending of the two ends of the semicircle, with some very slow footing, and now and then a hop.

But in the handkerchief dance which, is accompanied by a song from themselves, or which is, more properly speaking, only dancing to a song, they are very violent. It is upon the leader of the string that the principal movements devolve, and all the party take this place by turns. He begins at first opening the song, and footing quietly from side to side; then he hops quickly forward, dragging the whole string after him in a circle; and then twirls round, dropping frequently on his knee, and rebounding from the ground with a shout; every one repeating the burden of the song, and following the example of the leader, who, after hopping, twirling, dropping on the knee, and bounding up again several times round and round, resigns his place to the man next to him. The new Coryphæus leads them through the same evolutions, but endeavours to exceed his predecessor in the quickness and violence of his measures; and thus they continue at this sport for several hours, with very short intervals; seeming to derive fresh vigour from the words of the song, which is perhaps changed once or twice during the whole time.

In order to give additional force to their vocal music, it is not unusual for two or three old men of the party to sit in the middle of the ring, and set the words of the song at the beginning of each verse, at the same time with the leader of the string; and one of them has often a lute to accompany their voices.

It should have been told, that the lute is a very simple instrument—a three-stringed guitar with a very long neck and a small round base, whose music is very monotonous, and which is played with, what I shall be excused for calling a *plectrum*, made of a piece of quill, half an inch in length. The majority of the Albanians can play on this lute, which, however, is only used for, and capable of those notes that are just sufficient for the accompaniment and marking the time of their songs.

The same dance can be executed by one performer, who, in that case, does not himself sing, but dances to the voice and lute of a single musician. We saw a boy of fifteen, who, by some variation of the figure, and by the ease with which he performed the *pirouette*, and the other difficult movements, made a very agreeable spectacle of this singular performance.

There is something hazardous, though alluring, in attempting to discover points of resemblance between modern and ancient customs; yet one may venture to hint, that the Albanians, from whomsoever they may have learnt the practice, preserve in this amusement something very similar to the military dances of which we find notice in Classical authors. At the same time, one would not, as several French travellers have done, talk of the Pyrrhic dance of the Arnoots. Let us look into Xenophon, for a description of the Greek and barbarian dances with which he entertained some foreign ambassadors, and we shall fix upon the Persian, as bearing the nearest resemblance to the modern dance; for in that, the performer *dropped on the knee and rose again, and all this he did in regular measure to the sound of the flute**.

---

* Τέλος δε τὸ Περσικὸν 'ωρχεῖτο κροτῶν τὰς πέλτας καὶ ὤκλαζε, και ἀνίστατο, και ταῦτα πάντα εν ρυθμῶ πρὸς τὸν αὐλὸν επόιει.—Lib. 6. Xenop. Cy. Anab. p. 426; where, in a note, there is a reference to Meursius' Laconian Miscellanies, book ii. chap. 12, which describes the armed dance performed—"cum omni corporum flexu ad inferendos et declinandos ictus." To learn the Pyrrhic dance, was part of the duty of the Roman legionary soldier.

In the account given of the armed dances of the Laconians, we might also recognise the curious contortions and twirlings of the Albanians, whose sudden inflexions of the body into every posture, seem indeed as if they were made to ward and give blows.

But to return to the characteristic of this nation. Their love of arms is so ardent, that those who may fear too long an interval of peace in their own country, enter into the service of the Pashas in every part of the Turkish empire. The guard of the sacred banner from Mecca to Constantinople, used to be entrusted to one hundred and fifty of them, armed and dressed in their own fashion. The traveller Brown saw them pass through Damascus in procession. Egypt is at present in their hands, under a Bey, a friend of Ali Pasha's; and it was, in a great measure, their troops who compelled our unfortunate army to retreat from that country.

The Stradiotes, or Albanian cavalry, made a conspicuous figure in the old Italian wars: and the coast, to this day, has furnished the Kings of Naples with a regiment. Some of them we have seen in our service at Malta.

The famous Ghalil, commonly called Patrona, was an Albanian. This man, though a common seaman and a pedlar, headed the insurrection of 1730, in which Sultan Achmet III. was dethroned, and with a success of which neither ancient nor modern history can furnish another instance, remained for three weeks absolute master of Constantinople. The Kioprili family, which furnished the Sultans with three Grand Viziers, was from Albania.

The Morea has been perpetually disturbed by those of this restless people, who have been either long settled in the country, or who (since they were called in to quell the insurrection of the

Greeks in the year 1770) have constituted the guard of the Pasha of Tripolizza. These formerly amounted to about six thousand; they are now under Veli Pasha, not quite so many. In the year 1799 they marched from Napoli di Romania, and were near surprising the city of Tripolizza itself.

The troops with which Mustapha Bairactar opposed and quelled the Janissaries, were principally Albanians; and since the death of that daring Vizier, the appearance of one of this nation in the streets of Constantinople, as it was once formidable, is now displeasing, to their late enemies. A man boasted, in my hearing, that a friend of his had made forty Janissaries fly before him, and that any Arnoot could do the same. Without believing the enormous superiority, we may by this form some notion of the spirit of the people.

But all these mountaineers who enter into service abroad, depend upon a return to their own country. Those belonging to the Pasha of the Morea have more than once attempted to force the guard of the Isthmus; and some, who were in a Sicilian regiment in our pay, on finding that they were enlisted for life, occasioned a very serious disturbance in the garrison at Malta.

It must be recollected, that what has been said of the Albanians, relates only to those who are natives, or, at least, immediately sprung from natives of Albania; for there are settlements of this people to be met with in other parts of Turkey in Europe, and in the islands, who are nothing but miserable labourers, employed to attend the flocks and till the grounds of the rich Turks and Greeks. There are many of them in the district of Livadia, and in that of Attica, who can speak no other language but their own, and are all Christians; their ancestors having, most probably, left the mountains when the Turks first entered into Albania, or having been settled there since the first irruption of the Sclavonians into Greece.

These have been improperly called Wallachians, by travellers, whose errors have been copied by more accurate writers*. Gibbon, in his Sketch of Modern Athens, gives them that name, although he might have rectified the mistake by looking into Chandler, who is, however, himself incorrect, in saying that they wear a different dress from the Greek peasants, and are of a distinguished spirit and bravery. The woollen jacket and loose brogues are common to both, though perhaps the cotton kilt may be occasionally found amongst the former people ; and as for their superiority to the other villages, it seemed to me that they had assimilated with the surrounding slaves.

We read in Tournefort, that Marco Sanudo, Duke of Nio, one of the small islands of the Archipelago, sent for Albanian families to cultivate his little dominions; and the same anecdote will serve to show, what sort of reputation all people of this name possess in the Levant ; for Mr. Sonnini, determined to find no fault with his favourite Greeks, and being obliged to own that the Archipelago is infested with pirates, can only account for the circumstance, by referring all the robberies to the Albanians settled by Duke Marco at Nio.

But the fact is, that these colonists, except in their patience of fatigue and frugality, have but little of the spirit of the mountaineers of Albania, and are looked upon by them as a different race of people. Some of them are to be found to this day in Calabria, whither they retired when the Castriotes were invested

---

* Yet the positive Mr. De Pauw insists that these people are Wallachians, and descended from the Roman colonies settled by Trajan in Dacia. In proof of this, he refers to a note of Mr. D'Anville, in vol. xxx, of the Academy of Inscriptions, and to a work called " Etats formés après la chute de l'Empire Romain en Occident." See Letter xxx. pp. 491, 492, 493, of this volume.

with a Neapolitan dukedom. They were seen by Mr. Swinburne, and were found to have preserved the language and manners of their nation. They amounted in his time, a little more than thirty years ago, to one hundred thousand, their ancestors having continued to emigrate as late as the reign of Charles the Fifth. They lived in about a hundred villages or towns, the chief of which was Bova, thirty miles from Reggio. The men were able to talk Calabrese; but the women, like those in Albania, were acquainted with no other than their own language. All but those in the province of Cosenza were of the Latin church; and a college founded by Pope Clement XII. at St. Benedetto Ullano, in Upper Calabria, supplied the priesthood with ministers. They wore the Albanian dress. The men were poor and industrious, the women modest. The priests were held in the highest reverence and estimation.

★　　★　　★　　★　　★

The descriptions of Rycaut (and much earlier writers might be mentioned) apply to the Mussulmans of Constantinople at this day, as much as to those of the seventeenth century, and the decay of their relative strength, as an European power, has but little affected their national character. The Mahometan religion has prevented, and ever will prevent, any material change in the individual condition, and consequently the character of the Turks.

The light thrown upon the manners and customs of this people during the last hundred years, has left it unnecessary to disabuse the world on the subject of the religion of Mahomet. The times are past, when the Mussulmans were charged with believing that God is a corporeal being, the author of evil, without providence, and not eternal; that the soul is mortal; that the devils are friends of Mahomet, and of God; that Venus is the proper object of worship; that man was created of a leach; and many other absurdities, originating only in the ignorance of their accusers*.

Into the doctrinal part of their religion the Turks do not enquire, but content themselves with an implicit faith in the one eternal Deity, in his angels, in the prophets, in the day of resurrection and judgment, in the decrees of God, and in the virtue of purification, prayer, alms and fasting. There are some of their priests, as might be expected, who disturb themselves with the subtleties of the controversialists, and engrafting upon the simplicity of the original law a variety of strange creeds, have established sects, the opinions of which, if we are to believe some writers, are not only different from, but altogether inconsistent with, the faith of Mahomet. Rycaut mentions one brotherhood, whose mystery, which it required a long noviciate to penetrate, consisted in a profession of atheism, and a practice of the most horrid de-

---

* Pope Pius II. in a letter to the Sultan of the Turks, made the first charge; Cedrenus the second, the same Pope the third, Bartholinus of Odessa the fourth and fifth, Polydore Virgil the sixth, Johannes Andreas the seventh, the great Selden, in his 4th chap. on the Syrian Deities, the eighth; and Euthemius Zigalenus the last. Sylburgius accuses Mahomet of having called the Blessed Virgin the sister of Moses; and Bartholinus of Odessa upbraids the Koran for saying that she was impregnated by eating dates. Those who would see the origin and refutation of these follies, may consult the second book of Adrian. Reland's System of the Mahometan Theology.

baucheries; but Islamism can no more be affected by such a perversity, than the religion of England by the monks of Medenham.

The sect does not, as far as I could learn, exist at this day, but institutions and practices no less foreign to the original faith, may still be found. Such are the invocations of dead and the reverence of living saints, a belief in prophecies* omens and dreams and the power of amulets and charms, and the admission of numerous orders of Dervishes; the removal of all which excrescences, and the restoration of the simple Unitarianism of the Koran, it is the professed object of the Wahaubees to effect. These powerful sectaries have taken the holy cities, and overrunning all Arabia, and part of Syria, have menaced at the same time the Sophi of Persia and the Sultan of Constantinople, peremptorily inviting them to recognise the divine commission of Wahaub, the Unitarian Chief, and restore the faith to its primitive purity. Should the mission of this reformer accomplish its aim, and meet with general success, we may then expect to become acquainted with Mahometanism, such as it was in its infancy.

Mr. Leibnitz says of it, that " 'tis a kind of deism joined to the belief of some facts, and to the observation of some performances, that Mahomet and his followers have added, sometimes unluckily enough, to natural religion, but that have been agreeable to the inclinations of several countries;" and he adds, " we

---

* The knowledge of future events is obtained, they think, by the constant practice of virtue, fasting, and humiliation. The *Etishmysklerden*, " the attainers to the fulness of divine fervour," pretend to visions; yet Mahomet is declared in the Koran *Achir Pergamber* the last of the prophets, which the modern Mahometans have explained, as usual, to suit their own notious.—See Cantemir, Ottoman Hist. book i. p. 39, Tindal's translation.

are obliged to that sect for the destruction of paganism in many parts of the world*."

To this brief and just exposition, and the subsequent eulogy of the religion, I shall only add, that its main doctrine has been allowed to be so similar to that of a great heretical Christian, that in times when theological controversies were more bitter than at present, sober treatises were written, to prove the conformity of the Mahometan belief with that of the Socinians; and that sect, on account of the irregularities of Adam Neuser, was charged with a conspiracy against Christianity, in conjunction with the Emperor of the Turks†. What was once thought a disgrace to Socinus, may now be considered an honour to the author of Islamism, who, when he declared *There is but one God, and Mahomet is his prophet*, may, considering the infirmities of human nature, be scarcely so much condemned for the imposture of the latter article, as praised for having promulgated the sublime truth contained in the first half of his concise creed. In short, of the prophet of Mecca we may say what Adrian Reland has pronounced of his commentator Kerabisensis, *This Arabian delivers some truth, covered over with a shell of fiction, being destitute of divine revelation.*

'Ουκ ἴδεν, ἀλλ' ἐδόκησεν ἰδεῖν διὰ νύκτα σελήνην.

---

* A Letter from Mr. Leibnitz to the author of the Reflections upon the Origin of Mahometanism, dated Berlin, 1706.

† See Historical and Critical Reflections upon Mahometanism and Socinianism, translated from the French, London, 1712. *A Turk hearing a Polish Socinian discourse on the Trinity and Incarnation, wondered he did not get himself circumcised.* See the Letter of Mr. Leibnitz, who, of the two, prefers the Mahometan, as more consistent than the Socinian.

The rapid progress of Islamism has been attributed to the vicious licence permitted and promised to its votaries; but an Arabian impostor, many years after the Hegira, allowed a much greater laxity of morals to his followers, and notwithstanding some success, his sect did not survive him. On the contrary, the Prophet, in forbidding the use of wine, created a restriction to which the Arabians were not before accustomed; nor will any religion owe its dispersion and prevalence to a declaration of freedom of action; for it is consonant to the genius of man, to admire and follow systems abounding with rules and regulations, and even prescribing a conduct which seems to do violence to all the natural feelings and unbiassed inclinations of the human breast. Were this not the case, Fakeers, Monks, and Dervishes, could never have existed: it would have been impossible that any man in the world should, like Uveis the Mahometan, have established a sect and met with proselytes, whose pretensions to piety were founded on the extraction of all their teeth.

Mahomet was too wise to omit the palpable parts and outward ceremonials, which are the life and soul of all superstitions; which, in fact, are the superstitions. He was too wise, to make his Koran a promulgation of licences instead of restraints; his fasts and abstinences, his ablutions, his pilgrimage to Mecca, are so many meritorious mortifications, which have all tended to the propagation of his doctrine. To the same knowledge of the human mind may be attributed the miraculous relations of the Koran.

It has been before hinted, that a variety of principles and articles of faith have been invented by the founders of different Mahometan sects, but that these heresies do not engage the attention of the great body of the people. Some persons are inclined to think, that many of the higher classes in Turkey are very. sceptical in matters of religion*. Of this I could form no judgment; but it was not difficult to see, that few except the lower orders retain that spirit of intolerance and bigotry which Mahometans are accused of displaying in all their commerce with Christians. A notion has very generally obtained, of their contempt and hatred of infidels so far prevailing, that it is established amongst them, that they may break any engagement with an unbeliever; but nothing is more unfounded than such a supposition, for the contrary conduct is expressly commanded by the Koran†, and they have been always notorious for their good faith in their commercial intercourse with other nations. "*How do we trade amongst the Turks,*" enquires Mr. Harley, who had fallen into the common error, "*and trust the Mahometans, one of whose doctrines in the Alcoran is, not to. keep faith with Christians? They have obtained it by a just, punctual, and honourable practice in trade, and you credit them without scruple, nay, rather than some Christians‡.*"

All the people of the East, except the Mahometans, as Montesquieu§ thought, look upon all religions in themselves as indifferent, and amongst the Calmucks, the admission of every kind of religion is a point of conscience. The truth is, the Mahometans themselves, whether originally from climate or otherwise,

---

* *It must, however, be confessed, that in so great a nation there are many of the learned Turks who do not implicitly believe all that is said in the Koran,*" &c. Cantemir, Ottoman Hist. book i. p. 31, Tindal.

† See A Short System of the Mahometan Theology, book ii. sect. xxv.

‡ Essay on Public Credit, 1710 (reprinted 1797), p. 17.

§ Liv. xxv. chapit. 15, de l'Esprit des Loix.

notwithstanding great apparent steadiness in their own faith, are perfectly tolerant in their practice; and I cannot help supposing that they entertain very charitable notions on this head, for I recollect a person of authority, to whom one of us had introduced our Albanian attendant Dervish, with the recommendation that he was a Mussulman, observing, that he did not enquire into a man's faith, but his character, and that he presumed Heaven would be wide enough for persons of all religions.[*] The generality of the Turks are at the same time exceedingly attentive to all the forms prescribed by their law, and perform their religious duties without either affectation or levity. The obligation to external piety is not confined to the priesthood. They pray in the streets and in their open shops at Constantinople, not for the sake of ostentation, since every one is equally pious, but to perform a portion of their civil duties. On the same principle, no one, whatever may be his private opinions, utters any sentiments disrespectful to the faith. Such a levity would be sedition, and a

[*] The Koran, Surat 2, verse 59, has these words: " *Verily, those who believe, both Jews and Nazareens (Christians), and Zabians (Gentiles in Arabia, or Ishmaelites), whosoever of these believe in God and the last day, and do good works, have their reward with their Lord, and no fear shall come upon them, neither shall they be affected with sorrow.*" Artus Thomas, in his Triumph of the Cross; Bellarmine, in his Controversies, vol. ii. p. 293, 294; and Thomas à Jesu on the Controversies of the Gentiles, p. 677, and others, cry scandal against this toleration, *the last dotage of Mahomet;* and Reland has, I fear, with some success, defended the Prophet against the heinous charge. A short System of Mahometan Theology, book ii. sect. 2.—The Cham of the Tartars told Rubruquis in 1253, " *Que comme Dieu avoit donné aux mains plusieurs doigts, ainsi avoit il ordonné aux hommes plusieurs chemins pour aller en Paradis.*"—Voyage en Tartarie, cap. 46, p. 119.

crime against the representative of the Prophet; for the Sultan is the Vicar of Mahomet, and is the supreme head of the government, which is not less a theocracy than the ancient Jewish monarchy.

It has been established beyond doubt, by the writer who, in my humble judgment, has given the truest and most satisfactory account of the Turkish government, I mean Mr. Thornton, that the Ulema, or ministers of the Mahometan law, at whose head is the Mufti, do not assume or exercise a power paramount to that of the Sultan, however they may have been resorted to, in order to sanction the Imperial edicts, or to join with the Janissaries, or general voice of the people, in deposing a cruel or incapable prince*. The Mufti, who has been likened to the Popes or Patriarchs of the Christian sects, but is in fact more similar to the Pontifex Maximus of ancient Rome, is in dignity, though not in power, the second person in the empire; but he is not, as some have endeavoured to prove, the first. To show this, it is sufficient to say that his continuance in office depends upon the will of the Sultan.

In a despotic monarchy nothing remains fixed but the religion†; the Mahometan law is unchangeable and all-powerful; but its immediate ministers possess neither the one nor the other attribute. If the *fetwa*, or decree, of the Mufti were a necessary sanction to every act of importance, which it seems not to be, the person who disposes of the office may be supposed capable of controuling the officer. The religion may be called supe-

* Present State of Turkey, p. 100 to p. 113.
† De l'Esprit des Loix.

rior to the Sultan, for by it he holds his power, but I cannot think that any opposition to the Imperial authority on the part of the Ulema, however long or successfully it may continue, can be adduced to show that the Sultan of the Turks is not a despotic prince, or can be considered in any other light than an insurrection, to which every absolute monarch must occasionally be subject.

It is the custom for the Grand Signior to back his ordinances relative to peace and war, and other state matters, by the *fetwa*, as it is for him to go to the mosck publicly on every Friday, and to attend in person at a conflagration; but the two latter obligations are equally strong with the former; nor are the three exceptions to the exercise of his own will and discretion, of sufficient importance to be mentioned as a proof of limitation in the Ottoman sovereignty, or of any other point, than that no prince is altogether superior to established usages. Nevertheless, Abu-Taleb, the traveller commonly going by the name of the Persian Prince, a much better judge than either De Tott, Sir James Porter, or other Europeans, who have adopted the same notion, informs us in his Travels, that he did not consider the power of the Grand Signior absolute, which I can only account for by supposing, that in the Asiatic governments to which he had been accustomed, insurrections were not so frequent, nor the influence of usage so apparent, as in the capital of Turkey.

The identity of law and religion gives a sanctity of character to the Mufti, the Cazy-askers of Roumelia and Natolia, the Istamboul-Effendi, the Mollahs, Cadis, Naibs, and all the administrators of justice in Turkey; but the ecclesiastics, or Murta-ziki, are, except in their education, a distinct body from the Ulema, and are not immediately dependent upon the Mufti, but upon the Kislar-Aga, or Chief of the Black Eunuchs*. The Santons, Alfaquis, and Sheiks, explain texts of the Koran, but their sermons are not given at any stated time, nor very frequently; the Talismans perform the same office, but are chiefly employed in transcribing the holy books; the Imaums recite the prayers, at stated hours of the day in the moscks, but not aloud, only animating the people by their example: on Friday, however, before prayers at noon, a reader or chanter (Nat' chon) sings the praises of Mahomet. To each mosck there is also a Haim, or overseer; Fermesh, a sweeper; and Abkesh, a water-drawer. One Muezzin, or chanter, will serve for several moscks. The burying-grounds are under the inspection of a Turba-dhar, or sexton. There is also a person whose business it is to attend to the innumerable lights with which the larger moscks are supplied, and to provide for the illuminations of the Rhamazan, when all the minarets are adorned with lamps, hanging not only round the galleries and to the tops of the spires, but upon strings from one turret to another, so as to form various figures, and verses from the Koran.

There is no part of the religious duties of a Mussulman which

---

* The Cazy-askers are chief justices: they sit not on the right, as Mr. Thornton says, but on the left hand, of the Grand Vizier in the Divan. The Istambol-Effendi is chief justice of Constantinople; the Mollahs, or Moulas, are presidents of great towns, to whom the ancient Ottoman kings paid five hundred aspers a day, but who now receive nothing from the government (Bobovius, a Treatise concerning the Turkish Liturgy, sect. ii.); the Cadis are judges of small towns; and the Naibs, puisne judges. Each court has a Katib, a secretary; a Mokaiyd, a clerk; and Muhzir, a crier. The Mufti's pension is five hundred zequins a day from the Seraglio. (Notice sur la Cour du Grand Seigneur, p. 141), requires the intervention of a priest; nor, although a reader and chanter are retained in some great families, is the distinction which separates the Christian laity and clergy, to be recognised amongst the Mahometans. There is nothing in the external behaviour of the Imaums, or others of the secular priesthood, which distinguishes them from their fellow-subjects: they assume no authority, either temporal or ecclesiastical; and are under the controul of the Cadis, or municipal judges: in short, they are the guardians of the moscks rather than of the Mussulmans. The Hogias, or schoolmasters (one of whom is attached to each of the great moscks in Constantinople), are in smaller parishes the only public readers of the Koran.

The extreme simplicity of this religion, and of the ordinances by which it is supported, has not, however, prevented all pretensions to extraordinary holiness, or the encouragement of several sects of fanatical impostors, to whom some allusion has before been made. The Christian recluses were the admiration of the Mussulmans before they had adopted the same practice; but since the first institution of religious orders in the reign, and by the patronage, of Nasser-Ben-Hamed, the third prince of the Samanide dynasty, in the year 331 of the Hegira, there has been a constant succession of saints, distinguished from their fellow-citizens by the title and profession of poverty, and supposed to be occupied in the perpetual contemplation of the more abstruse points of the Mahometan doctrine*. These saints have been

---

* D'Herbelot, Bibliotheque Orientale, Articles *Nasser-Ben-Hamed, Dervische, Sofi, Zaked, Fakir,* &c. Saadi, in the Ghulistan, relates, that the Christian monks of Mount Libanus in his time performed miracles; and Bokhari, in

known under the names of Calenders, Torlaquis, and other distinct appellations applied to particular sects, but are more generally spoken of under their original title of Dervish, a word
having the same signification in the Turkish and Persian language
as the Fakir of the Arabic, and denoting a poor man. They
have their travelling mendicants, fraternities of settled recluses,
and some few solitaries, amounting in all to thirty-two orders;
all of which differ from each other, and are distinguished also by
particular manners and appearance from the rest of the world.

Although it is expressly said in the Koran, that the vow of
celibacy is not received in Paradise, the Calenders do not admit
of marriage; but the generality of the orders are under no such
restriction. Some individuals amongst them have, like Haji
Bek-Tash, attained an extraordinary reputation; but the profession of piety, beyond the acquirement of alms, is not attended
with any advantages in Turkey. The Mussulmans consider themselves obliged to contribute to the support of the religious; at
the same time, that not only the more enlightened of them, but
the common people, regard the Dervishes with but little internal
reverence, and rather tolerate than approve of their institutions.
The *Seyeh*, or wanderers, who raise contributions by proclama-
tion, are relieved, but not respected*. Their *kirkah*, or torn
habit, notwithstanding its alleged descent from the ancient pro-

---

his book entitled Sahib, recounts the wonders of the Abyssinian, Saheb Gioraije,
a Christian solitary, with the good faith of a Capuchin. There is also an Arabic history of Christian monks.

* On coming into a town, a Seyeh cries aloud from the market place or
court of the mosck, "*Ya allah senden besh bin altùn jsterim*"—*O God, give me,*

phets, has been the subject of much sarcasm for the Oriental wits, and the vices which it is known to envelop, have not added to its respectability*.—A Dervish attempted to kill Sultan Mahomet the Second, and also Achmet the First; and in the reign of Osman the First another enthusiast ventured to disturb the peace of the empire, by foretelling the triumph of Christianity upon the strength of a vision seen at Mecca. The prophet was cudgelled to death †.

I pray, five thousand crowns—or some other sum or commodity, which he is to collect in the course of his journey. The *Seyehs* come even from India. One of them delivered to Kioprili Mustapha Pasha, Grand Vizier to Solyman the Second, letters from the Great Mogul, and told him that his master, hearing of the Sultan's distresses, had sent an offer of assistance to his brother Mussulman. To which Kioprili replied, *that Solyman would be ever grateful for the zeal and friendship of the great Padishah of India, but that his affairs just then being in a prosperous state,* " *he could be honoured with no greater favour from his Indian majesty, than his commanding his beggars not to enter the Ottoman dominions.*"—Cantemir, Ottoman Hist. Part I. book i. p. 40, of Tindal's translation.

* Sâadi, in the eighth chapter of his Ghulistan, addressing the religious, says, " *Possess the virtues of a true Dervish, and then, instead of a woollen cap, wear, if you will, a Tartar bonnet.*" Ebu-Cassab, one of their spiritual masters, calls their garments the mask of hypocrisy; and Hafiz prefers a goblet of wine to the blue mantle of the Dervish; which the Persians, who have given a mystical meaning to all the verses of this poet, explain as an attachment to divine love, and a hatred for hypocrisy. *Dervishlik khirkhaden bellu dogkil,* is a Turkish proverb, which answers to the *cucullus non facit monachum.* See D'Herbelot, Bibliotheque Orientale, Article Dervische.

† In the early ages of the Mahometan religion a Mahometan said that he was God. A man reminded him, that one who had called himself a prophet had been killed. " *They were right,*" said the other, " *for I did not give him his commission: he was no prophet of mine.*"—Paroles Remarquables des Orientaux, Galand.

The character of the mendicant Dervishes of Asia Minor has been already seen*. Yet the Santons and Sheiks, whose exhortations make most impression in the moscks, are the superiors of these fanatics; and a sermon preached by one of the former in St. Sophia, was the origin of the disgraceful expedition undertaken by Sultan Solyman against Malta in the year 1564†.

Attempts have been made to abolish the institution, but the Janissaries still retain eight Dervishes of the order of Bek-Tash, as chaplains to the army; and the people of Constantinople run in crowds to amuse themselves (for no other motive can be assigned to them) at the exhibitions of the turning and of the howling Dervishes, to which all strangers are carried, as to the theatre or other places of entertainment in the cities of Christendom.

There is a monastery of the former order, the *Mevlevi* (so called from Mevlana their founder) in Pera, and we were admitted to the performance of their ceremonies on Friday the 25th of May. We were conducted by a private door into the gallery of the place of worship, a single octagonal room, with the middle of the floor, which was of wood highly polished, railed off for the exhibitors. A red carpet and cushion were placed at the side opposite the great door near the rails, but there were no seats in any part of the chamber. We waited some time until the great door opened, and a crowd of men and boys rushed in, like a mob into a playhouse, each of them, however, pulling off his shoes as he entered. The place without the rails, and our gallery, were filled in five minutes, when the doors were closed. The Dervishes

---

* Letter xxxvi. p. 648, of this volume.
† Notice sur la Cour du Grand Seigneur, p. 148.

dropped in one by one, and each of them crossing his arms, very reverently and with the utmost grace bowed to the seat of the Superior, who entered at last himself, better dressed than the others, and with his feet covered. With him came in another man, who was also distinguished from the rest by his garments, and who appeared afterwards to officiate as a clerk. Other Dervishes arrived, and went into the gallery opposite to the Superior's seat, where there were four small cymbal drums. The Superior now commenced a prayer, which he continued for ten minutes; then a man stood up in the gallery, and sang for some time from a book: the cymbals began to beat, and four Dervishes taking up their *neih* or long cane pipes, called by Cantemir the sweetest of all musical instruments*, played some tunes which were by no means disagreeable, and were, indeed, something like plaintive English airs. On some note being struck, the Dervishes below all fell suddenly on their faces, clapping their hands with one accord upon the floor.

The music ceased, and the Superior began again to pray. He then rose, and marched three times slowly round the room, followed by the others, who bowed on each side of his cushion, the Superior himself bowing also, but not to the cushion, and only once, when he was half way across it. The Superior reseated himself, and said a short prayer. The music commenced a second time, all the Dervishes rose from the ground, and fourteen out of the twenty who were present, let drop a long coloured petticoat, round the rim of which there were apparently some weights; and throwing off their cloaks, they appeared in a tight vest

* Ottoman Hist. Part I. book ii. p. 40.

with sleeves. The clerk then marched by the Superior, and bowing, retired into the middle of the room. A Dervish followed, bowed, and began to whirl round, bis long petticoat flying out into a cone. The rest followed, and all of them were soon turning round in the same manner as the first, forming a circle about the room, with three or four in the middle. The arms of one man alone were held straight upwards, two of them crooked their right arms like a kettle-spout, the rest had both arms extended horizontally, generally with the palm of one hand turned upwards, and the fingers closed and at full length. A very accurate and lively representation of this curious scene may be found in Lord Baltimore's Travels.—Some of them turned with great speed; they revolved round the room imperceptibly, looking more like automatons than men, as the petticoat concealed the movement of their feet: the clerk walked with great earnestness and attention amongst them, but without speaking, and the Superior remained on his cushion moving his body gently from side to side, and smiling. The performers continued at the labour for twenty-five minutes, but with four short intervals; the last time they turned for ten minutes, and notwithstanding some of them whirled with such velocity that their features were not distinguishable, and two of them were boys of fifteen and seventeen, apparently no one was affected by this painful exercise. The clerk, after the turning and music ceased, prayed aloud, and a man walking round, threw a cloak upon the Dervishes, each of whom was in his original place, and bending to the earth. The Superior began the last prayer, and the company withdrew.

The ceremonies just described are said by Volney to have a reference to the revolution of the stars, and whether or not they are to have credit for any superior astronomical science, these Dervishes certainly possess some literary merit, as all of them are instructed in the Arabic language, and make it their study to become critically acquainted with its beauties. Their monasteries contain many rare books, collected at considerable pains and expence in all the countries of the East where they have any establishments, or which are visited by any of their fraternity.

It cannot be supposed that any set of men who are better instructed should be more superstitious than their fellow-citizens; but it is very probable that they may be aware of the awe and astonishment which any strange religious ceremony creates in the mind of the vulgar, and that without being in reality enthusiastic, they take advantage of the reputation sometimes attached, even amongst the Turks, to that character. They cannot be unwilling that the spectators of the performance should discover some mystical meaning in their revolutions, which it seems to me were in their first origin nothing but a sort of religious penance; but I cannot think that they are themselves deceived as to the efficacy or intention of the ceremonies. The Superior does not inflict upon himself the execution of so rigorous a duty, and it may be added, that there is a marked superiority, both in his appearance and that of the musicians, to the air and manner of the Dervishes employed in the exhibition, who may, after all, be retained to display their feats for the benefit of the institution.

The Mevlevi are, however, rational worshippers, when compared with the Cadrhi, or Howling Dervishes, whose exertions, if considered as religious ceremonies, are more inexplicable and disgusting than those of any enthusiasts in the known world, and if regarded merely as jugglers' feats, are legitimate objects of curiosity. A large party of our countrymen went to see them on the 26th of June.

From our lodgings we walked to the back of Pera, and keeping the suburbs of Cassim Pasha on our left, passed over the large plain and hill of the Ok-meidan, or archery ground, where there are many marble pillars erected as memorials of the distance to which some of the Sultans, and other distinguished Toxophilites, have shot their arrows; for the endeavour of the Turks is not to hit a mark, but to exceed each other by the range of their bows; and I think it is Olivier who mentions, that they have contrived an extravagant method of flattering their sovereigns and grandees, by placing in the Ok-meidan, signs of a prowess altogether impossible. I recollect perfectly well walking another time across the plain, quite unconscious of the sport, and being stopped by the shouts of some Turks on a neighbouring hill, and by a fellow who ran hastily up to me, and pointed to an arrow which had just lighted in the ground. The archers were amongst some large loose stones, and at a distance which rendered them scarcely discernible. Some of the Asiatic troops still carry bows and arrows.

After crossing the Ok-meidan, we waited an hour in the court-yard of a ruined mosck, shaded by large plane trees, and containing two dry fountains and a range of deserted cells. We were told that the ceremony never took place except with the attendance of a sufficient number of spectators, and after leaving the mosck we staid some time in an outward yard, until a crowd was collected, and we heard music and praying in an anti-chamber. We then entered, and found a large party singing, or rather bawling, in a dirty deal apartment, fitted up at the further end

with several flags, having axes, swords, pikes, and cymbal-drums
on one side, and a silk cloth inscribed with characters on the
other. This they said was a part of Mahomet's tent, the other
portion of this holy relic being at Vienna. On the left hand
corner was a latticed box for women, and next to it was an open
compartment railed off from the floor. In this place we seated
ourselves, and saw three principal personages of the sect kneeling
under the flags, and waving their heads sideways, keeping time
with the musicians, who were beating drums and singing at the
lower end of the room. In the corner under the latticed box, was
a black or tawny dwarf half naked, upon his knees, contorting
himself into many frightful and ridiculous gestures, now and then
becoming furious, and knocking his arms and head violently against
the ground. To him we directed our attention, until at last he
tore open his vest below his waist, and struggling on the ground,
was led off frothing at the mouth, and suffering apparently under
the convulsions of actual madness.

After this exhibition the principals advanced; the crowd ranged
themselves along three sides of the lower end of the room, and six
persons squatting down in the middle of the party, commenced
singing, and were joined by the remainder of the company in the
chorus, which was the repetition of the name of God. The whole
of the three lines, amounting in all to between thirty and forty persons, none of whom belonged to the fraternity, but were introduced
promiscuously by kissing the principal's hands, continued waving
backwards and forwards, and sideways close together, howling
and grunting to a tune, which was lost at last in a general and
continued exclamation of *Yallah-Illah! Yallah-Illah!* when they
jumped and jogged themselves into that which appeared to all of

us, from undoubted symptoms, to be that peculiar kind of artificial frenzy, which we learn was produced by the Sarmatian art of see-saw, or session on a cord *.

I should mention, that before the violent howling and jogging began, a Dervish perfectly mangy, and covered with filth and sores, came round, and reverently taking off every man's turban, placed it under the banners. The three principals only jogged their heads and moved on their heels. They seemed half in joke, as also did several of the party, especially a young Imaum of our acquaintance who had accompanied us to the place, and who, although he joined in the whole ceremony, was laughing heartily and winking towards our box. During the howling the Superior of the order, a red-faced, drunken-looking man, entered the room, and walking busily amongst the party, made various exclamations of ill temper and discontent, as if displeased with some parts of the ceremony.

After the howling, a prayer was recited, and all the company dispersed into the anti-chamber to take coffee and pipes to recruit themselves; but they soon returned, and a jug of water, into which the Superior had blown, and a consecrated shirt, were handed round the room. Two infants were also brought in and laid on a mat before the Superior, who stood first on their bellies, and then on their backs, and afterwards breathing upon them, delivered them to his attendants, cured, as we were told, of some complaint which this charm was calculated to remove.

The howling and jogging recommenced, and to this succeeded a prayer. The Superior then brought forward two men, and ran

---

* See Swift *On the Mechanical Operation of the Spirit*—Tale of a Tub.

long needles, like netting needles, with large handles, through their cheeks, pushing them out at their mouths, and also through the thick skin above the wind-pipe. After a short time he pulled the needles out, wetting the wound with his spittle, and so contriving the extraction that no orifice was visible, although it appeared that a hole had been made, and the performer brought the men close to our box, as if to convince us that there was no delusion in the operation. The feat was repeated, and a black curly-headed fellow, who they said was an Egyptián, on the needle being drawn out, appeared to faint, and falling down, lay for some time on the ground, until the superior puffed into his mouth, when he jumped up, screaming out Yollàh! in a convulsed but ridiculous tone, and recovered instantly. The boring was practised on several in the room, and the jogging and singing were continued by the crowd below. The Superior, having first drawn several rusty swords and returned them to their sheaths, now took an attaghan, and breathing upon it, gave it to a black Arab, who stripped to his waist, and, after crying several times on the name of God, applied it to the narrow part of his abdomen as tightly as possible, sawing it with the utmost violence upon his belly, but without leaving any marks, except a few bloody scratches : whilst he performed this frightful feat, he called out to us, *bono? bono?* as much as to ask if it was well done.

Another swarthy Arab then took the attaghan, which by the way was handed to us, and was as sharp as a razor, and lying on the ground, placed it with its edge downwards across his body, and suffered the Superior to stand with his whole weight upon the back of the knife. The same man then took two sharp iron spikes, headed with wooden globes, and a tassel of iron chains, and knobs, which were all breathed upon and blessed, and drove them repeatedly into each of his flanks, so as to make the pair nearly meet in his body. During this trial he seemed in a fury, calling loudly on God and Mahomet, and with a kind of enthusiastic coquetry, would scarcely suffer the spikes to be forced from his hands.

A brazier of burning charcoal was then brought in, and six or seven men, chosen promiscuously as it appeared from the crowd, were presented by the Superior with red hot irons, breathed upon and blessed like the other instruments, which, after licking them with their tongues, they put between their teeth. One fellow near us made many wry faces, and pulled the irons from his mouth; but the others, although they were in evident pain, and the water streamed from their lips, seemed as if they were loth to part with them, and, either from pretence or some actual convulsion, were with difficulty forced to open their jaws. One of the Arabs then swallowed several pieces of burning charcoal, after they had been blessed; and this, as well as holding the hot irons, whatever preparation may have been actually used, was performed without any visible trick or slight of hand. The charcoal and irons were certainly both at a red heat.

Whilst this business was transacting in the upper part of the room, several tambourines were handed down, and played upon by persons of the crowd, who seemed highly delighted with the scene; and during the whole ceremony, those below continued screaming and jumping, and shouldering each other in a mass, and at last huddled themselves together into a ring, leaping round and round, and squeezing those in the middle into a jelly, until the whole party was utterly exhausted, and the performance closed, having lasted for three hours.

We retired after paying for our seats, but were followed by the two Arabs; one of whom spoke a few words of English, and asked us for an additional present, on account of some unusual exertions with which we had that day been favoured. He told us he had played before the English at Alexandria.

The part performed by the two Arabs, and by the dwarf first mentioned, was clearly a juggle; and, notwithstanding the religious preparations, it appeared that no one regarded it, or wished us to think it supernatural; but I confess myself at a loss to account for the voluntary sufferings of the others, all of whom were common fellows taken from the spectators. It is to be remarked, that the Superior himself did not seem to be one of the order, but only to be chosen for the occasion as director of the magical rites; and that the Dervishes took very little share in any of the laborious part of the ceremony.

The women, and the very lowest of the vulgar, may be frightened into some religious feelings by these horrid and absurd mummeries, accompanied as they are with frequent prayers and religious rites, and a constant invocation of the Deity. The existence of the jumping sect of our own island, renders unreasonable all scepticism as to the follies of enthusiasts; but it did not appear that either the spectators or performers were under any delusion as to the motive or effect of this species of devotion. Having given the relation of the facts just as they happened, from a note taken on the spot, I shall leave every one to form his own conclusion on this extraordinary scene.

The Cadrhi were abolished by Kioprili Mustapha Pasha, but revived after the death of that Vizier.

Leblich:
Travels of Ali Bey

'Ali Bey' (Domingo Badiá y Leblich), *Travels of Ali Bey, in Morocco, Tripoli, Cyprus, Egypt, Arabia, Syria, and Turkey. Between the Years 1803 and 1807,* 2 vols (London: Longman & Co., 1816), vol. II, pp. 47–73, 94–104.

The Spanish adventurer Domingo Badiá y Leblich (1766–1818) travelled the Ottoman East during the early years of the nineteenth century, and in 1807 he reputedly became the first European since the seventeenth century to see Mecca. Like Johann Ludwig Burckhardt, who was to reach the holy city in 1814, Leblich assumed the identity of a Muslim during the period of his residence in the Levant, travelling and publishing his accounts under the name 'Ali Bey'.

As Ali Bey, Leblich toured Morocco, northern Africa, Syria and Arabia between 1803 and 1807, and in 1814 he published an account of these travels in French under the title *Voyage d'Ali Bey en Asie et en Afrique.* Translated into English in 1816, Leblich's narrative is representative of a genre of travel writing which was closely associated with the oriental tale and which became increasingly popular in the nineteenth century. Heir to the tradition of Galland's *Arabian Nights* (1704–8) and Montesquieu's *Lettres persanes* (1721), Leblich's narrative is told from the perspective of his invented Eastern self, and it is one of a handful of Romantic travel narratives to blend strategies of fact and fiction so dramatically. Received by many nineteenth-century readers as an authentic account of Muslim experience, the narrative offers important information both on European representations of oriental subjectivity and on the relationship between travel writing and literature in the Romantic period.

As a representation of oriental subjectivity, *Travels of Ali Bey* is particularly interesting for the manner in which it engages with the Wahabi controversy and with stereotypes of the Ottoman decline. A Muslim who has travelled in Europe, Ali Bey is poised to narrate authoritatively the internal affairs of the Ottoman state for a Western readership, and his memorable account of Mecca is interspersed with details that describe both the impotence of Ottoman rule and the brutality of Wahabi reform. The final picture represents the Islamic East as a region torn between corrupt rulers, but inhabited by a devout and compliant populace. As British imperial interests in the East became consolidated throughout the early nineteenth century, representations of this sort served to reconfirm European stereotypes of the Orient – and the legitimacy of its foreign policy in the region.

Most importantly, however, Leblich's work provides a significant insight into the evolving relationship between travel writing and the oriental romance as it developed in early nineteenth-century Britain. Although narrated as a 'documentary' account of the Islamic East, *Travels of Ali Bey* engages simultaneously with the literary conventions of romance established by Southey, Byron, Beckford and Moore. Yet while these early Romantic writers routinely drew upon exploration literature as documentary source material for their orientalist poetry, 'second generation' authors of Romantic oriental tales more frequently employed the travel journal itself as a narrative framework for their literary productions. Thus, as the Romantic period developed, travel writing became increasingly associated with fiction rather than fact, and Leblich's *Travels of Ali Bey*, along with Morier's *Adventures of Hajji Baba of Ispahan* (1824), represent the fullest exploration of this hybrid genre.

CHAP IV.

PILGRIMAGE TO MECCA. — EL HADDA. — ARRIVAL AT MECCA. — CEREMONIES OF
THE PILGRIMAGE TO THE HOUSE OF GOD, TO SAFFA, AND TO MERNA. — VISIT
TO THE INTERIOR OF EL KAABA, OR HOUSE OF GOD. — PRESENTATION TO THE
SULTAN SCHERIF. — VISIT TO THE CHIEF OF THE SCHERIFS. — PURIFICATION
OR WASHING OF EL KAABA. — HONOURABLE TITLE ACQUIRED BY ALI BEY. —
ARRIVAL OF THE WEHHABIS.

BEING a little recovered, though very weak, I set out for Mecca
on Wednesday the 21st of January, at three o'clock in the
afternoon.

I travelled in a machine made of sticks, and covered with cushions,
of the form of a sopha or cabriolet, roofed with boughs upon arches;
which they placed upon the back of a camel, and called * Schevria.
It was very convenient, as I was enabled to sit up or lie down in it;
but the motion of the camel, which I felt for the first time in my
life, completely exhausted me, in the feeble state that I was in.
My Arabs began to dispute before they left the town, and continued
during a whole hour, shouting and stunning every body. I thought
they had finished; but new disputes and cries arose when we were
outside the walls, which lasted another hour. At last a calm suc-
·ceeded to the storm ; and the camels being loaded, we set out upon
our way at five, in an easterly direction, across a large desert plain,
terminated at the horizon by groupes of small detached mountains,
the aspect of which gave a little variety to the picture.

At half-past eight in the evening we arrived at the mountains,
which are composed of bare stone, and do not produce any vegetation.

* See Plate LXIII.

LXIII .

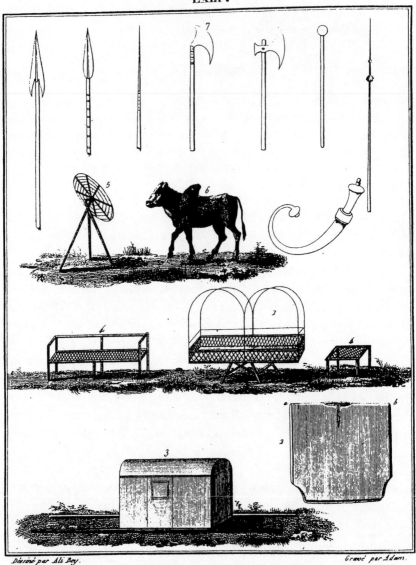

Dessiné par Ali Bey.   *Gravé par Adam.*

Published by Longman.Hurst.Rees.Orme & Brown.London.Nov.1.1815.

The serene atmosphere, and the moon, which shone bright above our heads, rendered our journey very agreeable. My Arabs sang and danced around me. For my part, I was far from being at my ease; the motion of the camel was insupportable. At length, stunned by their noise, exhausted by fatigue, and my weak state, I fell asleep during two hours. When I awoke my fever was increased; and I vomited some blood.

My Arabs having fallen asleep, we lost our way; but discovering about midnight that we directed our course to Mokha, we changed it to the north-east, passing between woody mountains of a certain height; and having found our road again, we continued eastward until six o'clock in the morning, when we halted at a small douar, called El Hadda, where there was a well of briny water.

I could not exactly estimate the distance we had gone; but I think we were about eight leagues to the east of Djedda.

The huts in this douar were all alike, quite round, about seven or eight feet diameter. The tops resemble cones, the summits of which are about seven feet high. They are formed with sticks like a cage, and covered with palm leaves and bushes. *

On the outside of the douar, which was encompassed by a hedge, were two circles of empty huts, which were destined to lodge the caravans; upon the arrival of which, the persons choose those that suit them best, without asking permission of any one.

Between the circles was the well, which was about two feet square and six fathoms deep. We judged that the soil was composed of moving sand to a great depth, by looking down the well, which was lined from top to bottom with boards to prevent its falling in.

There was some vegetation, but no flowers or fruit. This douar is situated in a sandy valley, which runs east and west, and is enclosed by mountains of red porphyry, of a colour more or less dark.

It appeared interesting to me to see the camels eat. The driver placed a mat of a circular form, about six feet diameter, upon the

* See the Plate.

ground, upon which he laid a pile of brambles and herbs, cut very small : he then permitted the camels to approach, when they immediately squatted themselves down upon the ground all round it, at regular distances, and began to eat with a sort of politeness and order which gave me pleasure. They each eat the herbs that were before them by a little at a time ; and if either of them left his place, his companion at his side appeared to scold him in a friendly manner, which made the other feel his fault, and return to it again. In a word, the camels' table is a faithful copy of their masters'.

We repeated the ceremony of purification, or maharmo, here, that we had performed already at Araboh. I made use of warm water, and repeated the prayer as usual whilst naked ; after which I covered myself with two napkins without seams, putting one round my loins, and the other round my body, passing it over the left shoulder and under the right arm, which remained naked, as also my head, legs, and feet. In this state I walked some steps in the direction of Mecca, reciting the invocation, " Li Beïk," &c. I retained this costume until the evening, according to the law, when I resumed my ordinary habit.

The inhabitants of the douar sell fresh water, which they bring from the neighbouring mountains to the southward.

Upon our departure, an Arab of the douar came to ask me for a remuneration for the lodging. I gave him a trifle.

At half-past three in the afternoon we took our leave, and set out in an easterly direction, by a very fine, broad, and straight road.

We began afterwards to see several little woods. After sun-set we passed between some volcanic mountains, covered with black lava, and perceived the shells of some houses that had been destroyed by the Wehhabites. We climbed over some small hills, and at eleven at night entered into a deep and narrow defile, in which the road was cut in steps through the different windings. This defile would make a strong military position.

At midnight, between Thursday and Friday the 23d of January 1807, or the 14th of the month Doulkaada, in the year 1221 of the Hegira, I arrived, through the favour of divine mercy, at the first houses of the holy city of Mecca, fifteen months after my departure from Morocco.

There were at the entrance of the town several Mogrebins, or Arabs of the West, who were waiting my arrival, with little pitchers of the water from the well of Zemzem, which they presented me to drink, begging me not to take it of any other person, and offering to supply my house. They told me secretly never to drink the water which the chief of the wells should offer to me.

Several other persons, who were also waiting, disputed between themselves which should have me for a lodger; for the lodgings are one of the principal speculations of the inhabitants. But the persons who were charged with providing every thing for me during my stay at Djedda, soon put an end to these disputes, by taking me to a house that had been prepared for me. It was situated near the temple, and the house inhabited by the Sultan Scherif.

Pilgrims ought to enter on foot into Mecca; but in consequence of my illness I remained upon my camel until I arrived at my lodging.

The moment I entered I performed a general ablution; after which I was conducted in procession towards the temple, with all my people, by a person appointed for that purpose, who, as he walked along, recited different prayers in a loud voice, which we repeated altogether, word for word, in the same tone. I was supported by two persons, on account of my extreme weakness.

In this manner we arrived at the temple, making a tour by the principal street to enter at the Beb-es-selem, or Gate of Health, which they look upon as a happy auspice. After having taken off our sandals we entered in at this blessed gate, which is placed near the northern angle of the temple. We had already traversed the portal or gallery, and were upon the point of entering the great

space where the house of God, or El Kaaba, is situated, when our
guide arrested our steps, and, pointing with his finger towards it,
said with emphasis, " Schouf, schouf, el beit Allah el Haram."
" Look, look, the house of God, the prohibited." The crowd that
surrounded me; the portico of columns half hid from view; the
immense size of the temple; the Kaaba, or house of God, covered
with the black cloth from top to bottom, and surrounded with a
circle of lamps or lanterns; the hour; the silence of the night; and
this man speaking in a solemn tone, as if he had been inspired; all
served to form an imposing picture, which will never be effaced
from my memory.

We entered into the court by a path a foot high, bordering
diagonally upon the northern angle of the Kaaba, which is nearly
in the centre of the temple. Before we arrived at it, we passed
under a sort of isolated triumphal arch, called Beb-es-selem, like
the gate by which we had entered. Being arrived at the house of
God, we repeated a little prayer, kissed the sacred black stone
brought by the angel Gabriel, named Hajera el Assouad, or the
heavenly stone; and, having the guide at our head, we performed
the first tour round the Kaaba, reciting prayers at the same
time.

The Kaaba is a quadrilateral tower, entirely covered with an
immense black cloth, except the base. The black stone is discovered through an opening in the cloth. It is encrusted on the
eastern angle. A similar opening to the former at the southern
angle discovers a part of it, which is of common marble. On the
north-west side rises a parapet about a leaning height, forming
nearly a semicircle, separated from the building, called El Hajar
Ismaïl, or the Stones of Ismael.

The following is a detail of the ulterior ceremonies which are
observed in this religious act, such as I performed them myself at
this period.

The pilgrims go seven times round the Kaaba, beginning at the
black stone, or the eastern angle, and passing the principal front,

in which is the door ; from whence turning to the west and south, outside of the stones of Ismael. Being arrived at the southern angle, they stretch out the right arm ; when, having touched the angular marble with the hand, taking great care that the lower part of their garment does not touch the uncovered base, they pass it over the face and beard, saying, " In the name of God, the greatest God, praises be to God ;" and they continue to walk towards the north-east, saying, " Oh great God ! be with me ! Give me the good things of this world, and those of the next." Being returned to the eastern angle, they raise their hands as at the beginning of the canonical prayer, and cry, " In the name of God, the greatest God." They afterwards say, with their hands down, " Praises be to God ;" and kiss the black stone. Thus terminates the first tour.

The second is like the first, except that the prayers are different from the angle of the black stone to that of the south ; but they are the same from the latter to the former, and are repeated with the same forms during the seven rounds. The traditional law orders that the last rounds should be made in a quick step ; but in consequence of my weak state we went very slowly.

At the end of the seventh, and after having kissed the black stone, they recite in common a short prayer, standing near the door of the Kaaba, from whence they go to a sort of cradle called Makam Ibrahim, or the place of Abraham, situated between the Kaaba and the arch Beb-es-selem, when they recite a common prayer. They then go to the well Zemzem, and draw buckets of water, of which they drink as much as they can swallow. After this they leave the temple by El Beb Saffa, or the gate of Saffa, from whence they go up a small street facing, which forms what is called Djebel Saffa, or the hill of Saffa.

At the end of this street, which is terminated by a portico composed of three arches upon columns, ascended by steps, is the sacred place called Saffa. When the pilgrims have arrived there, they turn their faces towards the gate of the temple, and recite a short prayer standing.

The procession then directs its course through the principal street, and passes a part of Djebel Meroua, or the hill of Meroua, the pilgrims reciting some prayers at the end of the street, which is terminated by a great wall. They then ascend some steps ; and, turning their faces towards the temple, the view of which is interrupted by the intervening houses, recite a short prayer standing, and continue to go from the one hill to the other seven times, repeating prayers in a loud voice as they proceed, and short ones at the two sacred places, which constitute the seven journeys between the two hills.

These being completed, there are a number of barbers in waiting to shave the pilgrims' heads, which they do very quickly, at the same time saying prayers in a loud tone, which the former repeat after them word for word. This operation terminates the first ceremonies of the pilgrimage to Mecca.

It is generally known that almost all Mussulmen let a tuft of hair grow upon the crown of their head. The reformer Abdouluehab declared this to be a sin ; and as the Wehhabites govern the country, every body is obliged to shave his head. In consequence of this, my long tuft was swept away by the inexorable barber.

The day beginning to dawn when I had finished these first ceremonies, they told me I might retire to take a little rest ; but as the hour for morning prayer was not far distant, I preferred to return to the temple, notwithstanding my weakness, which was increased by fatigue ; and I did not return home until six o'clock in the morning, after prayers.

I went to the temple again at noon, to the public Friday prayer, after having a second time made the seven turns round the Kaaba, recited a particular prayer, and drank largely of the water of Zemzem.

The next day, Saturday the 24th of January 1807, the 15th of the month Doulkaada, in the year 1221 of the Hegira, they opened the door of the Kaaba, which is shut the whole year, except three days ; on the first of which, all the men who are at Mecca may go in and say their prayers. On the second and following day it is dedicated to the women, who go to pray ; and the third, five days afterwards, is appropriated to washing and purifying it. It is on this account that the pilgrims, who generally stay only eight days at the period of the pilgrimage to Aarafat, return without having visited the inside of the Kaaba.

The door is in the north-east front, at a small distance from the black stone, and is six feet above the level of the court : they therefore placed, on the days when it was open, a handsome wooden staircase, mounted upon six bronze rollers.

I was carried to the temple on those days ; and as there was an immense crowd, they made me sit down in a kind of bower belonging to the guard, which is composed of black eunuchs.

The crowd being a little diminished, my guide and some guards conveyed me to the Kaaba. They took great care to make me put my right foot upon the first step in ascending.

Having entered the only hall in the Kaaba, I was immediately conducted to the southern corner, where, placing my body and face as close as possible to the wall, I repeated a prayer in a loud voice, and afterwards the ordinary prayer. I went successively to the west and north corners, repeating the same prayers as before in each. Being come at last to the east corner, I said a short prayer standing, and kissed the silver key of the Kaaba, which one of the Scherif's children, who was seated in an armed chair, held for that purpose. After this I withdrew, escorted by the eunuchs, who made their way through the crowd, by striking the people with their fists. As soon as I got outside I kissed the black stone ; took seven more turns round the building ; went into a small ditch, which is close to the door, where I said the ordinary prayer ; and, after having drank some water of the blessed Zemzem, I returned home.

I received an order in the afternoon to hold myself in readiness to present myself to the Sultan Scherif.

The Nekib el Ascharaf, or chief of the Scherifs, came to conduct me to the palace. He entered, but I waited at the door for the order to go in. A moment after, the chief of the well, who was already my friend, came to meet me. We ascended the staircase in the middle of which was a door that stopped our passage. My guide knocked at it, when two armed servants opened it. We continued to ascend; we traversed a dark gallery; and, after having left our sandals in this place, we entered into a fine saloon, in which was the Sultan Scherif (named Scherif Ghaleb), seated near a window, surrounded by six persons who were standing.

After I had saluted him, he asked me the following questions :

Do you speak Arabic ? *
Yes, sire.
And Turkish ?
No, sire.
Arabic only ?
Yes, sire.
Do you speak any Christian languages ?
Some.
Of what country are you ?
Haleb, or Alep.
Did you leave it when young ?
Yes, sire.
Where have you been since ?

I related my history to him. The Scherif then said to him who was on his left, " He speaks Arabic very well ; his accent is pure ;" and addressing himself to me, he cried, " Come near to me." I approached a little. He repeated, " Come near to me." I then went close to him. He said, " Sit down." I hasted to comply ; and immediately he made the person upon his left sit down. " You have without doubt," said the Scherif, " some news from the Christian lands. Tell me the last you have heard." I related to him briefly the actual state of Europe. He asked me if I could read and write

---

* The Scherif thought that I was a Turk.

French. " A little, sire," I replied. " A little, or well ?" " A little, and incorrectly, sire." " Which are the languages that you speak and write the best ?" " Italian and Spanish." We continued this conversation during an hour. At length, after having made him my present, and delivered the firman of the Captain Pacha, I retired, accompanied by my friend the chief of Zemzem, who conducted me to my house.

Before I proceed, I must give a description of this interesting person, the Chief of the Well.

He is a young man, about twenty-two or twenty-four years of age, extremely handsome, with very fine eyes. He dresses remarkably well, and is very polished. He has an air of sweetness, which is seducing, and appears to be endowed with all the qualities which render a person amiable. As he possesses the entire confidence of the Scherif, he fills the most important place. His title is, The Poisoner. Take courage, reader, lest I should make you tremble for me. This dangerous man was known to me the first time I went to the well of Zemzem, when he made his court assiduously to me. He gave me a magnificent dinner, and sent me every day two small pitchers of the water of the miraculous well. He even watched the moments when I went to the temple, and ran with the most winning grace and sweetness to present me a handsome cup filled with the same water, which I drank to the last drop, because it would have been considered a sort of crime or impiety to have refused it.

This wretch observes the same conduct to all the Pachas and important personages who come here. Upon the slightest suspicion, or the least caprice that may arise in the mind of the Scherif, he orders, the other obeys, and the unhappy stranger ceases to exist. As it is reckoned impious not to accept the sacred water presented by the chief of the well, this man is arbiter of the lives of every one, and has already sacrificed many victims.

From time immemorial the Sultan Scherifs of Mecca have had a poisoner at their court ; and it is remarkable that they do not try to conceal it, since it is well known, in Egypt and Constantinople, that the Divan has several times sent to Mecca, Pachas, or other persons, to be sacrificed in this manner.

This was the reason why the Mogrebins or Arabs of the West, who are entirely devoted to me, hasted to warn me to be upon my guard upon my arrival in the city. My servants wished this traitor at the devil; but I myself treated him with the greatest marks of confidence. I accepted his water and his entertainments with an unalterable serenity and coolness. I took the precaution, however, to keep three doses of vitriolated zinc, a much more active emetic than tartar emetic, always in my pocket, to take the instant I should perceive the least indication of treason.

The Scherif appeared to me to be about thirty-six or forty years of age : he is of a brown complexion, rather lusty ; has fine large eyes, and a regular beard. His dress consists of a benisch, or outer caftan, with an under one, bound with a cashmire shawl : of another his turban is composed. He had a large cushion placed behind him, a second at his side, and a third at his feet, upon which he leaned frequently. There was no other furniture besides these in the saloon, except a large carpet that covered the floor. He smoked his Persian pipe, or nerguilé, during my visit ; but the pipe itself was in another room, from which a tube of leather passed to his mouth, through a hole in the wall. The reformer Abdoulwehhab having proclaimed the use of tobacco to be a sin, and his sectaries who govern Arabia being generally formidable, they smoke with great circumspection, and mostly out of sight.

The next day, Sunday the 25th of January, I paid a visit to the Nekib el Ascharaf, or chief of the Scherifs, and made him a little present. He received me with much friendship, and shewed me as much attention as I could desire. This was the second day of the opening of the Kaaba, which was, as I have already remarked, set apart for the women. They entered it in crowds to say their prayers, and went seven times round it, the same as the men.

On Thursday the 29th of January, and the 20th of the month Doulkaada, the Kaaba was washed and purified, with the following ceremonies :

Two hours after sun-rise, the Sultan Scherif went to the temple, accompanied by about thirty persons, and twelve Negro and Arabian guards. The door of the Kaaba was already open, and surrounded with an immense number of people. The staircase was not placed. The Sultan Scherif got upon the shoulders and heads of the multitude, and entered with the principal Scheiks of the tribes. Those below wished to do the same ; but the guards prevented them, by beating them with their sticks. I staid at a distance from the door, to avoid the crowd, and in a short time received an order from the Scherif of the well to advance to the door, where he stood, making signs to me. But how could I get through the crowd that stood between us ?

All the water carriers in Mecca were advancing with their vessels full of water, which they passed from hand to hand, until they reached the guards at the door. They also passed a great number of very small brooms, made of the leaves of palm trees, in the same manner. The negroes began to throw the water upon the marble pavement of the Kaaba : they also cast rose water upon it, which, flowing out at a hole under the door, was caught with great avidity by the faithful. But as it did not run out fast enough to satisfy the wants of those at a distance, who were desirous to obtain it, they cried out for some of it to drink, and to wash themselves with : the negroes, with cups, and with their hands, threw it in quantities over them. They were civil enough to pass a small pitcher and a cup full of it to me, of which I drank as much as possible, and poured the rest over myself; for although this water is very dirty, it is a benediction of God, and is besides much perfumed with rose water.

I at last made an effort to approach : several persons raised me up ; and, after walking upon the heads of several others, I arrived at the door, where the negro guards helped me to get in.

I was prepared for the operation; for I had on only my shirt, a caschaba, or a shirt of white wool without sleeves, my turban, and the hhaik that covered me.

The Sultan Scherif swept the hall himself. Immediately after I entered, the guards took off my hhaik, and presented me a bundle of small brooms, some of which I took in each hand; and at the instant they threw a great deal of water upon the pavement, I began my duty by sweeping with both hands, with an ardent faith, although the floor was quite clean, and polished like glass. During this operation, the Scherif, who had finished, began to pray.

They gave me afterwards a silver cup, filled with a paste made of the saw dust of sandal wood, kneaded with the essence of roses; and I spread it upon the lower part of the wall, that was incrusted with marble, under the tapestry which covered the walls and the roof; and also a large piece of aloe wood, which I burned in a large chafing-dish, to perfume the hall.

After I had finished all these things, the Sultan Scherif proclaimed me Hhaddem-Beit Allah el Haram, or Servant of the forbidden house of God; and I received the congratulations of all the assistants.

I recited my prayers in the three first corners, as upon my first entering; and thus entirely completed my duties, whilst I attended to this pious work. The Sultan withdrew a short time after.

A great number of women, who were in the court at some distance from the door of the Kaaba, uttered from time to time shrill cries of rejoicing.

They gave me a small quantity of the sandal wood paste, and two of the small brooms, as interesting relics, which I kept most carefully.

The negroes helped me down upon the people, who also assisted me to reach the ground, and addressed compliments of felicitation to me. I then went to the Maham Ibrahim to say a prayer. They returned me my hhaik; and I went home completely wet.

The other assistants of the temple brought me, in their turns, some of the water which had been used to wash the Kaaba; and the Scherif's son, who had held the key, also sent me a small pitcher full, as also a horn of sandal wood paste, one containing other aromatics, a wax taper, and two brooms; and I made returns for all these favours in the best manner I could.

On Tuesday the 3d of February, 25th of the month Doulkaada, they cut that part of the black cloth that surrounded the door and the bottom of the building, which completed the ceremony, which is called Iaharmo el Beit Allah, or The Purification of the House of God. *

During this operation, all the assistants of the temple tried to obtain some bits of this cloth, which they divided into smaller ones, to make a sort of relic to give to the pilgrims as a present, who are expected to return the favour by some gratification. I received so much of it, that ———— God be thanked.

On the same day a part of the army of the Wehhabites entered Mecca to fulfil the duties of pilgrimage, and to take possession of this holy city. It was by chance I saw them enter.

I was in the principal street, about nine o'clock, when I saw a crowd of men coming; but what men! We must imagine a crowd of individuals, thronged together, without any other covering than a small piece of cloth round their waist, except some few who had a napkin placed upon the left shoulder, that passed under the right arm, being naked in every other respect, with their matchlocks upon their shoulders, and their khanjears or large knives hung to their girdles.

All the people fled at the sight of this torrent of men, and left them the whole street to themselves. I determined to keep my post, not being in the least alarmed; and I mounted upon a heap of rubbish to observe them better.

I saw a column of them defile, which appeared composed of five

* See Plate LVI.

or six thousand men, so pressed together in the whole width of the street, that it would not have been possible to have moved a hand. The column was preceded by three or four horsemen, armed with a lance twelve feet long, and followed by fifteen or twenty men mounted upon horses, camels, and dromedaries, with lances like the others ; but they had neither flags, drums, nor any other instrument or military trophy during their march. Some uttered cries of holy joy, others recited prayers in a confused and loud voice.

They marched in this manner to the upper part of the town, where they began to file off in parties, to enter the temple by the gate Beb-es-selem.

A great number of children belonging to the city, who generally serve as guides to strangers, came to meet them, and presented themselves successively to the different parties, to assist them as guides in the sacred ceremonies. I remarked, that among these benevolent guides there was not one man. Already had the first parties began their turns round the Kaaba, and were pressing towards the black stone to kiss it, when the others, impatient no doubt at being kept waiting, advanced in a tumult, mixed among the first ; and confusion being soon at its height, prevented them from hearing the voices of their young guides. Tumult succeeded to confusion. All wishing to kiss the stone, precipitated themselves upon the spot ; and many of them made their way with their sticks in their hands. In vain did their chiefs mount the base near the stone, with a view to enforce order : their cries and signs were useless ; for the holy zeal for the house of God which devoured them, would not permit them to listen to reason, nor to the voice of their chiefs.

The movement of the circle increased by mutual impulse. They resembled at last a swarm of bees, which flutter confusedly round their hive, circulating rapidly and without order round the Kaaba, and by their tumultuous pressure breaking all the lamps which surrounded it with their guns, which they carried upon their shoulders.

After the different ceremonies round the house of God, every party ought to have drank and sprinkled themselves with the water of the miraculous well; but they rushed to it in such crowds, and with so much precipitation, that in a few moments the ropes, the buckets, and pullies, were ruined. The chief, and those employed at the Zemzem, abandoned their post: the Wehhabites alone remained masters of the well; and, giving each other their hands, formed a chain to descend to the bottom, and obtained the water how they could.

The well required alms, the house of God offerings, the guides demanded their pay, but the greater part of the Wehhabites had not brought any money with them. They acquitted themselves of this obligation of conscience, by giving twenty or thirty grains of a very coarse powder, small pieces of lead, or some grains of coffee.

These ceremonies being finished, they commenced shaving their heads; for they all had hair an inch long. This operation took place in the street; and they paid the barbers in the same coin that they had paid the guides, the officers of the temple, &c.

These Wehhabites, who are from Draaïya, the principal place of the reformers, are of a copper colour. They are in general well made, and very well proportioned, but of a short stature. I particularly remarked some of their heads, which were so handsome, that they might have been compared with those of Apollo, Antinous, or the Gladiator. They have very lively eyes, the nose and mouth well formed, fine teeth, and very expressive countenances.

When we represent to ourselves a crowd of naked armed men, without any idea of civilization, and speaking a barbarous language, the picture terrifies the imagination, and appears disgusting; but if we overcome this first impression, we find in them some commendable qualities. They never rob either by force or stratagem, except when they know the object belongs to an enemy or an infidel. They pay with their money all their purchases, and every service that is rendered them. Being blindly subservient to their chiefs, they support in silence every fatigue, and would allow themselves to be led to the opposite side of the globe. In short, it may be perceived that they are men the most disposed to civilization, if they were to receive proper instruction.

Having returned home, I found that fresh bodies of Wehhabites were continually arriving, to fulfil the duties of their pilgrimage. But what was the conduct of the Sultan Scherif during this period? Being unable to resist these forces, he hid himself, fearing an attack from them. The fortresses were provisioned, and prepared for defence; the Arabian, Turkish, Mogrebin, and Negro soldiers, were at their posts; I saw several guards and centinels upon the forts; several gates were walled up; all was ready, in short, in case of aggression; but the moderation of the Wehhabites, and the negociations of the Scherif, rendered these precautions useless.

CHAP. V.

PILGRIMAGE TO ARAFAT. — GREAT MEETING OF THE PILGRIMS. — DESCRIPTION
OF ARAFAT. — SULTAN AND ARMY OF THE WEHHABIS. — CEREMONIES AT
ARAFAT. — RETURN TO MOSDELIFA. — RETURN TO AND CEREMONIES AT MINA.
— RETURN TO MECCA, AND END OF THE PILGRIMAGE. — APPENDIX TO THE
PILGRIMAGE.

THE grand day of the pilgrimage to Mount Arafat being fixed
for Tuesday the 17th February, I left the city the preceding
afternoon, in a schevria, placed upon a camel.

At two o'clock I passed the barracks of the Negro and Mogrebin
guards, which are situated at the northern extremity of the * town.
Afterwards, turning to the east, I saw a large country house belonging to the Scherif, and soon obtained a view of the celebrated Djebel
Nor, or Mountain of Light. It was upon this spot that the angel
Gabriel brought the first chapter of the Kour-ann to the greatest of
prophets. This mountain, which presents the appearance of a sugar
loaf, rises alone above the others that surround it. There was a
chapel formerly upon its summit, which was an object that the pilgrims visited; but the Wehhabites, having destroyed it, have placed
a guard at the foot of the mountain, to prevent them from ascending
and saying their prayers, which Abdoulwehhabb has declared to be
superstitious. It is said there is a staircase cut in the rock to facili-
tate the ascent. As it was situated a quarter of a league to our left,
I only looked at it in passing with the crowd of pilgrims; but I took
a sketch of it. †

Upon turning the road to the east-south-east about three o'clock,
I saw a small spring of fresh water, with stone basons; and shortly

* See Plate XLVII. † See Plate XLVIII.

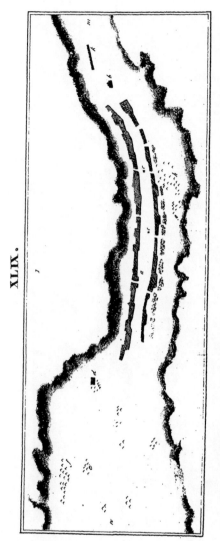

XLIX.

after I entered Mina, where the first thing I perceived was a fountain, in front of which is an ancient edifice, said to have been built by the devil.

The town of Mina, called by some Mona, is composed of a single street, which is so long, that it took me twenty minutes to pass through it. There are several handsome houses in it; but the greater number are in ruins, and without roofs. There are several dwellings of dry stone, about five feet high, which they let to pilgrims during the time of Easter. *

About four o'clock they pitched my camp upon the eastern side of Mina, in a little plain, where there was a mosque, surrounded by a wall that resembled a fortification.

The country lies in a valley, between mountains of granite rocks, that are perfectly bare. The road, which was very level, upon a sandy bottom, was covered with camels, with persons on foot or on horseback, and with a great number of schevrias, of the same form as my own.

A detachment of Wehhabites, mounted upon dromedaries, which I saw at the foot of Djebel, arrived, and encamped also before the door of the mosque. This was followed by several others also mounted; so that in a short time the plain was covered. About sun-set, the Sultan of the Wehhabites, named Saaoud, arrived; and his tents were pitched at the foot of a mountain, at a short distance from mine.

A caravan from Tripoli in Barbary; another from Yemen; a great number of Negro pilgrims from Soudan, or Abyssinia; several hundred Turks from Suez; a great many Mogrebins, who came by sea; a caravan from Bassora; others from the East; Arabs from Upper and Lower Egypt; those of the country in which we were; and the Wehhabites; were now all assembled, and encamped together, or rather one upon the other, in this little plain; where the pilgrims are obliged to encamp, because tradition relates,

* See Plates XLIX. and L.

that the holy Prophet always encamped here, when he went to Arafat.

The caravan from Damascus had not arrived; however, it had set out with troops, artillery, and a great number of women, to convey the rich carpet which is sent every year from Constantinople to the sepulchre of the Prophet at Medina; which present the Wehhabites look upon as a sin.

This caravan was close to Medina, when the Wehhabites went and met it, and signified to the Pacha of Damascus, Emir el Hage, that they could not receive the carpet, which was destined for the sepulchre, and that if he wished to continue his journey to Mecca, he must previously send back his soldiers, his artillery, and the women; so that by transforming themselves into true pilgrims, they would experience no impediment to the continuation of their journey. The Pacha, not willing to conform to these conditions, was desired to retrace his steps. Some pretend to say that they required a large sum of money from him, but others deny this fact.

On Tuesday the 17th February 1807, 9th Doulhagea, in the year 1221 of the Hegira, at six o'clock in the morning, we all set out towards the S. E. ¼ E. At a short distance we passed a house of the Scherif; and at seven we arrived at Mosdelifa, a small chapel with a high minaret, situated in a small valley *; after leaving which, we defiled through a very narrow passage between the mountains, and traversed a second valley to the south-east, which lay at the foot of Mount Arafat, where we arrived at nine.

Mount Arafat is the principal object of the pilgrimage of the Mussulmen; and several doctors assert, that if the house of God ceased to exist, the pilgrimage to the former would be completely meritorious, and would produce the same degree of satisfaction. This is my opinion likewise.

It is here that the grand spectacle of the pilgrimage of the Mussulmen must be seen—an innumerable crowd of men from all

* See Plate LI.

nations, and of all colours, coming from the extremities of the earth, through a thousand dangers, and encountering fatigues of every description, to adore together the same God, the God of nature. The native of Circassia presents his hand in a friendly manner to the Ethiopian, or the Negro of Guinea; the Indian and the Persian embrace the inhabitant of Barbary and Morocco; all looking upon each other as brothers, or individuals of the same family united by the bands of religion; and the greater part speaking or understanding more or less the same language, the language of Arabia. No, there is not any religion that presents to the senses a spectacle more simple, affecting, and majestic! Philosophers of the earth! permit me, Ali Bey, to defend my religion, as you defend spiritual things from those which are material, the plenum against a vacuum, and the necessary existence of the creation.

Here, as I remarked in the narrative of my voyage to Morocco, is no intermediary between man and the Divinity; all individuals are equal before their Creator; all are intimately persuaded that their works alone reconcile them to, or separate them from the Supreme Being, without any foreign hand being able to change the order of immutable justice! What a curb to sin! What an encouragement to virtue! But what a misfortune that, with so many advantages, we should not be better than the Calvinists!

Arafat is a small mountain of granite rock, the same as those that surround it: it is about 150 feet high, and is situated at the foot of a higher mountain to the E. S. E., in a plain about three quarters of a league in diameter, surrounded by barren mountains. *

It is inclosed by a wall, and is ascended by staircases, partly cut in the rock, and partly composed of masonry. † There is a chapel upon its summit, which the Wehhabites were then in the act of pulling to pieces in the interior. It was impossible for me to visit it, because individuals who follow the same rite as myself, that is to

* See Plate XLIX. † See Plate LII.

say, the Maleki, are forbidden to ascend the top, according to the instructions of the Imam, the founder of the rite. It was therefore that we stopped when we were half way up, to recite our prayer. At the foot of the mountain there is a platform erected for this purpose, called Djamáa Arrahma, or Mosque of Mercy, upon which, according to tradition, the Prophet used to say his prayer.

Near the mountain are fourteen large basons, which the Sultan Saaoud has put in repair. They furnish a great abundance of excellent water, very good to drink, and which serves also for the pilgrims to wash themselves with upon this solemn day. The Scherif has a house close to the south-west side of the mountain. Towards the north-west there is a second platform for offering up prayers, which is situated about a quarter of a league from the first, and is called Djamáa Ibrahim, or the Mosque of Abraham.

It was upon Mount Arafat that the common father of all mankind met Eve after a long separation; and it is on that account that it is called Arafat, that is to say, gratitude. It is believed that it was Adam himself who built this chapel.

The ritual commands, that after having repeated the afternoon prayer, which we did in our tents, we should repair to the foot of the mountain, and wait there the setting of the sun. The Wehhabites, who were encamped at great distances, with a view to obey this precept, began to approach, having at their head the Sultan Saaoud, and Abounocta their second chief; and in a short time I saw an army of forty-five thousand men pass before me, almost all of whom were mounted upon camels and dromedaries, with a thousand camels carrying water, tents, fire-wood, and dry grass for the camels of the chiefs. A body of two hundred men on horseback carried colours of different kinds, fixed upon lances. This cavalry, I was informed, belonged to Abounocta. There were also eight or ten colours among the camels, but without any other customary appendage. All this body of men, entirely naked, marched in the same order that I have formerly remarked.

It was impossible for me exactly to distinguish the Sultan and the second chief, for they were naked as well as the rest. However, I believe that a venerable old man, with a long white beard, who was preceded by the royal standard, was Saaoud. This standard was green, and had, as a mark of distinction, the profession of his faith, " La illahá ila Allah," " There is no other god but God," embroidered upon it, in large white characters.

I distinguished perfectly one of Saaoud's sons, a boy about seven or eight years old, with long and floating hair. He was brown like the rest, and dressed in a large white shirt. He was mounted on a superb white horse, upon a sort of pannel, without stirrups, according to their custom, for they are not acquainted with any other kind of saddle, and was escorted by a chosen troop. The pannel was covered with a red cloth richly embroidered, and spangled with gold stars.

The mountain and its environs were soon covered with Wehhabites. The caravans and detached pilgrims afterwards approached it. Notwithstanding the remonstrances of my people, I penetrated among the Wehhabites to their centre, to be able to obtain a nearer view of the Sultan ; but several of them with whom I conversed assured me that this was impossible, since the apprehension of a similar death to that which occurred to the unfortunate Abdelaaziz, who was assassinated, had occasioned Saaoud to multiply the number of his guard.

I must allow that I discovered much reason and moderation among the Wehhabites to whom I spoke, and from whom I obtained the greater part of the information which I have given concerning their nation. However, notwithstanding this moderation, neither the natives of the country nor the pilgrims could hear their name pronounced without trembling, and never pronounced it themselves but in murmurs. Thus they fly from them as much as possible, and shun conversation with them ; in consequence of which I had to encounter and overcome the different scruples of my people, who surrounded me whenever I wished to converse with any of them.

The Sultan Scherif had sent, according to annual custom, a part of his troops, with four small pieces of artillery. It was reported even that he would come in person; but I did not see him.

It is customary also, that an Imam of the Scherif should come every year and preach a sermon upon the mountain. The one that came this day was sent back by Saaoud before he commenced, and one of his own Imams preached in his stead; but I was too far off to be able to hear any thing. The sermon being over, I observed the Wehhabites make signs of approbation; and they cried outrageously.

I could easily have found means to introduce myself to the Sultan Saaoud, which I very much desired, so that I might have known him perfectly; but as it would have compromised me with the Sultan Scherif, who would have attributed this simple action of curiosity to some political motive, I abstained from effecting it.

We waited upon the mountain for the period of the sun's setting. The instant it occurred, what a tremendous noise! Let us imagine an assemblage of eighty thousand men, two thousand women, and a thousand little children, sixty or seventy thousand camels, asses, and horses, which at the commencement of night began to move in a quick pace along a narrow valley, according to the ritual, marching one after the other in a cloud of sand, and delayed by a forest of lances, guns, swords, &c.; in short, forcing their passage as they could. Pressed and hurried on by those behind, we only took an hour and a half to return to Mosdelifa, notwithstanding it had taken us more than two hours to arrive in the morning. The motive of this precipitation ordered by the ritual is, that the prayer of the setting sun, or Mogareb, ought not to be said at Arafat, but at Mosdelifa, at the same time as the night prayer, or Ascha, which ought to be said at the last moment of twilight, that is, an hour and a half after sun-set. These prayers are repeated by each group or family privately. We hastened to say them upon our arrival, before we pitched our tents ; and the day was terminated by mutual felicitations upon the happiness of our sanctification by the pilgrimage to the mount.

We set out the next day, Wednesday, 18th February, 10th of the month Doulhajea, and the first day of Easter, at five o'clock in the morning, to go to encamp at Mina.

We alighted immediately after our arrival, and went precipitately to the house of the devil, which is facing the fountain. We had each seven small stones of the size of grey peas, which we had picked up expressly the evening before at Mosdelifa to throw against the house of the devil. Mussulmen of the rite of Maleki like myself, throw them one after the other, pronouncing after every one these words, " Bism illah Allahuak'bar," which interpreted are, " In the name of God, very great God." As the devil has had the malice to build his house in a very narrow place, not above thirty-four feet broad, occupied also in part by rocks, which it was requisite to climb to make sure of our aim when we threw the stones over the wall that surrounded it, and as the pilgrims all desired to perform this ceremony immediately upon their arrival, there was a most terrible confusion. However, I soon succeeded in accomplishing this holy duty, through the aid of my people ; but I came off with two wounds in my left leg. I retired afterwards to my tent, to repose myself after these fatigues. The Wehhabites came and threw their little stones also, because the Prophet used to do so. We offered up the Paschal sacrifice this day.

I must praise the moderation and good order which reigned amidst this number of individuals, belonging to different nations. Two thousand women who were among them did not occasion the least disorder ; and though there were more than forty or fifty thousand guns, there was only one let off, which happened near me. At the same instant one of the chiefs ran to the man who had fired, and reprimanded him, saying, " Why did you do this ? are we going to make war here ?"

I met the eldest son of the Saaoud upon my way, in the morning. He was on horseback, at the head of a body of dromedaries, and arrived at Mina at the same time I did. At the moment of passing by my side, he cried to his company, " Come, children, let us approach." Then turning to the left, he galloped off, followed by his suite, to his father's tent, which was pitched, as before, at the foot of the mountain. Mine were situated opposite those belonging to the troops of the Scherif.

Having risen at break of day on Thursday the 19th to say my prayer, I perceived that my writing-desk, books, papers, and some clothes, had been stolen. My writing-desk contained my chronometer, some jewels, and other trifles, my great seal, and several astronomical observations and drawings.

My servants began to hunt on all sides, fearing the consequences of this robbery, because they had neglected to mount guard according to my desire ; but being much fatigued on the preceding days, and the guard of the Turkish and Mogrebin soldiers being close to my tents, they had been induced to take repose.

I finished my prayer, surrounded by my people ; and when it was completely daylight, they discovered papers scattered over the mountain. They ran to the spot, and found my writing-desk open, with the lock forced, and all my papers and books scattered about. The chronometer, jewels, and the tables of logarithms, which were bound, and which the thieves mistook for a Koran in the dark, were missing.

Before saying the noon prayer, we went to throw seven small stones against a little stone pillar, about six feet high and two square, which is placed in the middle of the street at Mina, and is said to have been built by the devil. We threw also seven stones against a pillar similar to the former, which is also reported to have been constructed by the same architect. It is placed at about forty paces distance from the other.

We set off on our return to Mecca, on Friday the 20th of February, the 12th of the month Doulhajea, and the third day of Easter, after having repeated the ceremony of the seven stones.

Upon our entering the town we went to the temple, where we took seven turns round the house of God ; and after having said the prayer, and drank of the water of Zemzem, we went out at the Saffa gate to complete our pilgrimage, by taking the seven journeys between Saffa and Meroua, as upon the night of our arrival; having completed which, we felicitated each other on having at last finished the holy pilgrimage.

This solemn act was formerly accompanied by several other customs and forms of devotion, added by different doctors or pious souls ; but the Wehhabites have suppressed them, thinking them superstitious. There remain now but a few, which I observed in all their extent.

On Sunday the 22d, almost all the pilgrims assembled at a spot about a league to the W. N. W. of Mecca, where there is a mosque, which is falling in ruins, called El Aamra. We first said the prayer, and then placed three stones one upon the other, in a devout manner, at a small distance from the mosque. We afterwards went to the spot where the infamous Abougehél, the furious enemy of our holy Prophet, resided, and threw seven stones upon it, with a holy fury, cursing it at the same time.

Being returned to the town, we again took seven turns round the house of God, and performed the seven journeys between Saffa and Meroua ; after which there remained nothing to add to the ceremony of pilgrimage for our sanctification.

Tradition says, that the above appendix was instituted by Ayéscha, the most beloved wife of our holy Prophet.

★   ★   ★   ★   ★

CHAP. VII.

DESCRIPTION OF MECCA. — ITS GEOGRAPHICAL POSITION. — TOPOGRAPHY. —
BUILDINGS. — PUBLIC MARKET PLACES. — PROVISIONS. —ARTS AND SCIENCES.
— TRADE. — MISERY. — DECLINE.

THE holy city of Mecca, the capital of Hedjaz, or the Arabia
Deserta of the ancient geographers, the centre of the Mussulman religion, in consequence of the temple which Abraham raised
to the Supreme Being, is the object of the affections of all true
believers.

A great number of observations of the passing of the sun through
the meridian, which I made, proved the latitude of Mecca to be
21° 28′ 9″ N. ; and several others of the lunary distances proved the
longitude to be 37° 54′ 45″ E. from the observatory of Paris. The
house in which I lived, and upon the flat roof of which I made my
observations, was situated almost in the middle of the city, at about
530 feet distance to the north from the Kaaba.

Having observed several azimuths, my magnetical declination
was 9° 43′ 52″ W.

The city of Mecca, called Mekka in Arabic, is situated in a very
narrow valley, the mean breadth of which may be about 155 toises;
that winds irregularly between mountains from the north-east to the
south-west ; so that the city, which follows the windings of the
valley, is quite irregular ; and the houses being also built upon the
sides of the mountains, render the plan of it still more so, which
is represented in plate LXII., where all the principal streets are
described ; but there are some little streets omitted, as I had not
time to include them. I much wished to have taken as complete a
view of Mecca as I did of Alexandria ; but it was impossible to find

a proper point of view, because the city, being confined between
the mountains, allowed me to discover only a few houses, if I went
out at one end of it; and if I went out at the sides, I found myself
upon the side of the mountains, from whence I could perceive
nothing but an irregular surface of flat roofs, without any perspective. I therefore found myself obliged to abandon the idea.
The view of Mecca, which is to be seen in the " Picture of the
Ottoman Empire, by Mr. Ohsson," might have had its merits,
when the city occupied but half the valley; but it is no longer like
that city. The fine fountain in Mr. Ohsson's drawing no longer
exists. The only water to be found at present is that of the
wells.

I shall not speak of the celebrated temple, because the plan and
profile which I have given of it prove the inaccuracy of the engravings
in the Picture of the Ottoman Empire. It would have been very
easy for me to have given an incorrect view of Mecca; but as I
wished absolutely to be as exact in my drawings as I endeavour to
be in my notes, I would not attempt it; for it would only have been
a picture of imagination, as any general view of this city must be.
In short, it may be considered as an assemblage of a great number
of houses grouped to the north of the temple, prolonging themselves in the form of a crescent from the N. E. to the S. W. by S.
It covers a line of 900 toises in length and 266 in breadth at its
centre, which extends from east to west.

The principal streets are regular enough; they may even be
called handsome, on account of the pretty fronts of the houses.
They are sanded, level, and very convenient. I had been so long
accustomed to live in the indifferent towns of Africa, that I was
quite surprised at the fine appearance of the buildings of Mecca.

I think they approach the Indian or Persian taste, which introduced itself during the time of the siege by the Caliph of Bagdad.
They have two rows of windows, as at Cyprus, with balconies covered with blinds. There are even several large windows, quite open,
as in Europe; but the greater number are covered by a species of

curtain like a Venetian blind, made of palm tree. They are extremely light, and screen the apartments from the sun, without interrupting the passage of the air. They fold up at pleasure at the upper part, exactly like the former.

The houses are solidly built with stone : they are three and four stories high, and even more sometimes. The fronts are ornamented with bases, mouldings, and paintings, which give them a very graceful appearance. It is very rare to find a door that has not a base with steps, and small seats on both sides. The blinds of the balconies are not very close ; and holes are cut besides in different parts of them.

The roofs form terraces, surrounded by a wall about seven feet high, open at certain spaces, which are occupied by a railing formed of red and white bricks, placed horizontally and symmetrically, leaving holes for the circulation of the air ; and at the same time that they contribute to the ornaments of the front, they skreen the women from being seen when they are upon the terraces.

All the staircases that I saw were narrow, dark, and steep. The rooms are well proportioned, long, broad, and lofty, and have, besides the large windows and balconies, a second row of smaller windows. They have also a shelf all round, as at Alexandria, which serves to place various things upon.

The beauty of the houses may be considered as the remains of the ancient splendour of Mecca. Every inhabitant has an interest in preserving his dwelling, to invite and excite the pilgrims to lodge with him ; because it is one of his principal resources, on account of the terms demanded, and other additional benefits.

There is no open place or square at Mecca, because the irregularity of the ground and the want of space would not permit it. The public markets are held in the principal streets ; and it may be said that the great street in the centre is a continued market from one end of the city to the other. The dealers expose their goods, &c. in slight sheds, built with sticks and mats, or under large umbrellas, supported by three sticks, which meet in the centre.

The markets are well provided with provisions and other articles, and are filled with people all day long, particularly at the period of the pilgrimage. There are also ambulatory restaurateurs, who sell ready-dressed victuals and pastry ; pewterers, shoemakers, and such like artizans.

All the provisions are dear, except meat, notwithstanding the abundance. A large sheep costs nearly seven francs. Fowls are very scarce, and consequently eggs. There is no game. The corn, or rather flour, comes from Upper Egypt; vegetables and rice from India. They obtain herbs, &c. from Taif; as also a small portion of corn, which is of an inferior quality to that of Egypt. Butter is kept in large pots, and is common in the country; but it is liquid like oil, on account of the heat of the climate. The prices vary extremely, in consequence of the want of safety in the commerce. The following were the prices of the articles opposite which they are placed, during my stay in 1807 :

	Turkish Piastres.
An oka of butter	5
A fowl	4
Six eggs	1
A camel load of fresh water	2
An oka of oil	4

	Paras.
An oka of bread	12
A bottle of the water of the well	15
An oka of fire wood	3
An oka of coals	20

The weights and measures are the same as in Egypt, but are so inexact, that it would be useless to look for a parallel to them.

This is also the case with the current money. The Spanish piastre goes in trade for five Turkish piastres of forty paras each; but in exchange it is only worth four and a half of them. There is every sort of money to be seen circulating in Mecca, as also money changers, who sit in the market behind a little counter, with a small pair of scales, who are occupied during the whole day in transacting their affairs in an incorrect way; but it may be imagined not to their own disadvantage.

All the productions of India and Persia, natural as well as artificial, may be bought here. Near my dwelling there was a double range of shops, exclusively destined to the sale of aromatic substances, of which I took the catalogue and description. *

At Mecca, as throughout all Arabia, they do not make bread, properly so called. They mix the flour with water, without any leaven (except a little very rarely), of which they make cakes of three or four lines thick, and eight or nine inches diameter, that they sell half baked, and as soft as paste. Such is their bread, which is called hhops.

The fresh water, which they bring from the neighbouring mountains, and from Mina, upon camels, is good. The well water, though a little brackish and heavy, is drinkable. The lower class of people never drink any other.

I examined all the wells particularly. They are all of the same depth; and the water is of the same temperature, taste, and clearness, as that of Zemzem. There are four that are public in the streets nearest to the temple, exactly like each other, and several in the most distant parts of the city. I am persuaded, from my observations, that the water which supplies all of them is one sheet, situated fifty-five feet under the surface of the ground, the quantity of which is owing to the filtration of rain water. The brackish taste it has is to be attributed to the decomposition of the saline particles mixed with the earth, from which it results, in the clearest manner, that as they have the same qualities, and spring from the same source as the water of Zemzem, they have the same virtue in drawing down the divine favour and blessing as the miraculous well. God be praised for it.

---

* It is to be regretted that this catalogue is lost.—Note of the Editor.

The meat at Mecca is of an inferior quality, the sheep being very large but very thin. They hardly know the existence of fish, though the sea is not more than a dozen leagues distant. The herbs, &c. which they bring from Taif, and other neighbouring places, but particularly from Setna Fathma, consist of onions, turnips, cucumbers, purslain, capers, and a sort of sallad composed of leaves like cow grass. This plant, which it was impossible for me to see in its whole state, is called corrát.

I never saw but one flower during the whole of my stay at Mecca, which was upon the way to Arafat. I ordered my servant to cut it and bring it to me ; but he was perceived by the pilgrims, who ran immediately to him, saying, it was a sin to pluck up or cut any plant during the pilgrimage to that place. I was therefore obliged to renounce the idea of obtaining the only flower I had seen.

They make several sorts of drink with raisins, honey, sugar, and other fruits. The vinegar is of a very bad quality. I was told they made it from raisins.

I believe there is no Mussulman city where the arts are so little known as at Mecca. There is not a man to be found that is capable of making a lock or forging a key. All the doors are locked with large wooden keys, and the trunks and cases with padlocks brought from Europe : I therefore was unable to replace the key of a trunk, and that of my telescope box, which were stolen at Mina.

The slippers and sandals are brought from Constantinople and Egypt ; for they know not how to make them at Mecca, except indeed those of wood or untanned leather, which are very bad.

There is not a single man to be found who knows how to engrave an inscription, or any kind of design upon a hewn stone, as formerly ; nor a single gun-smith or cutler able to make a screw, or to replace a piece of the lock of an European gun ; those of the country being only able to manufacture their rude matchlocks, their bent knives, lances, and halberds. Wherever they go, their shop is fitted up in a moment : all that is wanted for this purpose is a hole made in ground, which serves as a furnace : one or two goat skins, which one of them waves before the fire, serve them for bellows : two or three palm leaves, and four sticks, form the walls and the roof of the work-shop, the situation of which they change whenever occasion requires.

There is no want of braziers for vessels in copper ; but the original article comes from foreign manufactories. There are also tinmen, who make a kind of vase, which the pilgrims use to carry away some of the water of Zemzem. I discovered also a bad engraver of brass seals.

The sciences are found in the same state of perfection as the arts at Mecca. The whole knowledge of the inhabitants is confined to reading the Kourr-an, and to writing very badly. They learn from their infancy the prayers and the ceremonies of the pilgrimage to the house of God, to Saffa, and Meroua, in order to be able at an early age to gain money by officiating as guides to the pilgrims. Children of five or six years old are to be seen fulfilling these functions, carried upon the arms or shoulders of the pilgrims, who repeat the prayers which the children recite word for word, at the same time that they follow the path pointed out by them to the different places.

I wished to obtain a Kourr-an written at Mecca, but they are not numerous ; and they are so badly written, and so full of errors, that they cannot be of any use.

There are no regular schools, if we except those where they learn to read and write. In short, there are only a few talbes, or doctors, who, through caprice, vanity, or covetousness of obtaining something from their auditors, go and sit under the porticos of the temple, where they begin to read in a loud voice to draw a crowd of persons, who generally assemble pretty quickly, and arrange themselves round the doctor, who explains, reads, or preaches, whichever he can do, and go away or stay as they please. Such is the education of the people of this holy city, who are the most ignorant of mortals. It is true that their geographical situation contributes to it in a great measure.

Mecca, placed in the middle of a desert, does not resemble Palmyra, which the continual commerce between the East and the West elevated to the greatest degree of perfection and splendour, which we even admire in its ruins, and which would still have existed, but for the discovery of the Cape of Good Hope : on the contrary, it is not placed in any direct line of passage. Arabia is surrounded by the Persian Gulph to the east, the Red Sea to the west, the ocean to the south, and the Mediterranean Sea to the north. Its centre, therefore, cannot be in any direct line of communication with the neighbouring countries to which access may be had by sea. Its ports at most will only serve as sea-port towns to to trading vessels, as is the case with Djedda and Mokka upon the Red Sea, and Muscat, near the mouth of the Persian Gulph.

Mecca not being situated in the route to any country of consequence, nature has not designed it as a place of commerce, placed as it is in the middle of an extremely barren desert, which prevents its inhabitants from being either husbandmen or shepherds. What resources then remain to them for subsistence ? The force of arms, to oblige other countries to give them a part of their productions, or religious enthusiasm, to induce strangers to come and bring money to them, with which they may procure the necessaries of life.

In the time of the Caliphs, these two causes united rendered Mecca an opulent city ; but before and since that glorious period, it has had no other resource for its support than the religious enthusiasm of the pilgrims, which unfortunately begins to cool from day to day, through the effects of time, distance of place, and revolutions, that reduce this place to a mean and precarious existence. Such is its state at this moment, and such was it before the mission of the Prophet.

Mecca has always been the centre of the religious enthusiasm of different nations. The origin of pilgrimages, and the first foundation of its temple, are lost in the obscurity of ages, since they appear to be anterior to the period of history. The Prophet pulled down the idols which profaned the house of God.   The Koran confirmed the pilgrimage ; and it is in this manner that the devotion of other nations has been in all times the basis of the subsistence of the inhabitants of Mecca.   But as this could not alone suffice, they were very poor before the coming of the Prophet ; and now, after a short reign of glory and riches acquired by arms, it has relapsed into poverty.   How then can we hope to see the arts and sciences flourish ?   Separated by its situation from all commercial intercourse, it remains immersed in the most profound ignorance of all news, discoveries, revolutions, and the actions of other men. Hence it is that the people of Mecca will remain in stupidity and the grossest darkness, notwithstanding the concourse of strangers, who only remain there during the time absolutely necessary to fulfil the duties of their pilgrimage, to make some few commercial exchanges, and then prepare for their return to their own country.

Thus Mecca is so poor by nature, that if the house of God ceased to exist, it would be inevitably deserted in two years, or at least reduced to a simple douar or hamlet ; for the inhabitants in general subsist for the rest of the year upon what they accumulate during the time of the pilgrimage, at which period the place puts on a lively appearance, commerce is animated, and the half of the people are transformed into hosts, merchants, porters, servants, &c.; and the other, attached entirely to the service of the temple, live upon the alms and gifts of the pilgrims.

Such are their resources.   Deplorable opulence! which has stamped upon their countenances the mark of the extreme misery that surrounds them.

An Arab is by nature generally thin ; but those of Mecca, and above all those that serve in the temple, seem absolutely walking skeletons, clothed with a parchment that covers their bones.   I must own I was struck with astonishment when I saw them for the first time upon my arrival,   What I have advanced may be perhaps considered as an exaggeration ; but I protest to the truth of my assertions ; and may also add, that it is impossible, without seeing them, to form an idea of an assemblage of such lean and scraggy-looking men, as all of them are, with the exception of the chief of Zemzem, who is the only person that is at all lusty, and two or three eunuchs, a little less thin than the others. It appears even impossible that these skeletons, or shadows, should be able to stand so long as they do, when we reflect upon their large sunk eyes ; slender noses ; cheeks hollow to the bones ; legs and arms absolutely shrivelled up ; ribs, veins, and nerves, in no better state ; and the whole of their frame so wasted, that they might be mistaken for true anatomical models. Such is the frightful appearance of these unhappy creatures, that it is painful to be obliged to look at them. This is the existence which these servants of the temple enjoy ; but the pleasures that await them in Paradise are preferable to all the riches of the earth.

There are no people more dull and melancholy than these. I never once heard the sound of a musical instrument or song during the whole of my stay, that was executed by a man ; but my ears were struck once or twice by the songs of some women, which I set to music. * Plunged in a continual melancholy, the least contradiction irritates them ; and the few slaves they have are the most unhappy and wretched of all the Mussulman slaves, in consequence of the bad treatment they experience. I heard, in the house I lived in, a master beat his slave with a bastinado, during a quarter of an hour. He stopped every three or four minutes to allow his arm to rest, and then recommenced with new force.

It may be deduced, from these observations, that the population of Mecca diminishes sensibly. This city, which is known to have contained more than 100,000 souls, does not at present shelter more than from 16 to 18,000. There are some quarters of the suburbs entirely abandoned, and in ruins ; nearly two thirds of the houses that remain are empty ; and the greatest part of those that are

* See Plate LXIV.

inhabited are decaying within, notwithstanding the solidity of their construction; the fronts alone being kept in good order, to attract the pilgrims. In consequence of the inattention that is paid to repairs, the houses are falling down; and if there are no new ones erected (and I only saw one that was advancing slowly in the whole town) it will be reduced in the course of a century to the tenth part of the size it now is.

Elphinstone:
Account of the Kingdom of Caubul

Mountstuart Elphinstone, *An Account of the Kingdom of Caubul, and its Dependencies in Persia, Tartary, and India; Comprising a View of the Afghaun Nation, and a History of the Dooraunee Monarchy*, 2 vols (London: Longman, Hurst, Rees, Orme & Brown and J. Murray, 1819), vol. I, pp. 136–47, 237–52.

A prominent diplomat and administrator of British India, Mountstuart Elphinstone (1779–1859) published only a small portion of the journals he kept during his extensive travels in the East. First published in 1815, *An Account of the Kingdom of Caubul* nevertheless earned its author a formidable literary reputation, and his descriptions of the Caucasus region both guided British foreign policy and helped to shape the Romantic interest in the north-western provinces of the Empire.

Described by his nineteenth-century biographer as an administrator who 'exercised a decisive influence upon the fate of Western India' (see J. S. Cotton, *Rulers of India: Mountstuart Elphinstone* (Oxford, 1892), p. 9), Elphinstone's career with the East India Company was particularly distinguished, culminating with the Governorship of Bombay from 1819 to 1827. Sent to India in 1796, Elphinstone was first appointed as Assistant to the Secretary at Poona in 1801, and by 1804 he had been granted his own Residency at Nagpur. In 1808 he was promoted again and this time asked to lead an embassy into Kabul. Although the mission was ultimately unsuccessful, his experiences in Kabul were to shape Elphinstone's early public reputation and Romantic attitudes towards imperial expansion in the provinces.

The objective of the Kabul mission was part of Britain's larger policy of containment in the East. Napoleon was at the height of his power in Europe, and the French had gained influence with both the Ottoman and the Persian empires. Elphinstone was to ensure that French influence did not spread any further, and he was charged with negotiating a treaty with the Shah Shoja'. Few of these administrative details, however, found their way into Elphinstone's travel account of the embassy. For, while the narrative is full of the sort of geographical and cultural details that were valuable to subsequent diplomats and explorers, Elphinstone's central theme is the civilising Christian mission of imperialism. Casting himself as a Romantic Alexander, Elphinstone provides repeated points of comparison between the accounts of the classical historians and the East India Company's objectives in the Caucasus, in an effort to legitimise territorial expansion. When Percy Bysshe Shelley read *An Account of the Kingdom of Caubul* in 1817, he responded particularly to this Christian mythmaking, which he works to refute through intertextual engagement with Elphinstone's narrative in *Prometheus Unbound*.

BOOK I.

GEOGRAPHICAL DESCRIPTION OF AFGHAUNISTAUN.

CHAP. I.

SITUATION AND BOUNDARIES OF AFGHAUNISTAUN.

IT is difficult to fix the limits of the kingdom of Caubul. The countries under the sovereignty of the King of Caubul, once extended sixteen degrees in longitude from Sirhind, about one hundred and fifty miles from Delly, to Meshhed, about an equal distance from the Caspian sea. In breadth they reached from the Oxus to the Persian gulph, a space including thirteen degrees of latitude, or nine hundred and ten miles.

But this great empire has, of late, suffered a considerable diminution, and the distracted state of the goverment prevents the King's exercising authority even over several of the countries which are still included in his dominions. In this uncertainty I shall adopt the test made use of by the Asiatics themselves, and shall consider the King's sovereignty as extending over all the countries in which the Khootba * is read, and the money coined in his name.

In this view the present kingdom of Caubul extends from the west of Heraut in longitude 62°, to the eastern boundary of Cashmeer in longitude 77° east, and from the mouth of the Indus, in latitude 24°, to the Oxus, in latitude, 37° north.

The whole space included between those lines of latitude and longitude, does not belong to the King of Caubul, and it will hereafter appear, that of those which may be considered as annexed to his crown, many owe him but a nominal obedience.

This kingdom is bounded on the east by Hindostan, in which it however comprehends Cashmeer, and the countries on the left bank of the Indus. On the south it may be coarsely said to have the Persian gulph; and on the west a desart extends along the whole of the frontiers. Its northern frontier is formed by the mountains of the eastern Caucasus, which are, however, included within the western part of the boundary there formed by the Oxus.

According to the nomenclature of our latest

---

* The Khootba is a part of the Mahommedan service, in which the king of the country is prayed for. Inserting a prince's name in the Khootba, and inscribing it on the current coin, are reckoned in the East the most certain acknowledgments of sovereignty.

maps *, it comprehends Afghaunistaun and Se-
gistan, with part of Khorasan and of Makran;
Balk, with Tokarestaun and Kilan; Kuttore,
Caubul, Candahar, Sindy, and Cashmeer; together with a portion of Lahore, and the greater
part of Moultan.

The whole population of the kingdom cannot
be under fourteen millions. This was the number fixed by one of the gentlemen of the mission,
on a calculation of the extent and comparative
population of the different provinces. All extensive desarts were excluded; no greater rate
of population than one hundred to the square
mile, was allowed to any large tract except
Cashmeer, and sometimes (as in the whole country of the Hazaurehs) only eight souls were allowed to the square mile.

The different nations who inhabit the kingdom of Caubul were supposed to contribute to
the population in the following proportions:

Afghauns, - - - - - - -	4,300,000
† Beloches, - - - - - - -	1,000,000
† Tartars of all descriptions, -	1,200,000
Persians (including Taujiks), -	1,500,000
Indians (Cashmeerees, Juts, &c. &c.)	5,700,000
Miscellaneous tribes, - - - -	300,000

The principal part of my account of Caubul,

* Arrowsmith's Asia, 1801.
† I conceive the Beloches and Tartars to be much under-
rated in this table.

will be occupied by the Afghauns, but I shall
first give a sketch of the whole kingdom ; and,
as the surrounding countries may not be sufficiently familiar to my readers, to enable them
to understand the limits of the kingdom, or the
frequent allusions to its neighbouring states, I
shall begin with a slight account of the part of
Asia in which it is situated.

If we traverse the kingdoms of Hindostan
and Caubul, from the east of Bengal to Heraut,
we shall find them every where bounded on the
north by a chain of mountains which is covered
with perpetual snow, for almost the whole of
that extent, and from which all the great rivers
of both countries appear to issue. This chain
commences near the Burrampooter, and runs
nearly north-west, as far as Cashmeer : during
this part of its course it is called Hemalleh by
the natives of the neighbouring countries.
From Cashmeer its general direction is a little
to the south-west, as far as the high snowy peak
of Hindoo Coosh, nearly north of Caubul. From
this peak its height diminishes, it no longer
bears perpetual snow, and is soon after lost in a
groupe of mountains, which stretch in length
from Caubul almost to Heraut, and occupy
more than two degrees of latitude in their
breadth. Some ranges issue from this mass on
the west, and extend so far into Persia, as to
justify, if not completely to establish, the opi-

nion of the ancients, which connected the range
I have been describing, with mount Caucasus
on the west of the Caspian sea. *

From Cashmeer to Hindoo Coosh, the whole
range is known by the name of that peak. From
thence to the meridian of Heraut, the mountains
have no general name among the natives,
and I shall call them by that of Paropamisus,
which is already applied to them by
European geographers. But, although the
chain of mountains which I have described, appears
from the south to form the natural boundary
of Hindostan and Caubul, we must look
farther north for the ridge that terminates the
natural division, in which those countries are
situated, and contains the remotest sources of
their greatest rivers.

* The following passage in Arrian (book iii. chap. 28.)
will show the extent attributed by the Greeks to this mountain.
It is introduced when Alexander arrives at the foot
of mount Caucasus at a point which all geographers have
placed in the neighbourhood of Candahar. Ὁ δὲ ὄρος ὁ
Καύκασος ὑψηλὸν μὲν ἐστιν, &c. &c. &c. " The mountain of
" Caucasus is said by Aristobulus to be as high as any in
" Asia, but it is bare in most parts, and particularly in this
" place. It stretches for a great extent, so that mount
" Taurus, which divides Pamphylia from Cilicia, is said to
" be part of it, as well as other high mountains, distin-
" guished from Caucasus by various names, arising from the
" different nations to whose country they extend." A more
detailed account of this mountain will be found in the same
writer, book v. chap. 3. and 5. and in Pliny's Natural History,
book v. chap. 27.

Our geographers lay down a range of mountains under the name of Mus Tag, which seems to commence to the north of the eastern extremity of Hemalleh, and to run parallel to that mountain on the north, as far as the sixty-seventh degree of east longitude.

The inquiries made on the Caubul mission, have traced but a small part of the extent of this chain. Lieutenant Macartney could follow it with certainty no farther than from Auksoo to the west of Leh, or Ladauk, but the remaining part of its alleged course is probable, and though I have not access to the proofs of its existence, I have no reason to doubt it; I shall, therefore, take that part of the chain for granted, and include it in the name of Mooz Taugh. *

Though this mountain stands on higher ground than Hindoo Coosh, its height from its base, and

---

* This term, which in Turkish signifies ice-hill, is applied to one place in the range at least, where it is occasioned by a glacier near the road from Yarcund to Ladauk. This range, or a ſparticular pass in it, near the road just mentioned, is well known in Toorkistaun by the name of Karrakoorrum.

Since this note was published, I have been led by an examination of Izzut Oollah's route to believe that he crossed Mooz Taugh in long. 78° and lat. 39°. I have therefore put it down as it now stands in the map ; and I do not think it improbable that the Musart of Pallas, laid down by Mr. Arrowsmith between lat. 38° and lat. 40°, is a continuation of this mountain. 1816.

perhaps the absolute elevation of its summits, are inferior to those of the latter mountain.

It is in the southern side of Mooz Taugh, that the Indus appears to have its source, and on the opposite side the waters run north into Chinese Toorkistaun.

The slope of the countries on each side of the mountains, is pointed out by the direction of the streams; but on the north, the descent, as far at least as my information goes, is generally gradual and uninterrupted : while, on the south, there is a table land beneath Mooz Taugh, which is supported by Hemalleh and Hindoo Coosh, and from which the descent is comparatively sudden into the plains of Hindostan, and of the north-eastern part of the Caubul dominions.

The medium breadth of this Table Land may be about two hundred miles, but I have before said that I have no information about it east of the meridian of Ladauk. The eastern part of it is occupied by the extensive country of Tibet; west of which are Little Tibet and Kaushkaur, mountainous countries of no great extent. To the north-west of the last-mentioned country, is the plain of Pamere. Kaushkaur and Pamere are bounded on the west by a range of mountains, which runs from the chain of Mooz Taugh to that of Hindoo Coosh, and which supports the western face of the Table Land.

This range, though inferior in height to that of Hindoo Coosh, has snow on its summits throughout the most part of the year, at least as far as its junction with Mooz Taugh. It leaves the range of Hindoo Coosh in longitude 71° east, and runs in a direction to the east of north, till it meets Mooz Taugh : a range of mountains running also north and south, is crossed further north by the road from Kokaun to Cashgar, and may be considered as a continuation of this chain. It is there lower than before ; so that it is only in severe seasons that it retains its snow longer than the beginning of summer : a little to the north of this road, it gives rise to the Jaxartes ; and beyond this my information ceases. Our maps, however, continue it towards the north, till it reaches a range of mountains which divides Chinese Tartary from Siberia, and separates the waters of the former country from those that flow into the Arctic Ocean.

Our maps call the range which runs from Mooz Taugh to Hindoo Coosh, Belur Tag, which is evidently a corruption of the Turkish words *Beloot Taugh*, or Cloudy Mountains ; as I know of no general name applied by the people of Toorkistaun to this range, I shall use the term Beloot Taugh for it, on the few occa-sions I shall have for mentioning it.

Beloot Taugh forms the boundary between the political divisions of Independent Toorkistaun and Chinese Toorkistaun. It also forms these two countries into two natural divisions, since it separates their streams, and gives rise to rivers which water both countries.

I know of no branches sent out by Beloot Taugh towards the east. To the west it sends out several branches, which, with the valleys between them, form the hilly countries of Kurrateggeen, Shoghnaun, and Durwauz. The most southerly of them bounds Budukhshaun on the north, as Hindoo Coosh does on the south. I know little of the extent or direction of these branches, but one of them seems to stretch westerly to near Samarcand. These are the principal ranges of mountains north of Hindoo Coosh; but a few words are required respecting the rivers and countries between that range, Beloot Taugh, and the Caspian sea.

I have already mentioned the source of the Jaxartes. It holds a course to the north of west, till it falls into the Lake of Arul.

The Oxus rises in a glacier near Pooshtee Khur, a lofty peak of Beloot Taugh, in the most northerly part of Budukhshaun. Its general course is west as far as the sixty-third degree of longitude, from whence it pursues a north-westerly course, through a desart, to the lake of Arul. The rough country about the source of the Jaxartes is inhabited by wandering Kirghizzes; but, from the place where it

leaves the hills to longitude 66° or 67° east,
both banks are occupied by the Uzbek kingdom
of Ferghauna, called also Kokaun from the
residence of the sovereign. To the west of
longitude 66° east, the northern bank is inhabited, first by Kirghizzes, and then by Kuz-
zauks, both rude and pastoral nations. On the
southern bank, to the west of longitude 66° east,
is a desart, which extends in a south-westerly
direction to the inhabited country of Khorassaun. Its breadth varies, but in latitude 40°;
it is seven days' journey broad, and it there
separates the Uzbek kingdoms of Orgunge and
Bokhaura; the first of which lies on the Caspian,
and the other between the Oxus, the desart,
and the mountainous countries under Beloot
Taugh. The character of these kingdoms, or
at least of Bokhaura, is that of desart, enclosing
oases of various size and fertility. All the
country west of Beloot Taugh, and north of the
Oxus, is called Toorkistaun, a term which may
be extended to the east of Beloot Taugh, as far
as there is reason to think the Turkish language
is spoken; but when I have occasion to speak
of that division, I shall call it Chinese Toorkistaun, and the other Toorkistaun alone. The
name of Tartary is unknown in those regions.
There remains a tract, between the Oxus and
the Paropamisan mountains, which ought to be
mentioned with Toorkistaun (as its principal

population is Uzbek), though it is a province of Caubul. It has Budukshaun on the east; and the thinly inhabited country, which joins to its west, about Shibbergaun, is included in Khorassaun. The country slopes towards the Oxus. Small as it is, it includes several principalities; and is diversified with hill and plain, marsh and desart. Our geographers commonly call the whole division Bulkh, from the principal city it contains. This name is inaccurate; but* as I know no other general name for the whole tract, I shall continue to apply it to this division, with which I shall close my account of the country north of Hindoo Coosh.

---

* It might perhaps have been preferable to have used the name of Bactria, though that of Bulkh, from which it is derived, is now out of use, except in books.

★   ★   ★   ★   ★

BOOK II.

GENERAL ACCOUNT OF THE INHABITANTS OF AFGHAUNISTAUN.

CHAP. I.

INTRODUCTION, ORIGIN, AND EARLY HISTORY OF THE AFGHAUNS.

THE description, which I have attempted, of
the country of the Afghauns, has been rendered difficult by the great variety of the regions
to be described, and by the diversity even of contiguous tracts.   No less a diversity will be discovered in the people who inhabit it; and,
amidst the contrasts that are apparent, in the
government, manners, dress, and habits of the
different tribes, I find it difficult to select those
great features, which all possess in common, and
which give a marked national character to the
whole of the Afghauns.   This difficulty is increased by the fact, that those qualities which
distinguish them from all their neighbours, are
by no means the same, which, without reference
to such a comparison, would appear to Euro-

peans to predominate in their character. The
freedom which forms their grand distinction
among the nations of the East, might seem to an
Englishman a mixture of anarchy and arbitrary
power; and the manly virtues, that raise them
above their neighbours, might sink in his estimation almost to the level of the opposite defects.
It may, therefore, assist in appreciating their
situation and character to figure the aspects they
would present to a traveller from England, and
to one from India.

.If a man could be transported from England
to the Afghaun country, without passing through
the dominions of Turkey, Persia, or Tartary, he
would be amazed at the wide and unfrequented
desarts, and the mountains, covered with peren-
nial snow. Even in the cultivated part of the
country, he would discover a wild assemblage of
hills and wastes, unmarked by enclosures, not
embellished by trees, and destitute of navigable
canals, public roads, and all the great and ela-
borate productions of human industry and refinement. He would find the towns few, and
far distant from each other; and he would look
in vain for inns or other conveniences, which a
traveller would meet with in the wildest parts of
Great Britain. Yet he would sometimes be
delighted with the fertility and populousness of
particular plains and valleys, where he would
see the productions of Europe, mingled in pro-

fusion with those of the torrid zone; and the
land laboured with an industry and a judgment
no where surpassed. He would see the inhabitants, following their flocks in tents, or assembled in villages, to which the terraced roofs
and mud walls give an appearance entirely new.
He would be struck at first with their high, and
even harsh features, their sun-burned countenances, their long beards, their loose garments,
and their shaggy mantles of skins. When he
entered into the society, he would notice the
absence of regular courts of justice, and of
every thing like an organized police. He would
be surprised at the fluctuation and instability
of the civil institutions. He would find it difficult to comprehend how a nation could subsist in such disorder; and would pity those,
who were compelled to pass their days in such a
scene, and whose minds were trained by their
unhappy situation to fraud and violence, to rapine, deceit, and revenge. Yet he would scarce
fail to admire their martial and lofty spirit, their
hospitality, and their bold and simple manners,
equally removed from the suppleness of a citizen, and the awkward rusticity of a clown; and
he would, probably, before long discover, among
so many qualities that excited his disgust, the
rudiments of many virtues.

But an English traveller from India would
view them with a more favourable eye. He

would be pleased with the cold climate, elevated by the wild and novel scenery, and delighted by meeting many of the productions of his native land. He would first be struck with the thinness of the fixed population, and then with the appearance of the people; not fluttering in white muslins, while half their bodies are naked, but soberly and decently attired in dark-coloured woollen clothes; and wrapt up in brown mantles, or in large sheep-skin cloaks. He would admire their strong and active forms; their fair complexions and European features; their industry, and enterprise; the hospitality, sobriety, and contempt of pleasure, which appear in all their habits; and, above all, the independence and energy of their character. In India, he would have left a country where every movement originates in the government or its agents, and where the people absolutely go for nothing; and he would find himself among a nation where the controul of the government is scarcely felt, and where every man appears to pursue his own inclinations, undirected and unrestrained. Amidst the stormy independence of this mode of life, he would regret the ease and security in which the state of India, and even the indolence and timidity of its inhabitants, enable most parts of that country to repose. He would meet with many productions of art and nature that do not exist in India; but, in

general, he would find the arts of life less advanced, and many of the luxuries of Hindostan
unknown. On the whole, his impression of his
new acquaintances would be favourable; although he would feel, that without having lost
the ruggedness of a barbarous nation, they were
tainted with the vices common to all Asiatics.
Yet, he would reckon them virtuous, compared
with the people to whom he had been accustomed; would be inclined to regard them
with interest and kindness; and could scarcely
deny them a portion of his esteem.

Such would be the impressions made on an
European, and an Indian traveller, by their ordinary intercourse with the Afghauns. When
they began to investigate their political constitution, both would be alike perplexed with its
apparent inconsistencies and contradictions, and
with the union which it exhibits of turbulent independence and gross oppression. But the former
would, perhaps, be most struck with the despotic
pretensions of the general government; and
the latter, with the democratic licence, which
prevails in the government of the tribes.

Let us now try whether, in a particular examination of the history and present condition of
the Afghauns, some of the features exhibited in
these two pictures will not be softened down,
and some apparent inconsistencies reconciled
but, throughout the whole, let it be borne in

mind, that although I have endeavoured to measure them by the scale which will be applied in Europe, yet the first and most natural process by which I estimated their character was a comparison with their Indian and Persian neighbours.

The origin of the name of Afghaun, now so generally applied to the nation I am about to describe, is entirely uncertain ; but is, probably, modern. It is known to the Afghauns themselves only through the medium of the Persian language. Their own name for their nation is Pooshtoon ; in the plural, Pooshtauneh. The Berdooraunees pronounce this word Pookhtauneh ; whence the name of Pitan, by which the Afghauns are known in India, may probably be derived.

The Arabs call them Solimaunee ; but, whether from their possessing the mountains of Solimaun, from the name of some chief who may have headed them, when first invaded by the Arabs, or from some circumstances connected with their supposed descent from the Jews, is entirely uncertain. They have no general name for their own country ; but sometimes apply the Persian one of Afghaunistaun. Doctor Leyden has mentioned the name of Pooshtoon-khau, as bearing this sense ; but I never heard it used. The term Sirhud is sometimes made use of, but excludes the plains on the eastern side of the range of Solimaun; and is, in fact, nothing more than the Persian word for a cold country. The name most generally applied to the whole country by its inhabitants is *Khorassaun ;* but this appellation is obviously incorrect. For, on the one hand, the whole of the Afghaun country is not included within the strict limits of Khorassaun; and, on the other, a considerable part of that province is not inhabited by Afghauns. *

I know very little of the early history of the Afghauns. Their own accounts of their origin appear to me to be fabulous; and I shall therefore state the few facts to be found in foreign historians, before I proceed to those recorded or invented by themselves. †

* In some English books, I have seen the Afghaun country called Roh; a word which I understand means a hill in Punjauby, and which is only known to some of the Afghauns through the medium of books written in India.

† A diligent search into the Persian and Arabian histories would probably furnish more information concerning the antiquities of this people, and would, at least, enable us to trace the history of their country from the time of Mahmood of Ghuzni; but the necessary books are difficult to be procured, and would take a long time to explore. As I may have to refer hereafter to many facts in Asiatic history, I take this opportunity of acknowledging that I have scarcely any acquaintance with the writers on that subject but what I have derived from a few of those which have been translated into English or French, and a still smaller number in Persian and Pushtoo, which relate exclusively to the Afghauns.

All accounts agree that they inhabited the mountains of Ghore at a very remote period, and they seem early to have possessed the mountains of Solimaun; which term, in its most extended sense, comprehends all the southern mountains of Afghaunistaun. They also appear by Ferishta, to have been established in the north-eastern mountains of Afghaunistaun, in the ninth century. At that period, the greater part of the nation is said by the same author to have been subject to the Arabian dynasty of Samaunee. The Afghauns seem to have furnished a large part, and probably the principal part, of the army of Mahmood, and the other Ghuznevide kings; but those who inhabited the mountains of Ghore retained their independence, and were governed by a king of their own, who drew his descent through a long line of sovereigns, from Zohauk, one of the earliest kings of Persia. This genealogy, though asserted by Meer Khonde, and confirmed by Ferishta, may be considered as doubtful at least; but, it is certain, that the princes of Ghore belonged to the Afghaun tribe of Sooree, and that their dynasty was allowed to be of very great antiquity even in the eleventh century. Their principal cities seem to have been Ghore, Feerooz Coh, and perhaps Baumeean. *

* The last of these places is still the seat of a government to the north-west of Caubul. Feeroozcoh may be presumed

There are different accounts of the religion of the Afghauns of Ghore. Some say they were converted to the Mahomedan faith soon after the prophet; while others maintain that they were idolaters in the tenth century. The idols and caves of Baumeeaun appear to establish that the inhabitants of that country were at one time worshippers of Boodh.

---

to have given its name to the Emauks of Feeroozcohee; and, from the position of their residence, we should place it to the east of Heraut.   But there are three Ghorees, all within the borders of the Paropamisan mountains: and it is not very obvious which of the three was the seat of the Ghoree kings.   The first is to the south-east of Bulkh; the second, north-west of Ghuznee; and the third, east of Furra.   The few native opinions I have heard fix on the last-mentioned place; and I am strongly inclined to agree with them, from the consideration of a passage in D. Herbelot (Article Gaiatheddin), where one of the kings of Ghore is said to have reduced " Raver and Kermessir, which separate Ghore from Hindostan."   These countries must, therefore, have lain to the east of Ghore.   As *k* and *g* are expressed by the same letter in Persian, there can be no doubt that Gurmseer or Gurmeseer is meant by the second of these words; and Raver probably means the adjoining district of Dawer, or Zemeen Dawer (the land of Dawer).   The close resemblance between the Persian *d* and *r* may have led to this mistake, which has been carefully copied by other orientalists.   Certain it is, that the names of Raver and Kermessir are not now to be found.   Now of the three Ghorees, that near Furrah alone is to the west of Gurmseer and Dawer, and, consequently, it alone can be said to be separated from Hindostan by those districts.

This people was governed in the reign of Mahmood of Ghuzni, by a prince named Mahommed, who was defeated and taken prisoner by that conqueror. His descendants suffered many injuries from the House of Ghuznee, till the middle of the twelfth century, when they at last took up arms, defeated and dethroned the King of Ghuznee, and burnt that magnificent capital to the ground. They afterwards continued to extend their empire, and by degrees reduced under their government, the whole of the present kingdom of Caubul, India, Bulkh, Budukhshaun, and a great part of Khorassaun.

From that time till the invasion of Bauber, a period of three centuries, different dynasties of Afghauns reigned, with some interruptions, over India; but the other dominions of the House of Ghore were early wrested from them by the King of Khwarizm, from whom they were conquered by Jengheez Khaun; and the tribe of Sooree is now reduced to a few families in Damaun.

During the government of the descendants of Jengheez, and of Tamerlane, and his offspring, the Afghauns appear to have maintained their independence in the mountains; and at the time of Bauber, they seem to have been unconnected with all foreign powers. Bauber, the descendant of Timour, and the ancestor of the Great

Moguls, began his career by the conquest of Caubul, which was his capital till the end of his reign. On his death, Caubul remained subject to one of his sons, while the other was expelled from India by Sheer Shauh, who founded another Afghaun dynasty, of no long duration. At last the House of Timour was firmly established in India : the capital of their empire was transferred from Caubul to Delly; and the plains of Afghaunistaun were divided between the empires of Hindostan and Persia; but the mountains were never subjected to either.

In the beginning of the eighteenth century, the Afghaun tribe of Ghiljie founded an empire which included all Persia, and extended on the west to the present limits of the Russian and Turkish empires. Part only of Afghaunistaun, however, acknowledged their dominion. Naudir Shauh overthrew this dynasty, and annexed most of Afghaunistaun to Persia ; and, on his death, the present Afghaun monarchy was founded ; which at its height extended from the neighbourhood of the Caspian sea, to that of the river Jumna, and from the Oxus to the Indian ocean.

After this cursory notice of the facts relating to the Afghauns, which are ascertained by authentic history, we may now examine what they say of themselves. The account they give of their own origin is worthy of attention, and has already attracted the notice of an eminent orientalist. They maintain that they are descended from Afghaun, the son of Irmia, or Berkia, son of Saul, King of Israel; and all their histories of their nation begin with relating the transactions of the Jews from Abraham down to the captivity. Their narrative of those transactions appears to agree with that of the other Mahomedans; and though interspersed with some wild fables, does not essentially differ from Scripture. After the captivity, they allege that part of the children of Afghaun withdrew to the mountains of Ghore, and part to the neighbourhood of Mecca in Arabia.

So far this account is by no means destitute of probability. It is known that ten of the twelve tribes remained in the East after the return of their brethren to Judea; and the supposition that the Afghauns are their descendants, explains easily and naturally both the disappearance of the one people, and the origin of the other. The rest of the story is confirmed by the fact, that the Jews were very numerous in Arabia at the time of Mahomet, and that the principal division of them bore the appellation of Khyber, which is still the name of a district in Afghaunistaun, if not of an Afghaun tribe. The theory is plausible, and may be true; but when closely examined it will appear to rest on a vague tradition alone; and even that tradition

is clouded with many inconsistencies and contradictions.

The Afghaun historians proceed to relate,
that the children of Israel, both in Ghore and
in Arabia, preserved their knowledge of the
unity of God, and the purity of their religious
belief, and that on the appearance of the last
and greatest of the prophets (Mahomet), the
Afghauns of Ghore listened to the invitation of
their Arabian brethren, the chief of whom was
Khauled (or Câled), the son of Waleed, so famous for his conquest of Syria, and marched to
the aid of the true faith, under the command of
Kyse, afterwards surnamed Abdoolresheed. The
Arabian historians, on the contrary, bring the
descent of Khauled from a well-known tribe of
their own nation, omit the name of Kyse in
their lists of the prophet's companions, or allies *, and are entirely silent on the subject of
the Afghaun succours. Even the Afghaun historians, although they describe their countrymen as a numerous people during their Arabian
campaign, and though it appears from a sarcasm
attributed by those historians to the Prophet
(who declared Pushtoo to be the language of
hell), that they already spoke their national and
peculiar tongue, yet do not scruple in another
place, to derive the whole nation from the loins

* Ansaur " Assisters."

of the very Kyse who commanded during the period of the above transactions.

If any other argument were required to disprove this part of the history, it is furnished by the Afghaun historians themselves, who state that Saul was the forty-fifth in descent from Abraham, and Kyse the thirty-seventh from Saul. The first of these genealogies is utterly inconsistent with those of the Sacred Writings, and the second allows only thirty-seven generations for a period of sixteen hundred * years. If to these facts we add, that Saul had no son named either Irmia or Berkia, and that if the existence of his grandson Afghaun be admitted, no trace of that Patriarch's *name* remains among his descendants; and if we consider the easy faith with which all rude nations receive accounts favourable to their own antiquity; I fear we must class the descent of the Afghauns from the Jews, with that of the Romans and the British from the Trojans, and that of the Irish from the Milesians or the Bramins. †

* This number is from the Taureekhee Sheer Shauhee. The Taureekee Morussa gives a much greater number, but then it introduces forty-five generations between Abraham and Jacob.

† This subject is briefly discussed by Sir William Jones, in a Note on a Translation by Mr. Vansittart (Asiatic Researches, Vol. II. Article IV.) That elegant scholar is inclined to believe this supposed descent, which he strengthens by four reasons.

His first argument is drawn from the resemblance of the

name of Hazaureh to Arsareth, the country whither the
Jews are said by Esdras to have retired; but this reasoning,
which was never very satisfactory, is destroyed by the fact,
that the Hazaurehs are a *nation* who have but recently occupied and given their name to a part of Afghaunistaun.
The second argument is built on the traditions examined
in the text, and on the assertion of Persian historians, probably derived from those traditions, and at no time very
deserving of faith.

The third is founded on the Jewish names of the Afghauns; but those they probably have derived from the
Arabs, like all other Mahomedan nations. Their most ancient names have no resemblance to those of the Jews.

The last argument is founded on a supposed resemblance
between the Pushtoo and Chaldaic languages; of which the
reader will hereafter be enabled to judge. Many points of
resemblance between the manners of the Afghauns and
those of the Jews might be adduced, but such a similarity
is usual between nations in the same stage of society; and
if it were admitted as a proof of identity, the Tartars and
the Arabs, the Germans and the Russians, might be proved
to be the same. It is also maintained by more than one
European writer, that the Afghauns are a Caucasian tribe,
and particularly that they are descended from the Armenians. In the extent sometimes allowed to the name of Caucasus, the Afghauns still inhabit that celebrated mountain;
but if it be meant that they ever lived to the west of the
Caspian Sea, the assertion appears to be unsupported by
proof. Their Armenian descent is utterly unknown to themselves, though constantly in the mouths of the Armenians;
and the story told by the latter people, of the Afghauns
having become Mussulmans to avoid the long fasts prescribed by their own church, is too inconsistent with history to deserve a moment's consideration. I may add, that
I have compared a short Armenian vocabulary with the
Pushtoo, and could perceive no resemblance between the
languages; and that I once read a good deal of a Pushtoo
vocabulary to a well-informed Armenian, who, though he
strenuously asserted the descent of the Afghauns from his

countrymen, yet owned that he could not discover a word common to their language and his own. I have not had the same advantage with the languages of other Caucasian tribes, but I compared about two hundred and fifty Georgian words with the corresponding ones in Pushtoo, and nothing could be more different; and I know no ground for connecting the Afghauns with the western Caucasus, except the assertion of a German traveller, whose name I forget, that he saw Afghauns there during the last century, which proves too much.

Burckhardt:
Travels in Syria and the Holy Land

Johann Ludwig Burckhardt, *Travels in Syria and the Holy Land* (London: John Murray, 1822), pp. 457–8, 516–36.

Johann Ludwig Burckhardt (1784–1817) belongs, like Park or Cook or Stanhope, to that small group of Romantic travellers we might designate as 'legendary' – and like all figures of legend, he embodied a series of contradictions. A renowned explorer, Burckhardt failed his only commission. Opposed to slavery, he financed at least one tour through that trade. A European traveller in the biblical Holy Land, he spent part of his life as a Muslim. A figure of great romance and mystery, he wrote some of the most workmanlike travel accounts of the period and became famous for them.

Africa was Burckhardt's objective, but he was never to reach the interior. Swiss by birth, Burckhardt travelled in 1806 to England, where he met several men involved with the African Association and where he began to study Arabic in the hope of securing a position with this society. In 1809, as he had hoped, Burckhardt was formally commissioned by the Association as one of its explorers. Established in 1788 to advance British knowledge of the African interior and its trade routes, the Association commanded considerable resources. Burckhardt was to take the place of Mungo Park, who had recently disappeared on an expedition in search of the Niger and Timbuktu. As an employee of the Association, Burckhardt's relationship to British imperial interests was both contractual and direct. In the words of his nineteenth-century biographer, Burckhardt was 'so intimately associated with the exertions of British enterprise in the cause of physical and geographical discovery that England may justly claim him as her adopted son' (quoted in Katherine Sim, *Desert Traveller: The Life of Jean Louis Burckhardt*, p. 18). Indeed, his travels were amongst the most celebrated feats of British exploration during the Romantic period.

In preparation for his expedition into the African interior, Burckhardt was first sent to Syria to study Arabic, and the travels for which he became famous were undertaken during this period of extended preparation. Over the course of eight years, Burckhardt travelled throughout the Ottoman Near East, penetrating further into Syria, Egypt, Nubia and the Sinai peninsula than any other Romantic explorer. Here his accomplishments included the 'discovery' of Petra (1812) and of the temple of Ramses II in Abu Simbel (1813), the forbidden hajj to Mecca and Medina (1814) and a residence amongst the 'unknown' desert Bedouins (1816). His success as an adventurer in these regions fundamentally depended upon the disguise in which he travelled, which allowed him unprecedented access into the 'heart' of the Arabian East. Travelling under the assumed identity of 'Sheikh Ibrahim bin Abdullah', Burckhardt lived amongst the local populations as a poor man and a Muslim, and in this respect he was unlike the vast majority of European adventurers in the East.

While Burckhardt's personal 'conversion' to Muslim culture made him a more sensitive chronicler and, perhaps, a more respectful traveller than most, from an Arabian perspective his disguise was a fraud perpetrated upon the goodwill of his hosts. Although apparently a superb and careful actor, Burckhardt's identity was questioned in several instances and his travel account records at least one occasion on which his disguise was discovered. The reaction of his Bedouin companion underscores the complicated dynamics of imperialism that attend upon European desire for authentic penetration into the East. For Burckhardt's Bedouin guide understood clearly that travel writing and conquest were intimately related, when he expostulated that 'You write down our country ... our mountains, our pasturing places, and the rain which falls from heaven; other people have done this before you, but I at least will never become instrumental to the ruin of my country' (see below, p. 307).

Burckhardt's travels were to be published by the African Association only upon the completion of his commission, in order to preserve his anonymity and the integrity of his disguise. Ultimately, his fame would be posthumous. Burckhardt died at Cairo in 1817, in the final stages of preparation for his long-awaited expedition into the African interior. In the years following his death, Burckhardt's travel journals were published in successive volumes, under the titles: *Travels in Nubia* (1819); *Travels in Syria and the Holy Land* (1822); *Travels in Arabia* (1829); *Arabic Proverbs; or the Manners and Customs of the Modern Egyptians* (1830); and *Notes on the Bedouins and Wahabis* (1831). Reproduced below is a selection from Burckhardt's travels in the Holy Land, describing his expedition to Mount Sinai in 1816.

JOURNAL OF A TOUR

IN THE

PENINSULA OF MOUNT SINAI,

IN THE SPRING OF 1816.

About the beginning of April 1816 Cairo was again visited by the plague. The Franks and most of the Christians shut themselves up ; but as I neither wished to follow their example nor to expose myself unnecessarily in the town, I determined to pass my time, during the prevalence of the disease, among the Bedouins of Mount Sinai, to visit the gulf of Akaba, and, if possible, the castle of Akaba, to which, as far as I know, no traveller has ever penetrated. Intending to pass some days at the convent of Mount Sinai, I procured a letter of introduction to the monks from their brethren at Cairo ; for without this passport no stranger is ever permitted to enter the convent ; I was also desirous of having a letter from the Pasha of Egypt to the principal Sheikh of the tribes of Tor, over whom, as I knew by former experience, he exercises more than a nominal authority. With the assistance of this paper, I hoped to be able to see a good deal of the Bedouins of the peninsula in safety, and to travel in their company to Akaba. Such letters of recommendation are in general easily procured in Syria and Egypt, though they are often useless, as I found on several occasions during my first journey into Nubia, as well as in my travels in Syria, where the orders of the Pasha of Damascus were much slighted in several of the districts under his dominion.

A fortnight before I set out for Mount Sinai I had applied to the Pasha through his Dragoman, for a letter to the Bedouin Sheikh ; but I was kept waiting for it day after day, and after thus delaying my departure a whole week, I was at last obliged to set off without it. The want of it was the cause of some embarrassment to me, and prevented me from reaching Akaba. It is not improbable that on being applied to for the letter, the Pasha gave the same answer as he gave at Tayf, when I asked him for a Firmahn, namely, that as I was sufficiently acquainted with the language and manners of the Arabs, I needed no further recommendation.

The Arabs of Mount Sinai usually alight at Cairo in the quarter called El Djemelye, where some of them are almost constantly to be found. Having gone thither, I met with the same Bedouin with whom I had come last year from Tor to Cairo; I hired two camels from him for myself and servant, and laid in provisions for about six weeks consumption. We left Cairo on the evening of the 20th of April, and slept that night among the ruined tombs of the village called Kayt Beg, a mile from the city. From this village, at which the Bedouins usually alight, the caravans for Suez often depart; it is also the resort of smugglers from Suez and Syria.

★   ★   ★   ★   ★

May 10th,—early the next morning we again reached Noweyba, the place where we had first reached the coast. We here met Ayd's deaf friend. Szaleh had all the way, betrayed the most timorous disposition; in excuse for running away when we were attacked, he said that he intended to halt farther on in the Wady, in order to cover our retreat, and that he had been obliged to run after the camels, which were frightened by the firing; but the truth was, that his terrors deprived him of all power of reflection, otherwise he must have known that the only course to be pursued in the desert, when suddenly attacked, is to fight for life, as escape is almost impossible.

Having been foiled in my hopes of visiting Akaba, I now wished to follow the shore of the gulf to the southward; but Szaleh would not hear of any farther progress in that direction, and insisted upon my going back to the convent. I told him that his company had been of too little use to me, to make me desirous of keeping him any longer; he therefore returned, no doubt in great haste, by the same route we had come, accompanied by the deaf man; I engaged Ayd to conduct us along the coast, Hamd being very ignorant of this part of the peninsula, where his tribe, the Oulad Sayd, never encamp.

The date trees of Noweyba belong to the tribe of Mezeine; here were several huts built of stones and branches of the trees, in which the owners live with their families during the date-harvest. The narrow plain which rises here from the sea to the mountain, is covered with sand and loose stones. Ayd told me that in summer, when the wind is strong, a hollow sound is sometimes heard here, as if coming from the upper country; the Arabs say that the spirit of Moses then descends from Mount Sinai, and in flying across the sea bids a farewell to his beloved mountains.

We rode from Noweyba round a bay, the southern point of which bore from thence S. by W. In two hours and three quarters from Noweyba we doubled the point, and rested for the night in a valley just behind it, called Wady Djereimele (جريميلة), thickly overgrown with the shrub Gharkad, the berries of which are gathered in great abundance. Red coral is very common on this part of the coast. In the evening I saw a great number of shell-fish leave the water, and crawl to one hundred or two hundred paces inland, where they passed the night, and at sun-rise returned to the sea.

During the last two days of our return from the northward I had found no opportunity to take notes. I had never permitted my companions to see me write, because I knew that if their suspicions were once raised, it would at least render them much less open in their communications to me. It has indeed been a con-

stant maxim with me never to write before Arabs on the road ; at
least I have departed from it in a very few instances only, in Syria,
and on the Nile, in my first journey into Nubia ; but never in the
interior of Nubia, or in the Hedjaz.   Had I visited the convent of
Mount Sinai in the character of a Frank, with the Pasha's Firmahn, and had returned, as travellers usually do, from thence to
Cairo, I should not have hesitated to take notes openly, because
the Towara Arabs dread the Pasha, and dare not insult or molest
any one under his protection.   But wishing to penetrate into a
part of the country occupied by other tribes, it became of importance to conceal my pursuits, lest I should be thought a ne-
cromancer, or in search of treasures.   In such cases many little
stratagems must be resorted to by the traveller, not to lose entirely the advantage of making memoranda on the spot.   I had
accustomed myself to write when mounted on my camel, and
proceeding at an easy walk ; throwing the wide Arab mantle
over my head, as if to protect myself from the sun, as the Arabs do,
I could write under it unobserved, even if another person rode
close by me ; my journal books being about four inches long and
three broad, were easily carried in a waistcoat pocket, and when
taken out could be concealed in the palm of the hand ; sometimes
I descended from my camel, and walking a little in front of my
companions, wrote down a few words without stopping.   When
halting I lay down as if to sleep, threw my mantle over me, and
could thus write unseen under it.   At other times I feigned to go
aside to answer a call of nature, and then couched down, in the
Arab manner, hidden under my cloak.   This evening I had re-
course to the last method ; but having many observations to note, I
remained so long absent from my companions that Ayd's curiosity
was roused.   He came to look after me, and perceiving me im-
moveable on the spot, approached on tip-toe, and came close behind

me without my perceiving him. I do not know how long he had remained there, but suddenly lifting up my cloak, he detected me with the book in my hand. " What is this?" he exclaimed. " What are you doing? I shall not make you answerable for it at present, because I am your companion; but I shall talk further to you about it when we are at the convent." I made no answer, till we returned to the halting-place, when I requested him to tell me what further he had to say. " You write down our country," he replied, in a passionate tone, " our mountains, our pasturing places, and the rain which falls from heaven; other people have done this before you, but I at least will never become instrumental to the ruin of my country." I assured him that I had no bad intentions towards the Bedouins, and told him he must be convinced that I liked them too well for that; " on the contrary," I added, " had I not occasionally written down some prayers ever since we left Taba, we should most certainly have been all killed; and it is very wrong in you to accuse me of that, which if I had omitted, would have cost us our lives." He was startled at this reply, and seemed nearly satisfied. " Perhaps you say the truth," he observed ; " but we all know that some years since several men, God knows who they were, came to this country, visited the mountains, wrote down every thing, stones, plants, animals, even serpents and spiders, and since then little rain has fallen, and the game has greatly decreased." The same opinions prevail in these mountains, which I have already mentioned to be current among the Bedouins of Nubia; they believe that a sorcerer, by writing down certain charms, can stop the rains and transfer them to his own country. The travellers to whom Ayd alluded were M. Seetzen, who visited Mount Sinai eight years since, and M. Agnelli, who ten years ago travelled for the Emperor of Austria, collecting specimens of natural history, and who made some stay at Tor, from whence he sent Arabs to hunt for all kinds of animals.

M. Seetzen traversed the peninsula in several directions, and followed a part of the eastern gulf as far northward, I believe, as Noweyba. This learned and indefatigable traveller made it a rule not to be intimidated by the suspicions and prejudices of the Bedouins; beyond the Jordan, on the shores of the Dead sea, in the desert of Tyh, in this peninsula, as well as in Arabia, he openly followed his pursuits, never attempting to hide his papers and pencils from the natives, but avowing his object to be that of collecting precious herbs and curious stones, in the character of a Christian physician in the Holy Land, and in that of a Moslim physician in the Hedjaz. If the knowledge of the natural history of Syria and Arabia was the principal object of M. Seetzen's researches, he was perfectly right in the course which he adopted, but if he considered these countries only as intermediate steps towards the exploring of others, he placed his ultimate success in the utmost peril ; and though he may have succeeded in elucidating the history of the brute creation, he had little chance of obtaining much information on the human character, which can only be done by gaining the confidence of the inhabitants, and by accommodating our notions, views, and manners, to their own.   When M. Seetzen visited these mountains, the Towaras were not yet reduced to subjection by Mohammed Ali ; he was obliged, on several occasions, to pay large sums for his passage through their country, and the Mezeine would probably have executed a plot which they had laid to kill him, had not his guides been informed of it, and prevented him from passing through their territory.

I had much difficulty in soothing Ayd ; he remained quiet during the rest of the journey, but after our return to the convent, the report spread among the Arabs that I was a writer like those who had preceded me, and I thus completely lost their confidence.

May 11*th.*—We continued along the coast S. S. W. and at four hours passed a promontory, called Djebel Abou Ma (جبل ابو ما'), consisting of granite. From hence we proceeded S. W. by S. and at seven hours came to a sandy plain, on the edge of a large sheltered bay. We found here some Bedouin girls, in charge of a few goats; they told us that their parents lived not far off in the valley Omyle (عُميلة). We went there, and found two small tents, where three or four women and as many little children were occupied in spinning, and in collecting herbs to feed the lambs and kids, which were frisking about them. Ayd knew the women, who belonged to his own tribe of Mezeine. Their husbands were fishermen, and were then at the sea-shore. They brought us some milk, and I bought a kid of them, which we intended to dress in the evening. The women were not at all bashful; I freely talked and laughed with them, but they remained at several yards distance from me. Ayd shook them by the hand, and kissed the children; but Hamd, who did not know them, kept at the same distance as myself. Higher up in the Wady is a well of good water, called Tereibe (تريبة).

From hence we went S. W. by S. and at eight hours came to Ras Methna (راس مثنا), a promontory whose cliffs continue for upwards of a mile close by the water side. Granite and red porphyry here cross each other in irregular layers, in some places horizontally, in others perpendicularly. The granite of this peninsula presents the same numberless varieties as that above the cataract of the Nile, and near Assouan; and the same beautiful specimens of red, rose-coloured, and almost purple may be collected here, as in that part of Egypt. The transition from primitive to secondary rocks, partaking of the nature of grünstein or grauwacke, or hornstein and trap, presents also an endless variety in every part of the peninsula, so that were I even possessed of the requisite knowledge accurately to describe them, it would tire the patience of t he reader. Masses of black trap, much resembling basalt, compose several insulated peaks and rocks. On the shore the granite sand carried down from the upper mountains has been formed into cement by the action of the water, and mixed with fragments of the other rocks already mentioned, has become a very beautiful breccia.

At the end of eight hours and three quarters we rested for the night, to the south of this promontory, in a valley still called Wady Methna. From some fishermen whom we met I bought some excellent fish, of a species resembling the turbot, and very common on this coast These with our kid furnished an abundant repast to ourselves as well as to the fishermen. The love of good and plentiful fare was one of Ayd's foibles ; and he often related with pride that in his younger days he had once eaten at a meal, with three other Bedouins, the whole of a mountain goat; although his companions, as he observed, were moderate eaters. Bedouins, in general, have voracious appetites, and whoever travels with them cannot adopt any better mode of attaching them to his interests than by feeding them abundantly, and inviting all strangers met with on the road to partake in the repast. Pounds given as presents in money have less effect than shillings spent in victuals ; and the reputation of hospitality which the traveller thus gains facilitates his progress on every occasion. My practice was to leave the provision sack open, and at the disposal of my guides, not to eat but when they did, not to take the choice morsels to myself, to share in the cooking, and not to give any orders, but to ask for whatever I wanted, as a favour. By pursuing this method I continued during the remainder of the journey to be on the best terms with my companions, and had not the slightest altercation either with Hamd or Áyd.

On the eastern shore of the gulf, opposite the place where we rested, lies a valley called Mekna (مقنه), inhabited by the tribe of Omran. Close to the shore are plantations of date and other fruit-trees. The inhabitants of Mekna cross the gulf in small boats, and bring to this side sheep and goats for sale, of which they possess large flocks, and which are thus more plentiful in this part of the peninsula than in any other. The mountains behind Mekna recede from the sea, and further to the south take a more eastern direction, so as to leave a chain of hills between them and the shore, rising immediately from the water-side. The appearance of this gulf, with the mountains enclosing it on both sides, reminded me of the lake of Tiberias and of the Dead sea; and the general resemblance was still further heightened by the hot season in which I had visited all these places.

May 12th.—Our road lay S. S. W. along a narrow sandy plain by the sea side. In one hour and a half we reached Dahab (دهب), a more extensive cluster of date trees than I had before seen on this coast; it extends into the sea upon a tongue of land, about two miles beyond the line of the shore; to the north of it is a bay, which affords anchorage, but it is without protection against northerly winds. Dahab is, probably, the *Dizahab* mentioned in Deut. i. 1. There are some low hummocks covered with sand close to the shore of the low promontory, probably occasioned by the ruins of buildings. The plantations of date trees ar here enclosed by low walls, within many of which are wells of indifferent water; but in one of them, about twenty-five feet deep, and fifty yards from the sea, we found the best water I had met with on any part of this coast in the immediate vicinity of the sea. About two miles to the south of the date groves are a number of shallow ponds into which the sea flows at high-tide; here the salt is made which supplies all the peninsula, as well as the fishermen for curing their fish; the openings of the ponds being closed with sand, the water is left to evaporate, when a thick crust of salt is left, which is collected by the Bedouins. Dahab is a favourite resort of the fishermen, who here catch the fish called Boury (بورى) in great quantities.

The date trees of Dahab, which belong to the tribe of Mezeine and Aleygat, presented a very different appearance to those of Egypt and the Hedjaz, where the cultivators always take off the lower branches which dry up annually; here they are suffered to remain, and hang down to the ground, forming an almost impenetrable barrier round the tree, the top of which only is crowned with green leaves. Very few trees had any fruit upon them; indeed date trees, in general, yield a very uncertain produce, and even in years, when every other kind of fruit is abundant, they are sometimes quite barren. We met here several families of Arabs, who had come to look after their trees, and to collect salt. In the midst of the small peninsula of Dahab are about a dozen heaps of stones irregularly piled together, but shewing traces of having once been united; none of them is higher than five feet. The Arabs call them Kobour el Noszara, or the tombs of the Christians, a name given by them to all the nations which peopled their country before the introduction of the Islam.

We remained several hours under the refreshing shade of the palm trees, and then continued our road. In crossing the tongue of land I observed the remains of what I conceived to be a road or causeway, which began at the mountain and ran out towards the point of the peninsula; the stones which had formed it were now separated from each other, but lay in a straight line, so as to afford sufficient proof of their having been placed here by the labour of man. To the south of Dahab the camel road along the shore is shut up by cliffs which form a promontory called El She-djeir (شجير); we were therefore obliged to take a circuitous route through the mountains, and directed our road by that way straight towards Sherm, the most southern harbour on this coast. We ascended a broad sandy valley in the direction S. W.; this is the same Wady Sal in which we had already travelled in our way from the convent, and which empties itself into the sea. In the rocky sides of this valley I observed several small grottos, apparently receptacles for the dead, which were just large enough to receive one corpse; I at first supposed them to have been natural erosions of the sand-stone rock; but as there were at least a dozen of them, and as I had not seen any thing similar in other sand-rocks, I concluded that they had been originally formed by man, and that time had worn them away to the appearance of natural cavities.

We left the valley and continued to ascend slightly through windings of the Wady Beney (وادي بني) and Wady Ghayb (وادي غايب), two broad barren sandy valleys, till, at the end of four hours, we reached the well of Moayen el Kelab (معين الكلاب), at the extremity of Wady Ghayb, where it is shut up by a cliff. Here is a small pond of water under the shade of an impending rock, and a large wild fig-tree. On the top of a neighbouring part of the granite cliff, is a similar pond with reeds growing in it. The water, which is never known to dry up, is excellent, and acquires still greater value from being in the vicinity of a spacious cavern, which affords shade to the traveller. This well is much visited by the Mezeine tribe; on several trees in the valley leading to it, we found suspended different articles of Bedouin tent furniture, and also entire tent coverings. My guides told me that the owners left them here during their absence, in order not to have the trouble of carrying them about; and such is the confidence which these people have in one another, that no instance is known of any of the articles so left having ever been stolen : the same practice prevails in other parts of the peninsula. The cavern is formed by nature in a beautiful granite rock ; its interior is covered on all sides with figures of mountain goats drawn with charcoal in the rudest manner ; they are done by the shepherd boys and girls of the Towaras.

The heat being intense we reposed in the cavern till the evening, when, after retracing our road for a short distance, we turned into the Wady Kenney (قنّي), which we ascended ; at its extremity we began to descend in a Wady called Molahdje (ملاحجة), a narrow, steep, and rocky valley of difficult passage. Ayd's dog started a mountain goat, but was unable to come up with it. We slept in this Wady, at one hour and a half from Moayen el Kelab.

May 13th.—Farther down the Wady widens and is enclosed by high granite cliffs. Its direction is S. by W. Four hours continued descent brought us into Wady Orta (أرطب). The rocks here are granite, red porphyry, and grünstein, similar to what I had observed towards Akaba, at nearly the same elevation above the sea. At the end of six hours we left Wady Orta, which descends towards the sea, and turning to the right, entered a large plain called Mofassel el Korfa (مفصّل القرنا), in which we rode S. S. W. From the footsteps in the sand Ayd knew the individuals of the Mezeine, who had passed this way in the morning. The view here opened upon a high chain of mountains which extends from Sherm in the direction of the convent, and which I had passed on my return from Arabia, in going from Sherm to Tor. It is called Djebel Tarfa (جبل طرفة), and is inhabited principally by the Mezeine. At eight hours the plain widens ; many beds of torrents coming from the Tarfa cross it in their way to the sea. This part is called El Ak-ha (الاقيي), and excepting in the beds of the torrents, where some verdure is produced, it is an entirely barren tract. At nine hours we approached the Tarfa, between which and our road were low hills called Hodeybat el Noszara (حديبات النصارا), i. e. the hump backs of the Christians. The waters which collect here in the winter flow into the sea at Wady Nabk. At ten hours the plain opens still wider, and declines gently eastwards to the sea. To the left, where the mountains terminate, a sandy plain extends to the water side. At eleven hours is an insulated chain of low hills, forming here, with the lowest range of the Tarfa, a valley, in which our road lay, and in which we halted, after a fatigueing day's journey of twelve hours. As there were only two camels for three of us, we rode by turns; and Ayd regretted his younger days, when, as he assured us, he had once walked from the convent to Cairo in four days. The hills near which we halted are called Roweysat Nimr (رويسات نمر), or the little heads of the tiger.

May 14th.—We descended among low hills, and after two hours reached the harbour of Sherm (شرم). This is the only harbour on the western coast of the gulf of Akaba, which affords safe anchorage for large ships, though, by lying close in shore, small vessels might, I believe, find shelter in several of the bays of this gulf. At Sherm there are two deep bays little distant from each other, but separated by high land, in both of which, ships may lie in perfect safety. On the shore of the southern bay stands the tomb of a Sheikh, held in veneration by the Bedouins and mariners : a small house has been built over it, the walls of which are thickly hung with various offerings by the Bedouins; and a few lamps suspended from the roof are sometimes lighted by sailors. Sherif Edrisi, in his geography, mentions these two bays of Sherm, and calls the one Sherm el Beit (شرم البيت), or of the house, and the other Sherm el Bir (شرم البير), or of the well, thus accurately describing both;

for near the shore of the northern bay are several copious wells of brackish water, deep, and lined with stones, and apparently an ancient work of considerable labour. The distance from Sherm to the Cape of Ras Abou Mohammed is four or five hours; on the way a mountain is passed, which comes down close to the sea, called Es-szafra (الصفرة), the point of which bears from Sherm S. W. by S.

Bedouins are always found at Sherm, waiting with their camels for ships coming from the Hedjaz, whose passengers often come on shore here, in order to proceed by land to Tor and Suez. The Arab tribes of Mezeine and Aleygat have the exclusive right of this transport.   Shortly after we had alighted at the well, more than twenty Mezeine came down from the mountain with their camels; they claimed the right of conducting me from hence, and of supplying me with a third camel; and as both my camels belonged to Arabs of the tribe of Oulad Sayd, they insisted upon Hamd taking my baggage from his camel, and placing it upon one of theirs, that they might have the profits of hire.   After breakfasting with them, a loud quarrel began, which lasted at least two hours. I told them that the moment any one laid his hands upon my baggage to remove it, I should consider it as carried off by force, and no longer my property, and that I should state to the governor of Suez that I had been robbed here.   Although they could not all expect to share in the profits arising from my transport, every one of them was as vociferous as if it had been his exclusive affair, and it soon became evident that a trifle in money for each of them was all that was wanted to quiet them.   They did not, however, succeed; I talked very boldly; told them that they were robbers, and that they should be punished for their conduct towards me. At last their principal man, seeing that nothing was to be got, told us that we might load and depart.   He accompanied us to a short distance, and received a handful of coffee-beans, as a reward for his having been less clamorous than the others.

These people believed that my visit to Sherm was for the mere purpose of visiting the tomb of the saint. I had assigned this motive to Ayd, who was himself a Mezeine, telling him that I had made a vow to thank the saint for his protection in our encounter with the robbers; Ayd would otherwise have been much astonished at my proceeding to this distance without any plausible object. The nearest road from Sherm to the convent is at first the same way by which we came, and it branches off northward from Wady Orta; but as I was desirous of seeing as much as possible of the coast, I suggested to my guides, that if we proceeded by that route the Mezeine of Sherm might possibly ride after us, and excite another quarrel in the mountain, where we should find it more difficult to extricate ourselves. They consented therefore to take the circuitous route along the shore. Such stratagems are often necessary, in travelling with Bedouins, to make them yield to the traveller's wishes; for though they care little for fatigue in their own business, they are extremely averse to go out of their way, to gratify what they consider an absurd whim of their companion.

From Sherm we rode an hour and a quarter among low hills near the shore. Here I saw for the first and only time, in this peninsula, volcanic rocks. For a distance of about two miles the hills presented perpendicular cliffs, formed in half circles, and some of them nearly in circles, none of them being more than sixty to eighty feet in height; in other places there was an appearance of volcanic craters. The rock is black, with sometimes a slight red appearance, full of cavities, and of a rough surface; on the road lay a few stones which had separated themselves from above. The cliffs were covered by deep layers of sand, and the valleys at their feet were also overspread with it; it is possible that other rocks of the same kind may be found towards Ras Abou Mohammed, and hence may have arisen the term of black (μέλανα ὄρη), applied to these mountains by the Greeks. It should be observed, however, that low sand hills intervene between the volcanic rocks and the sea, and that above them, towards the higher mountains, no traces of lava are found, which seems to shew that the volcanic matter is confined to this spot.

We issued from the low hills upon a wide plain, which extends as far as Nabk, and is intersected in several places by beds of torrents. Our direction was N. E. by N. The plain terminates three or four miles to the east, in rocks which line the shore. At the end of three hours and a half we halted under a rock, in the bed of one of the torrents. The whole plain appears to be alluvial; many petrified shells are found imbedded in the chalky and calcareous soil. In the afternoon we again passed several low water-courses in the plain, and, at the end of five hours Wady Szygha (صيغة). At six hours and a half from Sherm we rested in the plain, in a spot where some bushes grew, amongst which we found a Bedouin woman and her daughter, living under a covering made of reeds and brush-wood. Her husband and son were absent fishing, but Ayd being well known to them, they gave us a hearty welcome, and milked a goat for me. After sunset they joined our party, and sitting down behind the bush where I had taken up my quarters, eat a dish of rice which I presented to them. The daughter was a very handsome girl of eighteen or nineteen, as graceful in her deportment and modest in her behaviour, as the best educated European female could be; indeed I have often had occasion to remark among the Bedouins, comparing them with the women of of the most polished parts of Europe, that grace and modesty are not less than beauty the gifts of nature. Among these Arabs the men consider it beneath them to take the flocks to pasture, and leave it to the women.

In front of our halting place lay an island called Djezyret Tyran (تيزان جزيرة): its length from N. to S. is from six to eight miles, and it lies about four miles from the shore. Half its length is a narrow promontory of sand, and its main body to the south consists of a barren mountain. It is not inhabited, but the Bedouins of Heteym sometimes come here from the eastern coast, to fish for pearls, and remain several weeks, bringing their provision of water from the spring of El Khereyde (الخريدة), on that coast, there being no sweet water in the island. Edrisi mentions a place on the western coast, where pearls are procured, a circumstance implied by the name of Maszdaf (مصدف), which he gives to it. The name is now unknown here, but I think it probable that Edrisi spoke of this part of the coast. The quantity of pearls obtained is very small, but the Heteym pick up a good deal of mother-of-pearl, which they sell to great advantage at Moeleh, to the ships which anchor there.

May 15th.—We continued over the plain in a direction N. by E. and in two hours reached Wady Nabk (وادي نبّق), which, next to Dahab and Noweyba, is the principal station on this coast. Large plantations of date trees grow on the sea-shore, among which, as usual, is a well of brackish water. The plain which reaches from near Sherm to Nabk is the only one of any extent along the whole coast; at Nabk it contracts, the western chain approaches to within two miles of the shore, and farther northward this chain comes close to the sea. The promontory of Djebel Abou Ma bore from Wady Nabk N. N. E ½ E. From hence to Dahab, as the Arabs told me, is about six hours walk along the shore. The highest point of the mountain upon the island of Tyran bore S. E. by S.

The opposite part of the eastern coast is low, and the mountains are at a distance inland. Near Nabk are salt-pits, similar to those at Dahab. Except during the date harvest, Nabk is inhabited only by fishermen ; they are the poorest individuals of their tribe, who have no flocks or camels, and are obliged to resort to this occupation to support themselves and families. We bought here for thirty-two paras, or about four-pence halfpenny, thirty-two salted fish, each about two feet in length, and a measure of the dried shell-fish, Zorombat, which in this state the Arabs call Bussra. For the smaller kinds of fish the fishermen use hand-nets, which they throw into the sea from the shore ; the larger species they kill with lances, one of which Ayd carried constantly with him as a weapon ; there is not a single boat nor even a raft to be found on the whole of this coast, but the Bedouins of the eastern coast have a few boats, which may sometimes be seen in the gulf. We saw here a great number of porpoises playing in the water close to the shore. I wished to shoot at one of them, but was prevented by my companions, who said that it was unlawful to kill them, as they are the friends of man, and never hurt any body. I saw parts of the skin of a large fish, killed on the coast, which was an inch in thickness, and is employed by these Arabs instead of leather for sandals.

We now turned from Nabk upwards to the convent, and in half an hour entered the chain of mountains along a broad valley called Wady Nabk, in which we ascended slightly, and rested at two hours and a quarter from Nabk under a large acacia tree. In the vicinity were three tents of Aleygat Arabs, the women of which approached the place where we had alighted, and told us that two men and a child were there ill of the plague, which they had caught from a relative of theirs, who had lately come from Egypt with the disease upon him, and who had died. At that time they were in a large encampment, but as soon as the infection shewed itself, their companions compelled them to quit the camp, and they had come to this place to await the termination of the disorder. My guides were as much afraid of the infection as I was, and made the women remain at a proper distance; they asked me for some rice, and sugar, which latter article they believe to be a sovereign remedy against diseases. I was glad to be able to gratify them, and I advised them to give the patients whey which is almost the only cooling draught the Arabs know; they conceive that almost all illnesses proceed from cold, and there- fore usually attempt to cure them by heat, keeping the patient thickly covered with clothes, and feeding him upon the most nou- rishing food they can afford.

Not far from our halting place, on the ascent of the mountain, is a reservoir of rain water, where we filled our skins. The acacia trees of the valley were thickly covered with gum arabic. The Towara Arabs often bring to Cairo loads of it, which they collect in these mountains; but it is much less esteemed than that from Soudan. I found it of a somewhat sweet and rather agreeable taste. The Bedouins pretend, that upon journeys it is a preven- tive of thirst, and that the person who chews it may pass a whole day without feeling any inconvenience from the want of water. We set out in the afternoon, and at the end of three hours and a half from Wady Nabk, passed the Mofassel el Korfa, which I have already mentioned. At four hours and a quarter we crossed Wady el Orta, the direction of our road N. W. by N., and at the end of five hours and a quarter we halted in Wady Rahab (وادي رحاب). All these valleys resemble one another; the only difference of ap- pearance which they afford, is that in some places the ground is parched up, while in others, where a torrent passes during the win- ter, the shrubs still retain some green leaves.

May 16th.—During the night we had a heavy shower of rain with thunder and lightning, which completely drenched both ourselves and our baggage. A beautiful morning succeeded, and the atmosphere, which during the last three days had been extremely hot, especially on the low coast, was now so much refreshed, that we seemed to have removed from a tropical to an alpine climate. We passed through several valleys emptying themselves into Wády Orta ; the principal of these is called Wady Ertama (ارتامة) . Route N. N. W. Although the rain had been heavy, the sands had so completely absorbed it, that we could scarcely find any traces of it. We started several Gazelles, the only game I have seen in the peninsula, except mountain-goats. Hares and wolves are found, but are not common, and the Bedouins sometimes kill leopards, of one of which I obtained a large skin at the convent. The Bedouins talk much of a beast of prey called Wober (وبر), which inhabits the most retired parts only of the peninsula ; they describe it as being of the size of a large dog, with a pointed head like a hog ; I heard also of another voracious animal, called Shyb (شيت), stated to be a breed between the leopard and the wolf. Of its existence little doubt can be entertained, though its pretended origin is probably fabulous, for the Arabs, and especially the Bedouins, are in the common practice of assigning to every animal that is seldom met with, parents of two different species of known animals. On the coast, and in the lower valleys, a kind of large lizard is seen, called Dhob (ضب), which has a scaly skin of a yellow colour ; the largest are about eighteen inches in length, of which the tail measures about one-half. The Dhob is very common in the Arabian deserts, where the Arabs form tobacco purses of its skin. It lives in holes in the sand, which have generally two openings ; it runs fast, but a dog easily catches it. Of birds I saw red-legged partridges in great numbers, pigeons, the Katta, but not in such large flocks as I have seen them in Syria, and the eagle Rakham. The Bedouins also mentioned an eagle whose outspread wings measure six feet across, and which carries off lambs.

After four hours and a half we reached Wady Kyd (كيد), and rested at its entrance under two immense blocks of granite, which had fallen down from the mountain; they form two spacious caverns, and serve as a place of shelter for the shepherdesses; we saw in them several articles of tent furniture and some cooking utensils. On the sides figures of goats are drawn with charcoal; but I saw no inscriptions cut in the rock. The blocks are split in several places as if by lightning. We followed the Wady Kyd, continuing on a gentle ascent from the time of our setting out in the morning. The windings of the valley led us, at the end of five hours and a half, to a small rivulet, two feet across, and six inches in depth, which is lost immediately below, in the sands of the Wady. It drips down a granite rock, which blocks up the valley, there only twenty paces in breadth, and forms at the foot of the rock a small pond, overshadowed by trees, with fine verdure on its banks. The rocks which overhang it on both sides almost meet, and give to the whole the appearance of a grotto, most delighful to the traveller after passing through these dreary valleys. It is in fact the most romantic spot I have seen in these mountains, and worthy of being frequented by other people than Arabs, upon whom the beauties of nature make a very faint impression. The camels passed over the rocks with great difficulty; beyond it we continued in the same narrow valley, along the rivulet, amidst groves of date, Nebek, and some tamarisk trees, until, at six hours, we reached the source of the rivulet, where we rested a little. This is one of the most noted date valleys of the Sinai Arabs; the contrast of its deep verdure with the glaring rocks by which it is closely hemmed in, is very striking, and shews that wherever water passes in these districts, however barren the ground, vegetation is invariably found.   Within the er closures of the date-groves I saw a few patches of onions, and (hemp; the latter is used for smoking;' some of the small leav(which surround the hemp-seed being laid upon the tobacco in tl pipe, produces a more intoxicating smoke.   The same custom pr(vails in Egypt, where the hemp leaves as well as the plant itself ar called Hashysh.   In the branches of one of the date-trees sever: baskets and a gun were deposited, and some camels were feedin upon the grass near the rivulet, but not a soul was to be seen in th valley; these Bedouins being under no'fear of robbers, leave thei goods and allow their beasts to pasture without any one to watc them; when they want the camels they send to the springs in searc of them, and if not found there, they trace their footsteps througl the valleys, for every Bedouin knows the print of the foot of hi own camel.

FURTHER READING

INTRODUCTION TO VOLUME 4

Judy Bieber, *Plantation Societies in the Era of European Expansion* (Brookfield, 1997).

Tarek Bishti, *Orientalism and Nineteenth-Century English Travellers to the Middle East* (Dublin, 1990).

Jeremy Black, *Britain as a Military Power, 1688–1815* (London, 1999).

George Brodrick and J. K. Fotheringham, *The History of England from Addington's Administration to the Close of William IV's Reign, 1801–1837* (London, 1906).

Michael Broers, *Europe Under Napoleon, 1799–1815* (New York, 1996).

George Gordon, Lord Byron, *The Works of Lord Byron*, eds Hartley Coleridge and Rowland Prothero (London, 1898–1905).

Virginia Childs, *Lady Hester Stanhope: Queen of the Desert* (London, 1990).

John Corrigan, Frederick Denny, Carlos Eire and Martin Jaffee, *Jews, Christians, Muslims: A Comparative Introduction to Monotheistic Religions* (Princeton, 1998).

Ralph Davis, *Aleppo and Devonshire Square: English Traders in the Levant in the Eighteenth Century* (London, 1999).

Michael Duffy, *Soldiers, Sugar, and Seapower: The British Expeditions to the West Indies and the War against Revolutionary France* (Oxford, 1987).

John Esposito, *Oxford History of Islam* (Oxford, 1999).

K. E. Fleming, *The Muslim Bonaparte: Diplomacy and Orientalism in Ali Pasha's Greece* (Princeton, 1999).

Brian Fothergill, *Sir William Hamilton: Envoy Extraordinary* (New York, 1969).

Desmond Gregory, *Malta, Britain, and the European Powers, 1793–1815* (London, 1996).

Isobel Grundy, *Lady Mary Wortley Montagu* (Oxford, 1999).

William Hunt and Reginald Poole, *The Political History of England* (London, 1906).

Edward Ingram, *Britain's Persian Connections, 1798–1828: Prelude to the Great Game in Asia* (Oxford, 1992).

———, *In Defence of British India: Great Britain in the Middle East, 1775–1842* (London, 1984).

Christopher Lloyd, *The Nile Campaign: Nelson and Napoleon in Egypt* (New York, 1973).

Philip Mansel, *Constantinople: City of the World's Desire, 1453–1924* (London, 1995).

Charles Lewis Meryon, *Travels of Lady Hester Stanhope* (Salzburg, 1983).

Mary Wortley Montagu, *Letters of the Right Honourable Lady M—y W—y M—e: Written during her Travels in Europe, Asia, and Africa* (Dublin, 1763).

David Morgan, *Medieval Persia, 1040–1797* (London, 1988).

Sari Nasir, *The Arabs and the English* (London, 1976).

E. H. Nolan, *The Illustrated History of the British Empire in India, and the East* (London, [1857–9]).

James S. Olson and Robert Shadle, eds, *Historical Dictionary of the British Empire* (Westport, Connecticut, 1996).

Rodney Pasley, *'Send Malcolm!' The Life of Major-General Sir John Malcolm, 1769–1833* (London, 1982).

Thomas Philipp and Ulrich Haarmann, eds, *The Mamluks in Egyptian Politics and Society* (Cambridge, 1998).

Stefanaq Pollo and Arben Puto, *The History of Albania from its Origins to the Present Day*, trans. Carol Wiseman and Ginnie Hole (London, 1981).

Holland Rose, A. P. Newton and E. A. Benians, *The Cambridge History of the British Empire* (Cambridge, 1961).

Alan Schom, *Napoleon Bonaparte* (New York, 1997).

Sarah Searight, *The British in the Middle East* (London, 1979).

Katherine Sim, *Desert Traveller: The Life of Jean Louis Burckhardt* (London, 1969).

Adam Smith, *An Inquiry into the Nature and Causes of the Wealth of Nations* (Oxford, 1993).

Donald Sultana, *Samuel Taylor Coleridge in Malta and Italy* (Oxford, 1969).

——, *The Siege of Malta Rediscovered: An Account of Sir Walter Scott's Mediterranean Journey and his Last Novel* (Edinburgh, 1977).

Constantin François de Volney, *The Ruins; or, Meditations on the Revolutions of Empires: and the Law of Nature* (London, 1787).

Shelagh Weir, *The Bedouin* (London, 1990).

Denis Wright, *The English amongst the Persians during the Qajar Period, 1787–1921* (London, 1977).

M. E. Yapp, *The Making of the Modern Near East, 1792–1923* (New York, 1987).

VOLNEY: TRAVELS THROUGH SYRIA AND EGYPT

Anon, 'Constantin Volney', in *Columbia Encyclopedia* (New York, 2000).

Count Daru, 'Life of Volney', in *The Ruins, or, Meditation on the Revolutions of Empire* (New York, 1926).

Charles Durozoir, trans., *A Life of Volney* (London, 1840).

Nanette LeCoat, 'Allegories Literary, Scientific, and Imperial: Representation of the Other in Writings on Egypt by Volney and Savary', *Eighteenth-Century Literature and Interpretation*, 38. 1 (Spring 1997), pp. 3–22.

Abraham Marcus, *The Middle East on the Eve of Modernity: Aleppo in the Eighteenth Century* (New York, 1989).

Alan Schom, *Napoleon Bonaparte* (New York, 1997).

Robert Sole, *Les savants de Bonaparte* (Paris, 1998).

Timothy Wilson-Smith, *Denon and the Art of Conquest* (London, 1996).

NIEBUHR: TRAVELS THROUGH ARABIA

Sarah Austen, *Life of Carsten Niebuhr* (London, 1833).

Petter Forskal, *Flora aegyptiaco-arabica*, ed. Carsten Niebuhr (Copenhagen, 1775).

———, *Resa till Lycklige Arabien. Dagbok 1761–1763* (*Journey to Felix Arabia*; Uppsala, 1950).

Thorkild Hansen, *Arabia Felix. The Danish Expedition of 1761–1767*, trans. James and Kathleen McFarlane (New York, 1964).

Frederik von Haven, *Tagebuch über eine Reise von Suez nach dem Djebel el-Mokateb*, ed. Johannes Buhle (Leipzig, 1795).

Barthold Niebuhr, *The Life of Carsten Niebuhr, the Oriental Traveller* (Edinburgh, 1836).

Carsten Niebuhr, *Beschreibung von Arabien* (Copenhagen, 1772).

———, *Reisebeschreibung nach Arabien und andern umliegenden Ländern* (Copenhagen, 1774–1837).

SONNINI: TRAVELS IN UPPER AND LOWER EGYPT

Cecilia Brightwell, *Lives of Labour; or, Incidents in the Career of Eminent Naturalists and Celebrated Travellers* (London, 1874).

David Knight, *Science in the Romantic Period* (Brookfield, 1998).

Emma Spary, *Utopia's Garden: French Natural History from Old Regime to Revolution* (Chicago, 2000).

Duncan Wu, *A Companion to Romanticism* (Oxford, 1998).

WOOD: IMPORTANCE OF MALTA

Roderigo Cavaliero, *The Last of the Crusaders: the Knights of St John and Malta in the Eighteenth Century* (London, 1960).

Collected Letters of Samuel Taylor Coleridge, ed. E. L. Griggs (Oxford, 1956–71).

Albert Ganado, *Malta in British and French Caricature, 1798–1815* (Malta, 1989).

Desmond Gregory, *Malta, Britain, and the European Powers, 1793–1815* (London, 1996).

Alethea Hayter, *A Voyage in Vain: Coleridge's Journey to Malta in 1804* (London, 1973).

Frederick Ryan, *'The House of the Temple': A Study of Malta and its Knights in the French Revolution* (Malta, 1998).

Alan Schom, *Napoleon Bonaparte* (New York, 1997).

Donald Sultana, *Samuel Taylor Coleridge in Malta and Italy* (Oxford, 1969).

Charles Tweedie, *Reflections on the Present Crisis of Public Affairs* (London, 1803).

Thomas Walsh, *Journal of the Late Campaign in Egypt; Including Descriptions of that Country, and of Gibraltar, Minorca, Malta, Marmorice, and Macri* (London, 1803).

POUQUEVILLE: TRAVELS THROUGH THE OTTOMAN EMPIRE

Julien Bessières, *Mémoire sur la vie et la puissance d'Ali Pacha, visir de Janina* (Paris, 1820).

K. E. Fleming, *The Muslim Bonaparte: Diplomacy and Orientalism in Ali Pasha's Greece* (Princeton, 1999).

Fatma Gocek, *East Encounters West: France and the Ottoman Empire in the Eighteenth Century* (New York, 1987).

Philip Mansel, *Constantinople: The City of the World's Desire* (London, 1995).

Patrick Manning, ed., *Slave Trades, 1500–1800: Globalization of Forced Labour* (Brookfield, 1996).

Robert W. Olson, *Imperial Meanderings and Republican By-ways: Essays on Eighteenth Century Ottoman and Twentieth Century History of Turkey* (Istanbul, 1996).

F. C. H. L. Pouqueville, *Histoire de la régénération de la Grèce, comprenant le précis des évènements depuis 1740 jusqu'en 1824* (Paris, 1824).

MORIER: JOURNEY THROUGH PERSIA

M. S. Anderson, *The Eastern Question, 1774–1823* (New York, 1996).

Peter Avery, *The Cambridge History of Iran: from Nadir Shah to the Islamic Republic* (Cambridge, 1991).

Ayten Coskunoglu, *A Critical Survey of the Life and Works of James Justinian Morier, 1780–1849* (Istanbul, 1967).

Henry McKenzie Johnston, *Ottoman and Persian Odysseys: James Morier, Creator of Hajji Baba of Ispahan, and his Brothers* (London, 1998).

Denis Wright, *The English amongst the Persians during the Qajar Period, 1787–1921* (London, 1977).

——, *The Persians amongst the English: Episodes in Anglo-Persian History* (London, 1985).

Karl Zeidler, *Beckford, Hope, und Morier als Vertreter des orientalischen Romans* (Leipzig, 1908).

HOBHOUSE: JOURNEY THROUGH ALBANIA

John Baggally, *Ali Pasha and Great Britain* (Athens, 1937).

Auguste Boppe, *L'Albanie et Napoleon* (Paris, 1914).

John Cam Hobhouse, Baron Broughton, *Recollections of a Long Life*, ed. Lady Dorchester (London, 1909–11).

Byron's Bulldog: the Letters of John Cam Hobhouse to Lord Byron, ed. Peter Graham (Columbus, 1984).

K. E. Fleming, *The Muslim Bonaparte: Diplomacy and Orientalism in Ali Pasha's Greece* (Princeton, 1999).

Michael Joyce, *My Friend H: John Cam Hobhouse, Baron Broughton de Gyfford* (London, 1948).

Kyriakos Metaxas, 'Byron's Intelligence Mission to Greece', *Byron Journal*, 10 (1982), pp. 72–4.

Mohammad Sharafuddin, *Islam and Romantic Orientalism: Literary Encounters with the Orient* (London, 1994).

Eric Vincent, *Byron, Hobhouse, and Foscolo: New Documents in the History of a Collaboration* (Norwood, 1978).

Robert Zegger, *John Cam Hobhouse, a Political Life, 1819–1852* (Columbia, 1973).

LEBLICH: TRAVELS OF ALI BEY

Anon, 'Domingo Badiá y Leblich', in *Columbia Encyclopedia* (New York, 2000).

Srinivas Aravamudan, *Tropicopolitans: Colonialism and Agency, 1688–1804* (Durham, 1999).

Syrine Hout, *Viewing Europe from Outside: Cultural Encounters and Critiques in the Eighteenth-Century Pseudo-Oriental Travelogue and the Nineteenth-Century 'Voyage en Orient'* (New York, 1997).

ELPHINSTONE: ACCOUNT OF THE KINGDOM OF CAUBUL

Shiri Ram Bakshi, *British Diplomacy and Administration in India, 1807–13* (New Delhi, 1971).

Rustom Choksey, *A History of British Diplomacy at the Court of the Peshwas, 1786–1818* (Poona, 1951).

——, *Mountstuart Elphinstone: the Indian Years, 1796–1827* (Bombay, 1971).

T. E. Colebrooke, *Life of the Honourable Mountstuart Elphinstone* (London, 1884).

J. S. Cotton, *Rulers of India: Mountstuart Elphinstone* (Oxford, 1892).

John Drew, *India and the Romantic Imagination* (New York, 1987).

Edward Ingram, *In Defence of British India: Great Britain in the Middle East, 1775–1842* (London, 1984).

Efraim Karsh and Inari Karsh, *Empires of the Sand: The Struggle for Mastery in the Middle East, 1789–1923* (Cambridge, 1999).

Sir John William Kaye, *Lives of Indian Officers* (London, 1889).

BURCKHARDT: TRAVELS IN SYRIA AND THE HOLY LAND

Robin Hallett, *Records of the African Association, 1788–1831* (London, 1964).

Daniel Masse, *Burckhardt, le bédouin de Petra* (Toulon, 1996).

James St John, *Egypt and Nubia, their Scenery and People: Being Incidents of History and Travel* (London, 1845).

Katharine Sim, *Desert Traveller: The Life of Jean Louis Burckhardt* (London, 1969).

NOTES

p. 5, l. 15: *Carmania*] a satrapy of ancient Persia, in the modern region extending from south-eastern Iran into Afghanistan.

p. 7, l. 5: *Chaldean Berosus*] fourth-century BC Babylonian historian, author of *Babyloniaca* (also known as *Chaldaica*).

p. 7, ll. 5–6: *Armenian Maribas*] not further identified.

p. 7, l. 6: *Moses Chorenensis*] fifth-century Armenian historian and author of *History of Armenia Major*, to which Volney refers here.

p. 7, l. 8: *Xisuthrus*] antediluvian king of Babylon, associated with the biblical tradition of Noah.

p. 7, l. 13: *Zenophon*] Xenophon, fifth-century BC Athenian historian, whose travels into the Persian Empire are described in *Anabasis*.

p. 7, l. 23: *Niebuhr*] Carsten Niebuhr (1733–1815), author of *Reisebeschreibung nach Arabien* (1774) and *Beschreibung von Arabien* (1772), translated into English under the title *Travels through Arabia and Other Countries in the East*; selections from Niebuhr's account are reproduced above (pp. 45–68).

p. 7, n. 1, l. 1: *Strabo*] (63 BC–AD 21), Anatolian historian and author of *Geographika*, describing his travels in Asia, Europe and Africa.

p. 8, l. 3: *Druzes*] Mowahhidoon, a fiercely independent and secretive Islamic sect in Lebanon, dating from the ninth century.

p. 8, ll. 10–12: *Diarbekir … Damascus*] The region Volney describes extends from Syria into eastern Turkey, including the region that comprised late eighteenth-century Armenia.

p. 8, ll. 17–18: *Zoroaster*] Zarathustra, sixth-century BC Persian prophet, founder of the Zoroastrian religion, now Parsi. Often called the 'fire-worshippers', Zoroastrians flourished in the Persian empire until the period of Alexander's invasion in the fourth century.

p. 9, ll. 20–1: *Orosmades…Typhon*] Ahura Mazda, Persian sun god and force of good, worshipped by Zoroastrians. In Zoroastrian scripture (the Avedas), Ahriman is the fallen twin of Ahura Mazda, leader of the daevas or daemon gods. Ahriman is associated with darkness, serpents and evil. Osiris is the murdered man-god of ancient Egyptian religion, associated with cyclical regeneration and the Nile. 'Typhon' or Set is the twin brother of Osiris, the personification of evil in ancient Egyptian mythology.

p. 9, l. 24: *Darius Hystaspes*] Darius Hystaspis, Emperor of Persia from 521 to 485 BC, who famously extended the boundaries of the Persian Empire as far as Greece.

p. 10, n. 2, l. 2: *Dr. Pallas*] Peter Simon Pallas (1741–1811), German scientist, naturalist and traveller in the employ of Empress Catherine the Great. His travel publications included *Description of Tibet*; *Travels through the Southern Provinces of the Russian Empire*; *Travels through Siberia and Tartary*; and *Views of Eighteenth-Century Russia*.

p. 31, n. 1, ll. 2–3: *M. Chenier*] Louis de Chénier (1722–95), author of *Recherches historiques sur les Maures: et histoire de l'empire de Maroc* (1787).

p. 42, n. 1, l. 1: *Niebuhr*] Carsten Niebuhr's *Reisebeschreibung nach Arabien* (1774) was first translated into French under the title *Description de l'Arabie: d'après les observations and recherches faites dans le pays même* (1774).

NIEBUHR: TRAVELS THROUGH ARABIA

p. 51, ll. 5–20: *Harbour of Tor ... Jebil*] The region Niebuhr describes extends along the shores of the Gulf of Suez and the coast of the Red Sea, from Suez in the north as far south as Jiddah, located on the Arabian peninsula west of Mecca. The harbours of Tor and Ras Mohammad are located in the Gulf of Suez, along the western coast of the Sinai peninsula. All the other locations lie along Niebuhr's itinerary south along the Red Sea coast to Jiddah.

p. 52, l. 3: *Mr Forskal*] Petter Forskal (1732–63), Niebuhr's travelling companion.

p. 57, l. 24: *Ihhram*] ihram, the state of ritual consecration undertaken by pilgrims to Mecca, symbolised by the white cotton vestments worn by male participants.

p. 61, l. 22: *Mr Gæhler*] not further identified.

p. 66, l. 2: *Mr Von Haven*] Niebuhr's travelling companion, Frederik Christian von Haven (1727–63).

p. 66, l. 24: *Sultan El Guri*] Qansuh II al Ghawri, Mameluke Sultan of Egypt from 1501 to 1516.

p. 68, l. 21: *Pococke*] Richard Pococke (1704–65), explorer and author of *A Description of the East, and Some Other Countries* (1743).

SONNINI: TRAVELS IN UPPER AND LOWER EGYPT

p. 71, l. 4: *M. Pauw*] Cornelius de Pauw (1739–99), traveller and author of *Philosophical Dissertations on the Egyptians and Chinese* (1795), which was originally published in French under the title *Recherches philosophiques sur les Égyptiens et les Chinois* (1773).

p. 71, l. 9: *Dr. Samoilovitz*] Danilo Samoilovich (1742–1805), author of numerous works on the plague, including *Mémoire sur la peste qui, en 1771, ravagea Moscou* (1783), *Mémoire sur l'inoculation de la peste* (1782) and *Lettre sur les expériences des frictions glaciales pour la guérison de la peste* (1782).

p. 71, l. 12: *travels of Savary and of Citizen Volney*] references to Claude Etienne Savary (1750–88), author of *Lettres sur l'Égypte* (1785) and to Constantin François de Volney (1757–1820), author of *Voyage en Syrie et en Égypte pendant les années 1783, 84, & 85* (1799); see above, pp. 1–2.

p. 71, n. 1, ll. 1–2: *Journal de Physique*] *Journal de physique, de chimie, d'histoire naturelle et des arts*, published monthly in Paris from 1773 to 1793.

p. 76, ll. 1–2: *Est elephas morbus ... praetera usquam*] Lucretius, *De Rerum Natura*, VI. 1114: 'There is an elephant disease which is generated beyond the rivers of the Nile, and nowhere apart from there'.

p. 77, l. 22: *Hasselquitz*] Frederik Hasselquist (1722–52), author of *Voyages dans le Levant* (1769).

p. 77, n. 1: *William Hillary*] author of *A Treatise on ... the Yellow Fever, and such Diseases as are Most Frequent in or are Peculiar to the West-India Islands* (1766).

p. 79, n. 1: *Multiplicatio coïtûs est nocibilior res oculo*] Abu-'Ali al-Husayn ibn Sina (Avicenna), *Work*, III. 5: 'the multiplication of sex is a more harmful thing than the [evil] eye'.

p. 80, l. 17: *my Travels in Turkey*] Sonnini also wrote a travel account of Greece and Turkey, published under the title *Voyage en Grèce et en Turquie: fair part ordre de Louis XVI, et avec l'autorisation de la cour ottomane*.

p. 81, ll. 12–13: *James Bruce*] (1730–94), prominent explorer and author of *Travels to Discover the Source of the Nile, in Egypt, Arabia, Abyssinia, and Nubia* (1790). Extracts from this work are reproduced in volume 5 of this edition.

p. 82, l. 8: *Niebuhr*] Carsten Niebuhr's *Reisebeschreibung nach Arabien* (1774), translated into French as *Description de l'Arabie*.

p. 84, l. 18: *Buffon*] Georges Louis Leclerc (1707–88), comte de Buffon, naturalist and author of *Histoire naturelle générale et particulière: des quadrupèdes, des singes et de l'homme*.

p. 84, ll. 22–4: *Thevenot ... Tachard ... kolben*] The allusions here are to the scientific works of: Jean de Thévenot (1633–67), author of *Relation d'un voyage fair au Levant* (1665); Guy Tachard (1651–1712), author of *Voyage de Siam des pères jésuites* (1686) and *Second voyage du père Tachard et des Jésuites* (1689); and Peter Kolb (1675–1726), author of *The Present State of the Cape of Good Hope, or, a Particular Account of the Several Nations of the Hottentots* (1731).

p. 85, l. 7: *Le Vaillant*] François le Vaillant (1753–1824), author of *Voyage de Monsieur le Vaillant dans l'intérieur de l'Afrique par le Cap de Bonne-Espérance dans les années 1780* and *Second voyage dans l'intérieur de l'Afrique: dans les années 1783, 84, & 85*.

p. 86, l. 11: *Psilli*] renowned race of Libyan serpent detectors and charmers, noted for their immunity to and ability to cure snake bites.

p. 88, l. 10: *Dr. Shaw*] Thomas Shaw (1694–1751), author of *Travels, or, Observations Relating to Several Parts of Barbary and the Levant* (1738).

WOOD: IMPORTANCE OF MALTA

p. 95, ll. 5–14: *Bonaparte's expedition ... blessing of peace*] As the initial stage of his Egyptian campaign, Napoleon took control of Malta on 11 June 1798. The island was surrendered to the British on 4 September 1800, after Napoleon's retreat from the Middle East. Malta's independence was restored to the Order of St John of Jerusalem by the Treaty of Amiens (25 March 1802); however, due to subsequent breaches of that treaty, which had been so unfavourably negotiated by the Addington administration, the island was ultimately retained by the British as a military base and later a colony.

p. 95, n. 1, l. 3: *present Chancellor of the Exchequer*] Henry Addington, Viscount Sidmouth, served as First Lord of the Treasury and Chancellor of the Exchequer from 1801 to 1804 and as Speaker of the House of Commons from 1790 to 1801.

p. 99, l. 6: *Knights of Malta*] formerly the Knights of Rhodes and members of the Order of St John of Jerusalem, to whom Malta had been granted in 1530 in recognition of the Order's service during the Crusades.

p. 99, l. 15: *Sir William Hamilton*] (1730–1803), British ambassador at Naples from 1764 to 1800; Sir John Jervis, naval officer, elevated to Earl of St Vincent after his victory at the Battle of Cape St Vincent (1797), First Lord of the Admiralty during the Addington administration.

p. 100, l. 12: *harbour of Trincomale*] located on the eastern coast of Ceylon (Sri Lanka). Ceylon's importance for securing the Cape Route to India led to the British capture of the island in 1796, and Trincomale was a harbour of significant strategic value throughout the Napoleonic Wars.

p. 100, l. 26: *the Porte*] usually 'The Sublime Porte', strictly the second, private court of the Sultan's palace in Constantinople, used metonymically to designate the Ottoman government.

p. 100, ll. 20–1: *Straits of Babel Mandel*] Bab el Mandeb, the straits connecting the Red Sea with the Gulf of Aden and the Arabian Sea, of great strategic value for maintaining access to the Indian subcontinent via the Middle East.

p. 104, n. 1, l. 1: *Treaty of Campo Formio*] Under the Treaty of Campo Formio, the French had gained several strategic territories, including Lombardy and the islands of Corfu, Zante and Cephalonia. In exchange for a significant portion of the Venetian republic, Austria had also acknowledged the cession of Holland and Belgium.

p. 104, n. 1, l. 9: *Tippoo Sultaun*] Tipu Sultan (1750–99), the formidable ruler of Mysore India during the period of the Third (1790–2) and Fourth (1799) Mysore Wars, which were fought against British imperialism. Tipu Sultan's resistance to British control of the Indian subcontinent was a significant factor in late eighteenth-century diplomatic machinations in the East. In order to defeat the Mysore, the British conspired with Tipu's traditional enemies, the Nizam and the Marathas, leading to Tipu's retaliatory negotiations with France and independent Afghanistan. 'Governor Malartic': Anne Joseph Hippolyte de Maures, comte de Malartic, served as the French Governor-General of Mauritius from 1792 to 1800.

p. 108, l. 21: *Volney*] Constantin François de Volney, *Travels through Syria and Egypt* (1787); see above, pp. 1–2.

p. 109, l. 16: *lord Minto*] Sir Gilbert Elliot (1751–1814), Baron Minto, served as Viceroy of Corsica (1794–6) and later as Governor-General of India (1807–13).

p. 112, l. 12: *Poonah*] Poona, a city in western India, the traditional homeland of the Marathas and their capital from 1714 until British occupation in 1817.

p. 112, ll. 16–17: *Zemaun Shaw*] Zeman Shah: ruler of independent Afghanistan from 1793 to 1800.

p. 112, l. 23: *monsieur Raymond*] Michel Joachim Marie Raymond (1755–98), French mercenary soldier, who entered the service of the Nizam of Hyderabad in 1786 and later commanded the Nizam's troops against the British.

p. 112, l. 25: *Scindeah*] Mahadaji Sindia, Maratha ruler who consolidated the confederacy's power at the end of the eighteenth century and who fought the British successfully during the first Anglo-Maratha War (1775–82). Sindia was recognised as the *de facto* ruler of northern India and as such he posed a significant obstacle to British imperial expansion.

p. 112, ll. 25–6: *general De Boigne*] Benoit Leborgne (1751–1830), comte de Boigne, French soldier who served with the British East India Company in Madras during the Hasting administration and who later, as a mercenary general, successfully commanded Sindia's Maratha armies during their resistance to British rule. De

Boigne's French successor, General Perror, later led Sindia's armies against Wellesley during the first months of the Second Anglo-Maratha War but resigned his command in September of 1803. Perror was briefly succeeded by another French officer, Louis Bourquain, who was captured by Lake and the British troops after a week in command. The significant French involvement in 'native' Indian and Persian resistance movements illustrates the complexity of Romantic-period politics in this region.

POUQUEVILLE: TRAVELS THROUGH THE OTTOMAN EMPIRE

p. 119, ll. 2–4: *two travellers…Gouffier…Beaujour*] Choiseuil Gouffier, not further identified, but most likely one of the anonymous authors affiliated with the Society of Dilettanti, which published numerous works on Greek antiquities matching this description. Also Louis-Auguste Felix (1765–1836), baron Beaujour, author of *Tableau du commerce de la Grèce, formé d'après une année moyenne, depuis 1787 jusqu'en 1797*.

p. 119, ll. 6–7: *Tournefort and Olivier*] Joseph Pitton de Tournefort (1656–1708), author of *Relation d'un voyage du Levant, fait par ordre du roy, contenant l'histoire ancienne & moderne de plusieurs isles de l'Achipel, de Constantinople, des côtes de la Mer Noire, de l'Armenie, de la Georgie, des frontieres de Perse & de l'Asie Mineure* and Guillaume Antoine Olivier (1756–1814), author of *Voyage dans l'empire othoman, l'Égypte et la Perse, fait par ordre du gouvernement, pendant les six premières années de la République*.

p. 121, l. 3: *Bessieres*] Julien Bessières (1770–1840), author of *Mémoire sur la vie et la puissance d'Ali Pacha, visir de Janina*.

p. 121, l. 20: *geographer*] Jean Denis (1760–1825), prominent cartographer whose works include *Recueil de cartes géographiques, plans, vues et médailles de l'ancienne Grèce, relatifs au Voyage du jeune Anacharsis* (1798).

p. 122, ll. 7–22: *we skimmed … that city*] Pouqueville's journey describes the sea-route north to Constantinople. Beginning in the north-eastern Aegean, he passed the islands of Chios, Psara and Tenedos and continued along the Turkish coast before entering the Dardanelles at the Bay of Chersonessus. This selection begins as he passed the Hellespont and crossed the Sea of Marmara, sailing towards Constantinople.

p. 122, l. 29: *Pera*] Galata, the foreign and merchant quarter of Constantinople, located outside the city proper.

p. 122, l. 36: *Tophana*] the entrance to the Galata quarter in Constantinople.

p. 122, l. 10: *Messrs. Beauvais and Gerard*] Both men had been part of the convey with which Pouqueville was travelling. Their vessel had become separated and captured, and the two Frenchmen had been placed in the prison at Constantinople six months prior to Pouqueville's detention.

p. 123, l. 22: *Seven Towers*] Yedi Kule, the chief fortress of Constantinople and a feared prison. Built in the fifteenth century, the citadel is located on the Sea of Marmara, just west of the city centre and at the mouth of the Bosporus.

p. 127, l. 22: *Mahomed II*] Mehmed II, 'the Conqueror', captured Constantinople on 29 May 1453, wresting control from the Roman Emperor Constantine XI and establishing the Ottoman Empire.

p. 128, l. 10: *Osman II*] reigned as Ottoman Sultan from 1618 to 1622. Osman took power after deposing Sultan Mustapha I and in 1622 was himself deposed by his predecessor. Osman's brief reign was marred by an unsuccessful Polish campaign.

p. 129, l. 6: *Candia*] Crete.

p. 129, l. 37: *Rodosto*] Tekirdag, a city in north-western Turkey on the Sea of Marmara.

p. 134, l. 31: *lady Montague*] Lady Mary Wortley Montagu, *Letters ... Written during her Travels in Europe, Asia, and Africa* (1763).

p. 135, l. 7: *authors of the Encyclopedie*] a reference to the *Encyclopédie, ou, Dictionnaire raisonné des sciences, des arts et des métiers* (1751), edited by Denis Diderot (1713–84) and Jean le Rond d'Alembert (1717–83).

p. 135, l. 19: *oulemas*] Muslim religious scholars.

p. 137, l. 35: *Procopius*] whose classical history of the Byzantine Empire included an account of the buildings of Justinian.

p. 137, l. 36: *Spon*] Jacob Spon (1647–85), author of *Voyage d'Italie, de Dalmatie, de Grece, et du Levant: fair aux années 1675 & 1676.*

p. 141, ll. 25–6: *Republic of the Seven Islands*] an independent republic of the Ionian islands, maintained as a Russian protectorate from 1800 to 1805 and established after French surrender in the War of the Second Coalition. It included the islands of Corfu, Paxos, Leukas, Ithaca, Cephalonia, Zante and Cerigo.

p. 145, l. 20: *Murad IV*] Ottoman sultan from 1623 to 1640.

p. 146, l. 23: *Frank*] formerly a generic term in the Middle East for European travellers.

p. 148, l. 44: *Messrs. Ruffin and Dantan*] the French chargé d'affaires at Constantinople and an interpreter attached to the French embassy during this period, respectively.

p. 149, l. 26: *M. Sevin*] François Sevin (1682–1741), author of *Lettres sur Constantinople*.

MORIER: A JOURNEY THROUGH PERSIA

p. 155, l. 2: *Tabriz to Arz-Roum*] Morier's journey took him westwards from Persia to Constantinople, and he describes in this section of his narrative the rural route from Persian Tabriz to Ottoman Erzurum. From Tabriz, Morier travelled north-west to Khvoy and onward out of Persia to Mount Ararat, passing through the territories of Azerbaijan and Armenia. From Ararat, he traced the Aras river valley south-west down into Erzurum.

p. 156, l. 6: *Mehmandar*] throughout Persia and India, an official courier attached to a traveller of distinction (*OED*).

p. 156, l. 31: *kanauts*] canauts, canvas enclosures or tents (*OED*).

p. 159, l. 4: *Bolouk of Aeenzaub*] not further identified.

p. 159, l. 8: *moss*] cakes or confections (*OED*).

p. 159, l. 17: *Aderbigian*] Azerbaijan.

p. 161, ll. 25–6: *Hossein Khan ... Aga Mohamed Khan*] Aga Mohammad Khan (1742–97) ruled Persia as the first Qajar Shah from 1779 until his assassination in 1797. Mohammad Khan was succeeded by his nephew, Fath Ali Shah (1771–1834), who ruled Persia during the time of Morier's travels.

p. 163, ll. 2–3: *Nejef Kooli Khan*] Najaf Kuli Khan, a Hindustani Afghan who rose to military power and political prominence as governor under the reign of Emperor

Fath Ali Shah. For details of Najaf's intricate relations with British imperial repre-
sentatives, see H. G. Keene, *The Fall of the Mogul Empire of Hindustane* (1887).

p. 166, l. 20: *Prince Abbas Mirza*] (1789–1833), Qajar crown prince and governor of
Azerbaijan, son of Persia's Fath Ali Shah.

p. 169, l. 70–p. 170, l. 1: *Ibrahim Pacha*] Ibrahim Pasha (1789–1848), viceroy of Egypt,
adopted son and successor of Mehemet Ali.

p. 173, ll. 11–12: *Abdulla Pacha, a rebel Courd*] not further identified.

p. 174, l. 33: *Timur Beg*] not further identified.

p. 178, l. 27: *Abdulla Aga*] not further identified.

HOBHOUSE: JOURNEY THROUGH ALBANIA

p. 187, l. 21: *the admirable Creichton*] James Crichton, 'the Admirable Crichton' (1560–
82), Scottish scholar and orator, subject of a famous painting by Thomas Urquhart.

p. 187, l. 26: *Sclavonian*] referring to the present-day Balkan countries.

p. 190, n. 1, l. 1: *Voyage en Albanie*] Presumably a reference to F. C. H. L. Pouqueville,
Voyage en Morée, à Constantinople, en Albanie (1805); see above, pp. 117–18.

p. 190, l. 7: *Lady M. W. Montague*] Lady Mary Wortley Montagu's *Embassy Letters*
(1763). Here, the letter 'To The Abbé Conti', 1 April 1717.

p. 192, ll. 25–6: *Metzovo … Agrapha*] a pass in and a region of the Greek Pindus range,
respectively.

p. 192, ll. 26–7: *Gulf of Arta*] a virtually landlocked inlet on the western coast of Greece,
connected to the Mediterranean by the Straits of Prévezis.

p. 194, l. 30: *Mouctar Pasha*] Muktar Pasha, eldest son of Albania's Ali Tepelene and
pasha of Lepanto. Muktar was known for an excessive degree of cruelty and violence. His massacre of Greek women by drowning in sacks, for example, was well
known during the Romantic period.

p. 197, l. 27: *Xenophon*] Hobhouse alludes here to Xenophon's descriptions of Eastern
military customs in *Anabasis*.

p. 198, n. 1, ll. 2–3: *Meursius' Laconian Miscellanies*] Joannes Meursius (1579–1639),
prominent seventeenth-century translator of numerous classical texts. Presumably
a reference to an unidentified eighteenth-century collection of these Laconian, i.e.
Greek, translations. The previous reference is to the fifth-century BC *Anabasis* of
Xenophon, which Hobhouse was clearly reading in a contemporary translation.

p. 198, l. 14: *traveller Brown*] a reference to John Campbell, *The Travels and Adventures
of Edward Brown, Esq., Containing his Observations on France and Italy; his Voyage to the
Levant; his Account of the Isle of Malta; his Remarks on his Journies thro' the Lower and
Upper Egypt; together with a Brief Description of the Abyssinian Empire* (1739).

p. 198, l. 23: *Ghalil … Patrona*] Patrona Halil or Khalil led a mob revolt against Sultan
Ahmed III in 1730, leading to the placement of Mahmud I on the throne.

p. 199, l. 1: *Kioprili family*] From 1656 to 1710, the Grand Viziers of the Koprulu family
included: Koprulu Mehmed Pasha (vizier 1656–61), Fazil Ahmed Pasha (vizier
1661–76), Fazil Mustafa Pasha (vizier 1689–91) and Fazil Numan Pasha (vizier
May–August 1710). Hobhouse appears not to have counted Fazil Numan Pasha
amongst the Koprulu viziers, probably due to the brevity of his appointment.

p. 199, ll. 5–6: *insurrection of the Greeks*] Hobhouse alludes here to the unsuccessful early Greek efforts to revolt against Ottoman rule. Tripolitza was the seat of Turkish rule in the Morea; Napoli di Romania refers to present-day Naupalia.

p. 199, l. 11: *Mustapha Bairactar*] Bayrakdar Mustapha Pasa, the Ottoman vizier who helped Mahmud II gain the throne in 1808. He was assassinated later that year by the janizaries, whom he had opposed.

p. 200, l. 6: *Wallachians*] Walachia, a principality of the lower Danube. Long under the power of the Otttoman Sultan, Walachia became a Russian protectorate in the settlement of the Russo-Turkish War (1768–74).

p. 200, l. 6: *travellers*] Hobhouse here lists several eighteenth- and nineteenth-century travel writers and historians. In addition to Edward Gibbon, his allusions include: Cornelius de Pauw (1739–99), traveller and author of *The Manners, Customs, and Private Life of the Greeks* (1793); Jean-Baptiste Bourguignon d'Anville (1697–1782), traveller, historian and cartographer; Richard Chandler (1738–1810), author of *Travels in Greece* (1776); Joseph Pittonde Tournefort (1656–1708), author of *A Voyage into the Levant* (1741); Henry Swinburne (1743–1803), author of *Travels in Two Sicilies in the Years 1777, 1778, 1779, and 1780* (1783); and Charles Sigisbert Sonnini de Manoncourt (1751–1812), author of *Travels in Greece and Turkey* (1801). Selections from Sonnini's earlier *Travels in Upper and Lower Egypt* are reproduced above (pp. 69–89).

p. 201, l. 21: *Rycaut*] Sir Paul Rycaut (1628–1700), author of *The Present State of the Ottoman Empire: Containing Maxims of the Turkish Politie, the Most Material Points of Mahometan Religion, etc.* (1670) and *The History of the Turkish Empire from the Year 1623 to the Year 1677* (1680).

p. 202, n. 1, ll. 1–9: *Pope Pius II … Mahometan Theology*] Here Hobhouse summarises the arguments outlined in Adrianus Reeland (1676–1718), *Four Treatises concerning the Doctrine, Discipline, and Worship of the Mahometans* (1712). Among these commentators, Hobhouse alludes to several figures of some historical significance, especially Pope Pius II (1405–64), pontiff from 1458 to 1464, the period immediately following the Muslim capture of Constantinople in 1453. Pius II led the last of the Crusades, directed against Islam. Polydore Vergil (*c.* 1470–*c.* 1555) was the author of the sixteenth-century *Twenty-Six Books of English History* (1534), the first critical history written in English. 'Selden' refers to John Selden (1584–1654), an important early orientalist and author of *De diis Syris Syntagmata* (1617).

p. 203, ll. 2–3: *monks of Medenham*] or Dashwood's Medenham Club, also known as the Hellfire Club. An eighteenth-century gentleman's club, hosting clerically themed orgies and black masses, founded by Sir Frances Dashwood (1708–81).

p. 203, l. 11: *Wahaubees*] Wahabis or al-Muwahhidun, an eighteenth-century militant sect of Islam, whose objectives were fundamentalist religious reform and independent rule. Followers called themselves 'unitarians'.

p. 203, n. 1, l. 6: *Cantemir, Ottoman Hist.*] Dimitrie Cantemir (1673–1723), Voivode of Moldavia, author of *Histoire de l'Empire Othoman* (1743).

p. 204, l. 9: *Adam Neuser*] Heidelbergian anti-Trinitarian dissenter, whose history is outlined in *Reflections on Mahometanism and Socianism*, published as one of the four treatises included in Reeland's edition.

p. 204, l. 8: *Socinians*] a sixteenth-century rationalist Christian sect, important for its subsequent influence on English Unitarian theology, developed by the Italian

Laelius Socinus (1525–62) and expanded by his nephew Faustus Socinus (1539–1604).

p. 204, l. 22: Ὀυκ 'ιδεν, αλλ' εδοκησεν ιδειν δια νυκτα σεληνην] 'not seen, but imagined seen by the night moon'.

p. 204, l. 13: *Fakeers … Dervishes*] both Muslim mystics and members of the Sufi sect, the characteristic ritual of which entails whirling and dancing. The fakir were mendicant dervishes and often esteemed as holy men.

p. 205, l. 15: *Uveis the Mahometan*] not further identified.

p. 206, l. 13: *Mr. Harley*] Robert Harley (1661–1724), Earl of Oxford, published *An Essay upon Publick Credit: Being an Enquiry into How the Publick Credit Comes to Depend on the Change of the Ministry, or the Dissolutions of Parliaments* in 1710. The work has often been attributed to Daniel Defoe.

p. 207, n. 1, l. 5: *Artus Thomas*] late sixteenth-century sieur d'Embry and author of *Description de l'isle des hermaphrodites* (1605). The reference to the Triumph of the Cross has not been further identified.

p. 207, n. 1, l. 6: *Bellarmine*] Saint Roberto Francesco Romolo Bellarmino (1542–1621), author of *Disputationes de controversiis Christianae* (1586–93).

p. 207, n. 1, ll. 6–7: *Thomas à Jesu*] (1564–1627), Carmélite mystic and author of voluminous treatises, most notably the *Stimulus missionum* (1610). A complete edition of his works was published in 1684, under the direction of Pope Urban III, but the reference here has not been further identified.

p. 207, n. 1, l. 11: *Rubruquis*] Guillaume de Rubruquis, thirteenth-century French monk and ambassador to Tartary and China. *Relation de voyages en Tartarie de fr. Guillaume de Rubruquis* appeared in several seventeenth- and eighteenth-century editions.

p. 208, l. 7: *Mr. Thorton*] The reference here is to Thomas Thorton's *Present State of Turkey; or, a Description of the Political, Civil, and Religious, Constitution, Government, and Laws of the Ottoman Empire* (1809).

p. 208, ll. 9–12: *Janissaries … Mufti*] the élite army of the Ottoman Sultan and an Islamic legal authority, respectively.

p. 209, ll. 16–17: *Abu-Taleb*] The reference here is to *The Travels of Mirza Abu Taleb Khan, in Asia, Africa, and Europe, during the Years 1799, 1800, 1801, 1802, and 1803* (1810).

p. 209, l. 18: *De Tott*] François (1733–93), baron de Tott, author of *Memoirs of Baron de Tott: Containing the State of the Turkish Empire and Crimea, during the Late War with Russia* (1785).

p. 209, ll. 18–19: *Sir James Porter*] (1710–76), author of *Observations on the Religion, Law, Government, and Manners of the Turks* (1771).

p. 210, n. 1, ll. 5–6: *Bobovius*] Alberto Bobovii's *De Turcorumliturgia* (1690). This was translated as *Treatise of Bobovius (Sometimes First Interpreter to Mahomet IV) Concerning the Liturgy of the Turks, their Pilgrimage to Mecca, their Circumcision, Visitation of the Sick, &c.* and collected by Reeland for publication in his *Four Treatises Concerning the Doctrine … of the Mahometans*.

p. 210, n. 1, ll. 9–10: *Notice sur la Cour du Grand Seigneur*] a reference to Joseph Eugène Beauvoisin, *Notice sur la cour du grand-seigneur: son sérail, son harem, la famille du sang imperiale, sa maison militaire, et ses ministres* (1807).

p. 211, l. 21: *Samanide dynasty*] ruled Iran from 819 to 999.

p. 211, n. 1, l. 1: *D'Herbelot*] Barthelemy d'Herbelot (1625–95), author of *Bibliothèque orientale, ou Dictionaire universel, contentant généralement tout ce qui regarde la connoissance des peuples de l'Orient* (1697).

p. 211, n. 1, ll. 1–2: *Sâadi in the Ghulistan*] Sa'di, Musharrif Od-Din Muslih Od-Din (1213–91), author of the two greatest works of classical Persian poetry, *Bustan* and *Gulistan*.

p. 211, n. 1, l. 3–p. 212, n. 1, l. 1: *Bokhari...Sahib*] Al-Bukhari (810–70), Islamic traditionalist and author of the *Sahib*, a contemporary compilation of the sayings of the prophet Muhammad, considered by Sunni Muslims a canonical text.

p. 213, n. 2, l. 4: *Hafiz*] Mohammad Shams Od-Din Hafez (1325–89), Persian lyric poet and author of the *Divan*.

p. 213, n. 3, l. 5: *Galand*] Antoine Galland (1646–1715), author of *Les paroles remarquables, les bon mots, et les maximes des Orientaux* (1694).

p. 214, ll. 5–6: *expedition undertaken by Sultan Solyman against Malta*] Sultan Suleiman I (c. 1495–1566) attempted to capture Malta for the Ottoman Empire in 1564–5, without success. Granted to the Order of St John of Jerusalem in 1530, the island remained under the control of the Knights of Malta until Napoleon's invasion in 1798.

p. 214, l. 14: *Mevlevi*] an Islamic and Sufi order, often identified by European travellers as the 'whirling dervishes'.

p. 216, ll. 11–12: *Lord Baltimore's Travels*] Frederick Calvert (1731–71), Baron Baltimore, author of *A Tour to the East, in the Years 1763 and 1764: with Remarks on the City of Constantinople and the Turks* (1767).

p. 216, l. 28: *Volney*] Constantin François de Volney, *Travels through Syria and Egypt*. Ten years later, in *Ruins of Empire*, Volney further developed his ideas about the astrological origins of religion.

p. 218, l. 3: *Pera*] Galata, the foreign and merchant quarter of Constantinople, located on the northern shore of the Golden Horn, opposite the Islamic city proper.

p. 218, l. 10: *Olivier*] a reference to Guillaume Antoine Olivier (1756–1814) and his *Travels in the Ottoman Empire, Egypt, and Persia* (1801).

LEBLICH: TRAVELS OF ALI BEY

p. 229, l. 12: *douar*] a small encampment of Arab tents, arranged in circular fashion (*OED*).

p. 231, l. 8: *Zemzem*] Zamzam, the well of Abraham, located in Mecca. Drinking from the well constitutes one of the central rites of hajj.

p. 234, l. 17: *Abdoulwehab*] Muhammad Ibn Abd al-Wahhab (1703–91), founder of a militant and fundamentalist Islamic reform movement. Throughout the Romantic period, the Wahabis fought to establish independent control the Arabian peninsula and, particularly, Mecca and Medina. Their success in disrupting authority from Constantinople is demonstrated by Ali Bey's subsequent description of the Sultan's failed caravan to Medina.

p. 235, l. 32: *Sultan Scherif*] Sultan Sharif Ghalib Effendi, Governor of Jidda and semi-autonomous ruler of Mecca and Medina at the end of the eighteenth century. A title of nobility, indicating descent from the clan of the Prophet Muhammad, the Aschraf (plural) were recognised by Constantinople as the princes of Mecca.

p. 249, l. 22: *Sultan of the Wehhabites, named Saaoud*] referring to the Saudi dynasty of the Arabian Najd and, presumably, to Sa'ud ibn 'Abd al-Aziz, in particular. Since the mid-eighteenth century, the Saudi Emirs had been closely affiliated with the Wahabi movement.

p. 254, l. 1: *Maleki*] Maliki, one of the four principal schools of Sunni Muslim practice, founded in the eighth century by the Iman Maliki ibn Anas.

p. 255, l. 22: *Abdelaaziz*] presumably Abd al-Aziz, the assassinated son of Muhammad ibn Sa'ud, the first Wahabite Saudi Emir.

p. 259, l. 27: *Ayéscha*] 'A'ishah (614–78), the third and 'most beloved' wife of Muhammad.

p. 263, l. 11: *Taif*] Tayif, located south-east of Mecca; the city was the site of brutal Wahabite reform in the first years of the nineteenth century. The massacre at Tayif, along with the interruption of the caravan from Damascus described here, were amongst the most shocking contemporary events in the Islamic Middle East.

ELPHINSTONE: ACCOUNT OF THE KINGDOM OF CAUBUL

p. 289, l. 27: *Doctor Leyden*] John Leyden (1775–1811), traveller. Presumably a reference here to Leyden's *An Historical and Philosophical Sketch of the Discoveries and Settlements of the Europeans in Northern and Western Africa at the Close of the Eighteenth Century* (1799).

p. 290, ll. 4–5: *Khorassaun*] The Khorasan is the region representing the historical boundaries of the Parthian empire, which stretched from the Oxus River to the Iranian desert, as far west as the Caspian Sea and as far east as the Hindu Kush.

p. 290, n. 2, l. 1: *Persian and Arabian histories*] Among the most important translations from Asiatic history in this period were Muhammad Qasim Hindushah, Ferishtah, *History of Hindustane* (1768), trans. Alexander Dow, and Mahdi Khan Astarabadi, *History of the Life of Nadir Shah, King of Persia* (1773), trans. Sir William Jones. Elphinstone later cites Ferishtah's history as particularly influential (see p. 311).

p. 291, l. 2: *Ghore*] The al-Ghawr plain extends along the Jordan River.

p. 291, ll. 14–15: *Mahmood … Ghuznevide kings*] a tenth-century dynasty, begun when the former Turkish slave Alptegin seized control of Ghazna. Power soon came into the hands of another former slave, Subuktigin, whose son was Mahmud of Ghazna. Mahmud was responsible for extending the Ghaznavide empire as far as central India, and his descendants ruled until 1150.

p. 291, l. 12: *Samaunee*] presumably a reference to the tenth-century Samanide dynasty, founded by Isma'il Samani. The Samanides governed Transoxania during a period of transition from a dominant Persian culture to an increasingly Turkish and Arabic society.

p. 291, l. 19: *Zohauk*] Zohak, a mythological Arabic king of the Persian heroic age. Closely associated with Aji-Dahak, the serpentine spirit of evil, Zohak reigned over Asia, Arabia, Persia and Afghanistan for 1,000 years before being chained eternally at the foot of Mount Davand.

p. 291, l. 21: *Meer Khonde*] Persian historian Mir Khvand, Muhammad ibn Khavandashah (1433–98), author of *Raudat al-safa*, a history of the early kings of Persia. Silvestre de Sacy, *Mémoires sur diverse antiquitiés de la Perse: et sur les médailles des rois de la dynasties des Sassanides* (1793) includes a French translation of Mir Khvand's account.

p. 292, l. 6: *Baumeenaun*] Bamian, located north-west of Kabul. This important Buddhist site includes two immense figures of the Buddha dating from the fifth century and a series of (once frescoed) caves.

p. 292, n. 1, l. 10: *D. Herbelot*] Barthélemy d'Herbelot (1625–95), author of *Bibliotheque Orientale, ou Dictionnaire universel contentant tout ce qui fair connoître les peuples de l'Orient.*

p. 293, l. 15: *invasion of Bauber*] A descendent of Genghis Khan and Timur, Babur invaded regions of Afghanistan and India in the sixteenth century and established the Mogul empire. The Mogul empire continued its rule of the area throughout the Romantic period.

p. 293, ll. 20–1: *Khwarizm ... Jengheez Khaun*] Sultan 'Ala ad-Din Muhammad, the Khwarezm Shah, ruled after the collapse of the Ghurid empire in 1206. He was deposed by the invading Genghis Khan in 1219.

p. 293, l. 25: *Tamerlane*] Timur, conqueror of large parts of Afghanistan at the end of the fourteenth century.

p. 294, l. 5: *Sheer Shauh*] Sher Shah Sur, the founder of the Islamic Sur dynasty, who ruled northern India from 1540 to 1556.

p. 294, l. 14: *Ghiljie founded an empire*] The Ghilzai tribe, descendants of the Khilji Turks, ruled parts of Afghanistan intermittently from the tenth to the eighteenth centuries. They were one of the three major tribes of Afghanistan, along with the Pashtun and the Abdali.

p. 294, ll. 18–19: *Naudir Shauh*] Nader Ooli Beg or Nader Shah, who drove the Afghans from Persia and expanded the Mogul empire. He ruled as Shah of Persia from 1736 until his assassination in 1747.

p. 295, l. 3: *Afghaun, son of Irmia*] According to Pashtun tradition, the tribe descends from Afghana, a grandson of King Saul of Israel.

p. 296, l. 11: *Khauled ... son of Waleed*] A general in the service of the Prophet Muhammad, Khalid ibn al Walid led the invasion into Syria in 633–4, bringing the region under the control of the Muslim caliphate.

p. 296, n. 1, l. 1: *Ansaur*] Al-Ansar, 'the helpers'. A reference to the people of Medina who first responded to the Prophet Muhammad's call to Islamic faith and government.

p. 297, n. 1, l. 1: *Taureekhee Sheer Shauhee*] Tarkih-e Firuz Shahi (*The History of Firuz Shah*); the first known Muslim history of India, written in the fourteenth century by Ziya'-ud-Din Barani.

BURCKHARDT: TRAVELS IN SYRIA AND THE HOLY LAND

p. 303, l. 6: *Akaba*] Al-Aqabah, a port town and its fortifications, located in Jordan on the eastern inlet of the Red Sea. It marked the southern terminus of the Syrian trade route and lay just beyond the north-eastern extremity of the Sinai peninsula.

p. 303, l. 12: *Pasha of Egypt*] Mehemet or Mohammed Ali (*c.* 1769–1849), viceroy and pasha of Egypt. 'Tribes of Tor': the Towara Bedouin tribes, which controlled the southern Sinai peninsula. The sheikh in question is presumably Hassan Ibn Amer, mentioned later in Burckhardt's account.

p. 303, l. 19: *journey into Nubia*] Burckhardt was the author of numerous exploration accounts, all published posthumously, including *Travels in Nubia* (1819) and *Travels in Syria and the Holy Land* (1822). His *Travels in Arabia* (1829) was also to become an important Romantic-period travel text.

p. 303, l. 23: *Dragoman*] an officially sanctioned intermediary of the Ottoman Empire, who could serve as translator, political minister or local guide. 'Bedouin Sheikh': the nomadic peoples of the Middle Eastern deserts of Syria, Jordan, Iraq and Arabia. Organised around tribal structures, the Bedouins were lead by a family elder or sheikh.

p. 304, l. 4: *Tayf*] Tayif, a settlement located in the mountainous area south-east of Mecca. 'Firmahn': an official edict, in this instance a passport.

p. 304, l. 8: *Noweyba*] port town of the Sinai peninsula, located on the western shore of the Gulf of Aqaba. After leaving Noweyba, Burckhardt travelled south along the eastern coast of the Sinai peninsula to Dj Abou Ma, Ras Methan, Dahab, Nabk, Sherm and the Cape of Ras Abou Mohammed, before turning inland along the Wadi Orta to Rahab, Kyd and the Convent of Mount Sinai.

p. 304, l. 22: *Wady*] wadi, a valley that during the flood season becomes a waterway.

p. 305, ll. 6–7: *Oulad Sayd*] one of the Towara Bedouin tribes. While the Towara tribes were generally known for their hospitality and integrity, other tribes had murderous reputations. The Huywat, Alowein, Mezeine and Omran were particularly feared by Burckhardt's guides and by Romantic-period travellers in the area.

p. 306, l. 4: *Hedjaz*] an area of the Arabian peninsula stretching south from Jordan along the coast of the Red Sea and located in present-day western Saudi Arabia.

p. 307, l. 16: *Taba*] a settlement just south-west of Aqabah, on the western shore of the Gulf.

p. 307, l. 28: *M. Seetzen*] traveller Ulrich Jaspar Seetzen (1767–1811), whose *Brief Account of the Countries adjoining the Lake of Tiberias, the Jordan, and the Dead Sea* appeared in 1810.

p. 307 l. 29: *M. Agnelli*] not further identified. The Austrian Emperor Francis I (1768–1835) was renowned for his interest in and support of the sciences, and Agnelli's research may have appeared as a state publication.

p. 311, l. 14: *lake of Tiberias*] the Sea of Galilee.

p. 315, l. 28: *Sherif Edrisi*] Al-Sherif, Al-Idrisi, al-'ali bi-Allah (*c.* 1100–66), medieval Arabic geographer, cartographer and author of *The Pleasure Excursion of One Who is Eager to Traverse the Regions of the World*, to which Burckhardt refers here.

INDEX